The Frontier Thesis
and the Canadas:
The Debate
on the Impact
of the Canadian
Environment

ISSUES IN CANADIAN HISTORY

General Editor
J. L. GRANATSTEIN

ISSUES
IN
CANADIAN
HISTORY

The Frontier Thesis and the Canadas: The Debate on the Impact of the Canadian Environment

Edited by
MICHAEL S. CROSS

THE COPP CLARK PUBLISHING COMPANY
TORONTO

For Reany
because she makes me happy

[1729]

The Publishers have made an honest attempt to secure permission from authors, publishers, and estates to reproduce all material used, and if any omissions have been made, these are wholly unintentional and the Publishers would be glad to learn of them.

Contents

PART IV: The Frontier Challenge to Institutions   79

PART V: The Frontier and the Class System   104

Introduction

"North American democracy was forest-born."[1] Thus, succinctly, did the leading Canadian exponent of the frontier thesis sum up the importance of the frontier wilderness to our development. Right or wrong, it was an exciting attempt to explain the peculiar pattern of social and political growth on this continent.

In the writing of history, as in politics, Canadians have been notable for their lack of grand ideas. Most Canadian historians have been reluctant to discuss publicly their philosophies of history or to identify themselves with particular 'schools' of historical writing. The frontier thesis was an important exception to this generalization. In the 1920's and 1930's it gained a group of enthusiastic and vocal adherents who ardently pressed its virtues as a means of explaining Canada's development. Like most schools of Canadian historiography, however, frontierism was imported rather than indigenous; its origins were in the United States, where the frontier hypothesis has been perhaps the most important tool of historical interpretation in the twentieth century. Like most schools of Canadian historiography, too, frontierism soon became more used than discussed. Today an avowed 'frontierist' is hardly to be found in a day's walk. Yet evidence of the frontier approach is to be discovered in the writings of a great many historians, many of whom would take umbrage at having this fact drawn to their attention.

But what is a frontier? A place, a thinly-settled place, a line where civilization ends, an area where man meets the wilderness. This is the frontier-as-location. But this is not what the so-called frontier school of history is really about. Frontierists have usually written about the frontier as a process, as a symbol of the continuing American commitment

---

1. A. R. M. Lower, *Colony to Nation*, (Toronto, 1946), p. 49.

1

to progress and improvement. It was an expression of the peculiar affinity of Americans for their land. Throughout the history of the United States the vastness of the land has exerted a strange power over the minds of its people. Their enthusiastic response to this vastness, their patriotic glorying in it, was perhaps a necessary response—otherwise the vastness might oppress and defeat the people who met it.

This powerful tradition was codified in the works of the Wisconsin historian, Frederick Jackson Turner. As he stood before a meeting of the American Historical Association in Chicago in 1893, Turner systematized for Americans their frontier ideology. "The existence of an area of free land," he told the generations, "its continuous recession, and the advance of American settlement westward, explain American development." In this address, reprinted in Part I below, Turner used both meanings of the word frontier, isolating it as a place, but more usually preferring the 'process' approach. Turner, like his followers to come, saw the American West as a great crucible, the original melting pot in which the European was stripped down to his vital human essences, these essences then being collected to form a new and better being—the American. It was an evolutionary process this, a series of reconstructions of social character. The pioneer in going to the frontier was overwhelmed by nature, his European social nature torn away. He reverted to savagery. But, in a generation or less, civilization was re-established. Yet it was inevitably different from the original European pattern. The major difference was democratization. Because each man had to cope with the wilderness substantially on his own, the tendency of the frontier was anti-social. The pioneer, forced into total reliance upon his individual initiative, developed confidence in his own ability to solve any problem, became antipath-

etic to any form of control—in short he became an individualist and a democrat.

The Turner thesis rapidly became a dominant school of American history, for it offered Americans not only a comprehensive explanation of their nation's development, but one that was highly complimentary. They were superior to other peoples, more democratic, more inventive, more ambitious. And they owed these virtues not to their European inheritance but to the American environment itself.

More than followers, historians became disciples of Turner. The reverence given the prophet was perhaps best summed up in the scriptural quality of the title of a memorial volume published in 1961—*Wisconsin Witness to Frederick Jackson Turner*. The theory also stimulated a large body of violent critics, who assaulted Turner and his thesis in damning terms. Like William Appleman Williams they might denounce frontierism as a romantic flight from reality and its responsibilities[2]; like Mody Boatright they might see the hypothesis as a smoke-screen for the exploitative capitalism of American business[3]; but all critics agreed that frontierism overemphasized the uniqueness of American development and oversimplified the process of that development. As the years passed, the critics began to outweigh the disciples. Nevertheless, the frontierist vein in American historiography still runs wide and rich, and the Turner hypothesis has affected the work of all American historians, be they frontierists or critics.

The frontier thesis presumably has less relevance to Canadian life, for the tradition has been much shorter and less deeply-

---

2. William Appleman Williams, *The Contours of American History*, (Cleveland, 1961), p. 377.
3. Mody C. Boatright, "The Myth of Frontier Individualism," *Southwestern Social Science Quarterly*, vol. XXII, no. 1, (1941), pp. 14-32.

rooted in Canadian historiography than in that of the United States. Frontierism at no time has gained a majority adherence among historians of Canada. Nor has the frontier ideology had the same influence on the public mind as in the United States. The Hollywood image of the Wild West has not had its parallel in Canada: there surely is some significance in the fact that Canada's western heroes have been not rugged individualist gunmen like Wyatt Earp or Jesse James, but rather a collective law-enforcement agency, the Mounties. In the 1920's and 1930's, however, the frontier theory did have wide acceptance among historians. Perhaps it was the climate of the times—the last mad flurry of the 'Roaring Twenties', and the onset of the Depression—which raised for historians fundamental questions about the origins of North American institutions and their ability to withstand rapidly changing conditions; perhaps it was this which made the mysticism of the frontier thesis attractive to Canadian scholars. Whatever the reason, this was the high point of frontierism in this country, with such eminent figures as A. R. M. Lower, A. L. Burt and Walter N. Sage in the forefront of the movement.

Both Sage and Burt applied the Turner thesis to the history of French Canada, seeing the *coureurs de bois* as the prototype of the new man produced by the wilderness environment. Other historians have attempted to use the frontier approach to explain the development of Canadian religion, literature, migration patterns. For most, however, frontierism was a passing stage. The most striking example of this was Professor Frank H. Underhill, then of the University of Toronto. Writing of pre-Confederation politics in 1927 and 1935, Underhill unequivocally explained the Clear Grits in Upper Canada in terms of frontier democracy and agrarian radicalism. By 1946, however, he largely had recanted his Turnerism and was no longer convinced

of the vitality and uniqueness of frontier political expressions. What remained of Underhill's once ardent frontierism was an emphasis on the similarity of Canadian and American development and on the difference between European and North American political patterns.

It was A. R. M. Lower who made by far the best use of the hypothesis. Like Turner he was most concerned with establishing the basic conditions which had nurtured democracy; like Turner he argued that democracy was a pragmatic response to the frontier environment. Much of Professor Lower's theorizing was adopted directly from the American frontier school. His writings in the period rarely attempted to establish the thesis deductively from evidence, but rather built on American frontierist literature as if it itself were data. Lower did, however, explore many areas of Canadian frontier history previously unresearched. He wrote extensively and well of the timber frontier, attempting to widen the application of the theory from purely agrarian frontiers to those of commerce. Like other Turnerians, Lower began to stray from the fold by the late 1930's. He had been deeply concerned about the continuing vitality of democracy, once the frontier which had given it birth was gone. His move away from frontierism may have begun in 1939 when he found an alternative, and new hope, in the Canadian North. He wrote then " 'The North'—in Canada the words are already charged with the mystery and magnetism that 'The West' once held for the United States—may keep her people fresh and young and adaptive long after their frontier of settlement has closed."[4] By the

4. A. R. M. Lower, "Geographical Determinants in Canadian History," in Ralph Flenley, ed., *Essays in Canadian Historiography Presented to George Mackinnon Wrong*, (Toronto, 1939), p. 233.

time *Colony to Nation*, his general textbook on Canadian history, appeared in 1946, Lower had come to a stronger recognition of the moderating influence of transatlantic traditions on the response to the wilderness. Still he could make his assertion that "North American democracy was forest-born."

Frontierism exerted an indirect influence on Canadian historiography which was more widespread than its direct influence. It helped focus attention on the influence of the physical environment on the development of Canadian society, economy and politics. The 'staple theory', perhaps the most important of all approaches to Canadian history, drew inspiration from Frederick Jackson Turner. The frontierist influence remains clear in the staple theory, and in the 'Laurentian school' of Canadian history which grew from the staple theory. These approaches reversed priorities, emphasizing the importance of urban centres rather than frontier outposts. Yet the view of the environment, and even of the role of the frontier, was often similar to that of the Turner thesis. The most striking difference lay in the moral judgments made about the frontier. For Turner, the frontier was the well-spring of all that was good in North American society; for Laurentians like D. G. Creighton, the frontier was the homeland of parochial farmers who failed to appreciate the commercial dynamism found in cities like Montreal, a dynamism essential for the growth of Canada.

How can we evaluate the usefulness of the frontier thesis in explaining Canadian history? It has stirred such emotional reactions that we must read both its adherents and its critics with considerable quantities of salt near at hand. The theory really can be tested only by a series of case studies, in which it is applied to various localities, under various circumstances. It is not enough to accept the overgeneralizations on either side. For example, Turner drew his theory from his own American Middle West; this was the frontier environment from which his examples were derived. But this environment, this agricultural small-farm frontier, was very different from the pattern found in many parts of Canada. Canada has been, for the most part, a country of *commercial* frontiers. Due to geographical immensity and difficulty, the American pattern of unassisted agricultural settlement in the first instance has rarely been possible. First the land had to be penetrated and transportation and markets provided. Thus the order of penetration for much of the country was fairly uniform; first came the exploiting business pioneers, often operating on an itinerant basis; then the government, organizing the territory, assisting transportation; finally came the permanent—usually agricultural—settler. Such has been the pattern, through the age of the fur trade, the days of timber, through the advance of the railway, the mining and petroleum industries. Clearly, then, it is not possible to accept uncritically either Turnerians or their opponents, both of whom have been chiefly concerned with agricultural frontiers. The situation on the frontier of commerce may be very different.

On any kind of frontier, however, there are certain common concerns with which the theory attempts to deal. Its usefulness is to be measured by its credibility in explaining these phenomena in any particular case. The most significant factor to be considered is that of social disorganization. Social upheavals, violence, anti-social behaviour, the breakdown of traditional institutions, these have fascinated students of the frontier, and have been viewed by them as the major agents of social change. For Turner, it was the destruction of European social patterns by the wilderness which liberated man and gave birth to American initiative and American democracy. For the Canadian sociologist, S. D. Clark (Part VII), the weakening of traditional institutions produced a new, pragmatic, individualistic and radical society. That social unrest of some kind did in fact occur on most frontiers is evident: Hollywood did grasp the core of the frontier experience. That its nature and cause have been the chief concern of frontier historians is equally clear. It would seem that if we can determine the kind of social disorganization which took place on any given frontier, its extent, and the ultimate causes of it, we have gone far towards discovering the nature of this frontier society and of the more mature societies which will grow out of it.

The selections that follow attempt to illustrate some of the kinds of problems of interpretation which arise in frontier studies. Since the frontier is, by definition, constantly moving, we are forced to pursue it as it recedes both in space and in time, and to be conscious that the effect of the environment may be different in different times and different places. We must take into consideration the impact of the frontier upon institutions as well as upon individuals, and investigate the interaction of institutions and individuals. Above all the problem of the frontier is compounded because we are concerned not only with the influence of the environment on social institutions and on the physical existence of men, but of the influence of the environment upon the minds of men. Clearly the problem of the frontier is not susceptible to clear-cut, conclusive answers.

* * *

The area in which the frontier problem will be investigated here is that of the two Canadas, in the period before Confederation. Upper and Lower Canada were created out of the old province of Quebec by the Constitutional Act of 1791. The Act of Union of 1840 reunited the two colonies in the Province of Canada, an entity which ceased to exist with Confederation, and the creation of the provinces of Ontario and Quebec.

Both of these colonies had large unsettled areas even in the 1860's. Despite two and a half centuries of colonization Lower Canada in 1791 was settled only in the St. Lawrence valley; the bulk of the province was densely forested wilderness. The frontier advanced very slowly in Lower Canada, for French Canadians showed a marked reluctance to leave the family homes along the St. Lawrence. When settlement did push into the back country, as it did with greater vigour by the late 1840's, it was often in groups, often under the leadership of priests. There is a problem here. The French Canadians were obviously in origin a frontier people. They had opened a primitive continent, had met the frontier in its most savage form. Yet the descendants of these pioneers clung to the security of their St. Lawrence womb; they clung to that prototype of European institutions, the Roman Catholic Church. Is this anomaly a refutation of the frontier thesis, or can it be explained within a frontierist approach? *YES*

Upper Canada would appear to conform more closely to a classic frontier pattern. Although there were group settlements in Glengarry County, Richmond, Peterborough, and elsewhere, the bulk of immigrants came as individuals or in family groups, and moved on to forest farms. Upper Canada saw the rise of movements that have been interpreted as expressions of the frontier spirit—the Methodist Church, a symbol of frontier religion; the backwoods rebellion movement in 1837; the Clear Grit radicals in the politics of the 1850's. But all of these have been discredited by some historians as genuine examples of the influence of the frontier. And it is obvious that Upper Canada *No* showed many tendencies alien to the frontier ideal. The vast majority of its people remained strongly loyal to the British connection, and to the cautious development of British political institutions. Only a minority of Upper Canadians appear to have been agitated over the achievement of political democracy, the very corner-stone of the frontier ideology.

Similar arguments arise in the discussion of the social history of Upper Canada. Contemporary travellers often commented on the "Yankee manners" of Upper Canadians. Many tourists from Britain deplored the rudeness and independence of the settlers, their refusal to pay respect to social rank. Upper Canadians, it seemed, were developing levelling social attitudes essentially similar to those of the United States. Many of the techniques of daily life were also similar. The logging bee, the building bee, the quilting bee: these communal approaches to work were carried on on both sides of the border. British travellers were often as alarmed by Upper Canadian farm techniques as by Upper Canadian manners. The American style of extensive agriculture, rather than European intensive agriculture, was practiced in the British colony, so that a Canadian field was indistinguishable from one in Pennsylvania, yet looked nothing like one in Yorkshire. On the other hand, there were many areas of Upper Canada in which the frontier stage was marked by local leadership elites, small groups which enjoyed the prestige of English gentry. The frontier had passed for most of Upper Canada before the Family Compact fell from power. While, as indicated, many travellers remarked on the 'Yankeefied' character of Upper Canada, as many were interested to note that Upper Canada was not as progressive or as hard-driving as bordering American states. They commented on the lack of ambition of the Canadians in contrast to their American neighbours, how Canadians were less willing to take chances financially, how Canadians

were less sensitive about their pride and their independence.

The lesson here is not only that contemporaries were as divided in their opinions as historians have been. It is, as well, that there were significant differences between Canada and the United States, and in how Canadians and Americans responded to similar environments. In studying the frontier, it is necessary not only to measure the impact of the frontier environment, but to explain the differences in its impact on the two countries. Is it, as a Laurentian School historian would say, because of Canada's strong economic ties to Britiain, ties which gave Britain a greater influence on Canada, in life style and politics as much as in economics? Or perhaps the explanation lies in the "hot house" nature of the Upper Canadian frontier. In the United States, the frontier advance was almost continuous from the beginning of the seventeenth century until the frontier passed away in the late nineteenth century. Generation after generation of Americans lived with the frontier experience as a continuing phenomenon. In Upper Canada, however, the frontier was more fleeting. A small number of settlers came into the province during and after the American Revolution of the 1770's, but large scale settlement did not begin until after 1815. By the late 1840's, the frontier had passed out of Old Ontario into the forbidding country of the Canadian Shield. A new frontier of acceptable agricultural land did not open until the railway opened the prairies after 1885. Clearly, then, the Upper Canadian frontier experience was much more compressed than that of the United States. Was it, therefore, less influential, and less lasting in its impact?

To make some determination about the value of the frontier thesis, it is essential to observe a broad spectrum of factors: democratization in politics; the social class system;

the functioning of institutions like the churches, police, and so on; the degree and causes of social disorder. These are some of the aspects of Upper Canadian life which must be investigated before it is possible to assess the applicability of the frontier hypothesis. The selections in this book are obviously only a starting point for this kind of assessment. But perhaps they do illustrate some of the variety of questions which must be asked in this process of evaluation. That in itself should be a step forward, given the way so many historians, on both sides of the debate—like Hollywood frontier heroes—have shot from the hip without adequately investigating the whole range of questions which together make up the problem of the frontier.

Clash of Opinion

There can be little question but that American democracy had a forest birth and there also can be little doubt of the validity of the larger thesis that the frontier environment, or life lived on the margins of civilization, tends to bring about an equality of which the political expression is democracy. . . . It may be concluded that our own pioneering era plus the influence of American pioneer life brought about political democracy in Canada.

A. R. M. LOWER

For a moment, at the frontier, the bonds of custom are broken and unrestraint is triumphant. There is not *tabula rasa*. The stubborn American environment is there with its imperious summons to accept its conditions; the inherited ways of doing things are also there; and yet, in spite of environment, and in spite of custom, each frontier did indeed furnish a new field of opportunity, a gate of escape from the bondage of the past; and freshness, and confidence, and scorn of older society, impatience of its restraints and its ideas, and indifference to its lessons, have accompanied the frontier.

FREDERICK JACKSON TURNER

The Turner thesis is increasingly viewed as an inadequate concept with which to "explain" American development, and by some even as a positive hindrance to sound inquiry into the American past. . . . It became plain, as new thought and research was brought to bear upon the problem, that the frontier theory, as an analytical device, was a blunt instrument.

RICHARD HOFSTADTER

. . . I don't think the frontier has been that important in Canadian history. I think the Americans had a frontier. I think they made an enormous amount of it. They have even created an historical theory on it which they call 'The Frontier Thesis' and by that historical theory they ascribe to the frontier the greatest formative influence in American history. I don't think the frontier in Canada has played any such part and I think that however useful the concept may be in the United States, and they are beginning to be a little doubtful about that now there too, it has only a very limited relevance to Canada.

D. G. CREIGHTON

From this analysis of the rebellion in Upper Canada, it is apparent that it was neither an accident nor an insignificant affair but rather a movement similar in many respects to the numerous frontier revolts in the history of the United States.

L. S. STAVRIANOS

. . . the essential thing about the *Globe* and the movement it led is that it represented the aspirations and general outlook on life of the pioneer Upper Canadian farmer. The "Clear Grit" party in Upper Canada was an expression of the "frontier" in our Canadian politics just as Jacksonian Democracy or Lincoln Republicanism was in the politics of the United States.

FRANK H. UNDERHILL

The final picture of the *Globe* should not be that of an agrarian radical oracle making common cause, on occasion, with the essentially foreign world of Toronto business; but rather one of an urban Liberal newspaper seeking to carry its viewpoint to the rural masses—and generally succeeding.

J. M. S. CARELESS

There was then no distinction, as is the case now a days. All were on an equality and ready to do any kind acts and services for one another. The happy meetings we often had, I look back to with much pleasure. I am decidedly of opinion that true happiness, as far as human nature has the privilege of enjoying it, was far more abundant then than the present frivolities of the age.

CAPT. JAMES DITTRICK, PIONEER

I never in my life have seen so much general distress and poverty as is daily exhibited here—but that is a subject too long to touch at present, it ought to discourage emigration, if anything can stop that unfortunate disposition. The indus-

trious do very well but the 9/10ths that come out are people who have not been industrious at home (to say the best of them) and cannot well be expected to change morals and manners and habits by a passage across the Atlantic.

THE EARL OF DALHOUSIE

. . . it is education and manners that must distinguish the gentleman in this country, seeing that the labouring man, if he is diligent and industrious, may soon become his equal in point of worldly possessions. The ignorant man, be he ever so wealthy, can never be equal to the man of education. It is the mind that forms the distinction between the classes in this country— "Knowledge is power!"

CATHERINE PARR TRAILL

. . . if we compare the results of the settlement of educated people and of the labouring classes, the former withering away and leaving no sign behind—the latter growing in numbers and advancing in wealth and position until they fill the whole land, it is impossible to avoid the conclusion, that except as leaders and teachers of their companies, gentlefolk of refined tastes and superior education, have no place in the bush, and should shun it as a wild delusion and a cruel snare.

SAMUEL THOMPSON

Part I

The Frontier Thesis:
The Historians Debate

There is only one starting point for any debate on the frontier hypothesis. This section, therefore, begins with Frederick Jackson Turner's monumental paper of 1893 in which the theory was first elaborated with Turner's characteristic vigour and sense of drama. Reading his work, and hearing of his influence upon his students, we get some understanding of why the violence and upheaval of the frontier captured his imagination: like his frontier and the dynamic pioneers with which he peopled it, Turner himself was somewhat larger than life. The text of his address presents no unusual problems of interpretation, for Turner was both forceful and lucid in making his case. There are two things worth noticing especially, however. One is the moral connotation the theory carries with it. Turner describes both the positive and negative qualities produced by the frontier, but there is never any doubt that he considers the overall effect to be good, that, indeed, he considers that the frontier has produced the finest of all human products in the American. This is environmentalism with a difference in which the operation of the particular environment is almost invariably for the good. The second consideration is the kind of problem which can spring from this kind of environmentalism. In addition to the exultation over the frontier-born greatness of America, there is in Turner a worried, brooding aspect. For, by the time he wrote, the frontier had passed. If America owed her success, and her democracy, to the frontier, what lay ahead if the frontier was gone? Was American democracy, and with it the United States itself, doomed with the passing of the frontier?

Any number of anti-frontierist statements exist. That chosen is by the eminent American historian, Richard Hofstadter, who has written a number of studies of the so-called Progressive era in which Turner lived and wrote. Hofstadter's article is a summary of the kinds of attacks made on Turner up to 1949, when the article was written. It is clear that Hofstadter's disenchantment with frontierism springs not only from his criticism of Turner's historical methods, but also from ideological considerations. A modern liberal critic of American society, Hofstadter is naturally hostile to Turner's glorification of the 'American dream' and of the traditional values of American life.

The debate has been perhaps a little more gentlemanly, and certainly less dogmatic, in Canada. The first Canadian selection demonstrates how a moderate frontierist blends the thesis with other factors to emerge with a general interpretation of the history of Upper Canada. Fred Landon, an important historian of Ontario and former librarian at the University of Western Ontario, wrote this summary as a foreword to a new edition of his book, *Western Ontario and the American Frontier*, which appeared in 1967. The book was first published in 1941, and it is interesting to see how little Dr. Landon's interpretation has changed over that period of time. Then two brief excerpts illustrate the rather noisy debate of the late 1920's. A. R. M. Lower was making a tentative statement about the influence of the frontier in Canada. He clearly was deeply impressed by Turner's writings, for he seemed surprised that the frontier impact had not been complete, and was struggling for explanations for this Canadian incompleteness. There is much of Turner here, even to the 'scientific'

biological approach Turner favoured—Lower spoke of human "types," and of "the biological law of dispersion." At the same 1929 meeting of the Canadian Historical Association at which Lower delivered his paper, J. L. McDougall launched a sharp and sarcastic attack on both Turner and his Canadian disciples. It must have been one of the more contentious meetings of that staid organization.

Part I is completed by an excerpt from a television interview with Canada's most acclaimed historian, Donald Creighton. Arguing that the frontier has not been "the main source of inspiration," Creighton advances his own interpretation of Canadian development, based on the 'Laurentian' approach—which emphasizes the importance of the St. Lawrence trade route and its links to Europe—and on the 'Metropolitan' approach —which stresses the flow of goods and ideas from cities to the countryside. There is special interest in this, as an example of how historical theories fade into one another. Metropolitanism is a grandson or great-grandson of the frontier thesis. Mackintosh derived the environmentalism of his staple approach from Turner; then Creighton's Laurentianism grew from the staple theory; and Metropolitanism carried it a stage further into a general theory of urban growth. Perhaps there is an ecumenical undercurrent in Canadian historiography.

In this section, as throughout, the authors' footnotes have been omitted.

The Frontier Thesis is Born

In a recent bulletin of the Superintendent of the Census for 1890 appear
these significant words: "Up to and including 1880 the country had a frontier of
settlement, but at present the unsettled
area has been so broken into by isolated
bodies of settlement that there can hardly
be said to be a frontier line. In the discussion of its extent, its westward movement, etc., it can not, therefore, any
longer have a place in the census reports."
This brief official statement marks the
closing of a great historic movement. Up
to our own day American history has
been in a large degree the history of the
colonization of the Great West. The existence of an area of free land, its continuous
recession, and the advance of American
settlement westward, explain American
development.

Behind institutions, behind constitutional forms and modifications, lie the vital
forces that call these organs into life and
shape them to meet changing conditions.
The peculiarity of American institutions
is, the fact that they have been compelled
to adapt themselves to the changes of an
expanding people—to the changes involved in crossing a continent, in winning a
wilderness, and in developing at each area
of this progress out of the primitive economic and political conditions of the frontier into the complexity of city life. Said
Calhoun in 1817, "We are great, and
rapidly—I was about to say fearfully—
growing!" So saying, he touched the distinguishing feature of American life. All
peoples show development; the germ
theory of politics has been sufficiently emphasized. In the case of most nations,
however, the development has occurred
in a limited area; and if the nation has
expanded, it has met other growing
peoples whom it has conquered. But in the
case of the United States we have a different phenomenon. Limiting our attention
to the Atlantic coast, we have the familiar
phenomenon of the evolution of institutions in a limited area, such as the rise of
representative government; the differentiation of simple colonial governments into
complex organs; the progress from primitive industrial society, without division of
labor, up to manufacturing civilization.
But we have in addition to this a recurrence of the process of evolution in each
western area reached in the process of expansion. Thus American development has
exhibited not merely advance along a
single line, but a return to primitive conditions on a continually advancing frontier
line, and a new development for that area.
American social development has been
continually beginning over again on the
frontier. This perennial rebirth, this fluid-
ity of American life, this expansion westward with its new opportunities, its continuous touch with the simplicity of primitive
society, furnish the forces dominating American character. The true point of view
in the history of this nation is not the

Atlantic coast, it is the Great West. Even the slavery struggle, which is made so exclusive an object of attention by writers like Professor von Holst, occupies its important place in American history because of its relation to westward expansion.

In this advance, the frontier is the outer edge of the wave—the meeting point between savagery and civilization. Much has been written about the frontier from the point of view of border warfare and the chase, but as a field for the serious study of the economist and the historian it has been neglected.

The American frontier is sharply distinguished from the European frontier— a fortified boundary line running through dense populations. The most significant thing about the American frontier is, that it lies at the hither edge of free land. In the census reports it is treated as the margin of that settlement which has a density of two or more to the square mile. The term is an elastic one, and for our purposes does not need sharp definition. We shall consider the whole frontier belt, including the Indian country and the outer margin of the "settled area" of the census reports. This paper will make no attempt to treat the subject exhaustively; its aim is simply to call attention to the frontier as a fertile field for investigation, and to suggest some of the problems which arise in connection with it.

In the settlement of America we have to observe how European life entered the continent, and how America modified and developed that life and reacted on Europe. Our early history is the study of European germs developing in an American environment. Too exclusive attention has been paid by institutional students to the Germanic origins, too little to the American factors. The frontier is the line of most rapid and effective Americanization. The wilderness masters the colonist. It finds him a European in dress, industries, tools, modes of travel, and thought. It takes him from the railroad car and puts him in the birch canoe. It strips off the garments of civilization and arrays him in the hunting shirt and the moccasin. It puts him in the log cabin of the Cherokee and Iroquois and runs an Indian palisade around him. Before long he has gone to planting Indian corn and plowing with a sharp stick; he shouts the war cry and takes the scalp in orthodox Indian fashion. In short, at the frontier the environment is at first too strong for the man. He must accept the conditions which it furnishes, or perish, and so he fits himself into the Indian clearings and follows the Indian trails. Little by little he transforms the wilderness, but the outcome is not the old Europe, not simply the development of Germanic germs, any more than the first phenomenon was a case of reversion to the Germanic mark. The fact is, that here is a new product that is American. At first, the frontier was the Atlantic coast. It was the frontier of Europe in a very real sense. Moving westward, the frontier became more and more American. As successive terminal moraines result from successive glaciations, so each frontier leaves its traces behind it, and when it becomes a settled area the region still partakes of the frontier characteristics. Thus the advance of the frontier has meant a steady movement away from the influence of Europe, a steady growth of independence on American lines. And to study this advance, the men who grew up under these conditions, and the political, economic, and social results of it, is to study the really American part of our history. . . .

At the Atlantic frontier one can study

the germs of processes repeated at each successive frontier. We have the complex European life sharply precipitated by the wilderness into the simplicity of primitive conditions. The first frontier had to meet its Indian question, its question of the disposition of the public domain, of the means of intercourse with older settlements, of the extension of political organization, of religious and educational activity. And the settlement of these and similar questions for one frontier served as a guide for the next. The American student needs not to go to the "prim little townships of Sleswick" for illustrations of the law of continuity and development. For example, he may study the origin of our land policies in the colonial land policy; he may see how the system grew by adapting the statutes to the customs of the successive frontiers. He may see how the mining experience in the lead regions of Wisconsin, Illinois, and Iowa was applied to the mining laws of the Sierras, and how our Indian policy has been a series of experimentations on successive frontiers. Each tier of new States has found in the older ones material for its constitutions. Each frontier has made similar contributions to American character, as will be discussed farther on.

But with all these similarities there are essential differences, due to the place element and the time element. It is evident that the farming frontier of the Mississippi Valley presents different conditions from the mining frontier of the Rocky Mountains. The frontier reached by the Pacific Railroad surveyed into rectangles, guarded by the United States Army, and recruited by the daily immigrant ship, moves forward at a swifter pace and in a different way than the frontier reached by the birch canoe or the pack horse. The geologist traces patiently the shores of ancient seas,

maps their areas, and compares the older and the newer. It would be a work worth the historian's labors to mark these various frontiers and in detail compare one with another. Not only would there result a more adequate conception of American development and characteristics, but invaluable additions would be made to the history of society.

Loria, the Italian economist, has urged the study of colonial life as an aid in understanding the stages of European development, affirming that colonial settlement is for economic science what the mountain is for geology, bringing to light primitive stratifications. "America," he says, "has the key to the historical enigma which Europe has sought for centuries in vain, and the land which has no history reveals luminously the course of universal history." There is much truth in this. The United States lies like a huge page in the history of society. Line by line as we read this continental page from West to East we find the record of social evolution. It begins with the Indian and the hunter; it goes on to tell of the disintegration of savagery by the entrance of the trader, the pathfinder of civilization; we read the annals of the pastoral stage in ranch life; the exploitation of the soil by the raising of unrotated crops of corn and wheat in sparsely settled farming communities; the intensive culture of the denser farm settlement; and finally the manufacturing organization with city and factory system. This page is familiar to the student of census statistics, but how little of it has been used by our historians. Particularly in eastern States this page is a palimpsest. What is now a manufacturing State was in an earlier decade an area of intensive farming. Earlier yet it had been a wheat area, and still earlier the "range" had attracted the cattle-herder. Thus Wisconsin, now developing manufacture, is a State with varied agricultural interests. But earlier it was given over to almost exclusive grain-raising, like North Dakota at the present time.

Each of these areas has had an influence in our economic and political history; the evolution of each into a higher stage has worked political transformations. But what constitutional historian has made any adequate attempt to interpret political facts by the light of these social areas and changes?

The Atlantic frontier was compounded of fisherman, fur-trader, miner, cattle-raiser, and farmer. Excepting the fisherman, each type of industry was on the march toward the West, impelled by an irresistible attraction. Each passed in successive waves across the continent. Stand at Cumberland Gap and watch the procession of civilization, marching single file—the buffalo following the trail to the salt springs, the Indian, the fur-trader and hunter, the cattle-raiser, the pioneer farmer—and the frontier has passed by. Stand at South Pass in the Rockies a century later and see the same procession with wider intervals between. The unequal rate of advance compels us to distinguish the frontier into the trader's frontier, the rancher's frontier, or the miner's frontier, and the farmer's frontier. When the mines and the cow pens were still near the fall line the traders' pack trains were tinkling across the Alleghanies, and the French on the Great Lakes were fortifying their posts, alarmed by the British trader's birch canoe. When the trappers scaled the Rockies, the farmer was still near the mouth of the Missouri....

... the frontier promoted the formation of a composite nationality for the American people. The coast was preponderantly English, but the later tides of continental immigration flowed across to the free lands. This was the case from the early colonial days. The Scotch-Irish and the Palatine Germans, or "Pennsylvania Dutch," furnished the dominant element in the stock of the colonial frontier. With these peoples were also the freed indented servants, or redemptioners, who at the expiration of their time of service passed to the frontier. Governor Spotswood of Virginia writes in 1717, "The inhabitants of our frontiers are composed generally of such as have been transported hither as servants, and, being out of their time, settle themselves where land is to be taken up and that will produce the necessarys of life with little labour." Very generally these redemptioners were of non-English stock. In the crucible of the frontier the immigrants were Americanized, liberated, and fused into a mixed race, English in neither nationality nor characteristics. The process has gone on from the early days to our own. Burke and other writers in the middle of the eighteenth century believed that Pennsylvania was "threatened with the danger of being wholly foreign in language, manners, and perhaps even inclinations." The German and Scotch-Irish elements in the frontier of the South were only less great. In the middle of the present century the German element in Wisconsin was already so considerable that leading publicists looked to the creation of a German state out of the commonwealth by concentrating their colonization. Such examples teach us to beware of misinterpreting the fact that there is a common English speech in America into a belief that the stock is also English.

In another way the advance of the frontier decreased our dependence on England. The coast, particularly of the South, lacked diversified industries, and was dependent on England for the bulk of its supplies. In the South there was even a dependence on the Northern colonies for articles of food. Governor Glenn, of South Carolina, writes in the middle of the eighteenth century: "Our trade with New York and Philadelphia was of this sort, draining us of all the little money and bills we could gather from other places for their bread, flour, beer, hams, bacon, and other things of their produce, all which, except beer, our new townships begin to supply us with, which are settled with very industrious and thriving Germans. This no doubt diminishes the number of shipping and the appearance of our trade, but it is far from being a detriment to us." Before long the frontier created a demand for merchants. As it retreated from the coast it became less and less possible for England to bring her supplies directly to the consumer's wharfs, and carry away staple crops, and staple crops began to give way to diversified agriculture for a time. The effect of this phase of the frontier action upon the northern section is perceived when we realize how the advance of the frontier aroused seaboard cities like Boston, New York, and Baltimore, to engage in rivalry for what Washington called "the extensive and valuable trade of a rising empire."

The legislation which most developed the powers of the national government, and played the largest part in its activity, was conditioned on the frontier. Writers have discussed the subjects of tariff, land, and internal improvement, as subsidiary to the slavery question. But when American history comes to be rightly viewed it will be seen that the slavery question is an incident. . . .

. . . The pioneer needed the goods of the coast, and so the grand series of internal improvement and railroad legislation began, with potent nationalizing effects. Over internal improvements occurred great debates, in which grave constitutional questions were discussed. Sectional groupings appear in the votes, profoundly significant for the historian. Loose construction increased as the nation marched westward. But the West was not content with bringing the farm to the factory. Under the lead of Clay—"Harry of the West"—protective tariffs were passed, with the cry of bringing the factory to the farm The disposition of the public lands was a third important subject of national legislation influenced by the frontier.

The public domain has been a force of profound importance in the nationalization and development of the government. The effects of the struggle of the landed and the landless States, and of the Ordinance of 1787, need no discussion. Administratively the frontier called out some of the highest and most vitalizing activities of the general government. The purchase of Louisiana was perhaps the constitutional turning point in the history of the Republic, inasmuch as it afforded both a new area for national legislation and the occasion of the downfall of the policy of strict construction. But the purchase of Louisiana was called out by frontier needs and demands. As frontier States accrued to the Union the national power grew. In a speech on the dedication of the Calhoun monument Mr. Lamar explained: "In 1789 the States were the creators of the Federal Government; in 1861 the Federal Government was the creator of a large majority of the States."

When we consider the public domain from the point of view of the sale and disposal of the public lands we are again brought face to face with the frontier. The policy of the United States in dealing with its lands is in sharp contrast with the European system of scientific administration. Efforts to make this domain a source of revenue, and to withhold it from emigrants in order that settlement might be compact, were in vain. The jealousy and the fears of the East were powerless in the face of the demands of the frontiersmen. John Quincy Adams was obliged to confess: "My own system of administration, which was to make the national domain the inexhaustible fund for progressive and unceasing internal improvement, has failed." The reason is obvious; a system of administration was not what the West demanded; it wanted land. Adams states the situation as follows: "The slaveholders of the South have bought the coöperation of the western country by the bribe of the western lands, abandoning to the new Western States their own proportion of the public property and aiding them in the design of grasping all the lands into their own hands. Thomas H. Benton was the author of this system, which he brought forward as a substitute for the American system of Mr. Clay, and to supplant him as the leading statesman of the West. Mr. Clay, by his tariff compromise with Mr. Calhoun, abandoned his own American system. At the same time he brought forward a plan for distributing among all the States of the Union the proceeds of the sales of the public lands. His bill for that purpose passed both Houses of Congress, but was vetoed by President Jackson, who, in his annual message of December, 1832, formally recommended that all public lands should be gratuitously given away to individual adventurers and to the States in which the lands are situated."

"No subject," said Henry Clay, "which has presented itself to the present, or perhaps any preceding, Congress, is of greater magnitude than that of the public lands." When we consider the far-reaching effects of the government's land policy upon political, economic, and social aspects of American life, we are disposed to agree with him. But this legislation was framed under frontier influences, and under the lead of Western statesmen like Benton and Jackson. Said Senator Scott of Indiana in 1841: "I consider the preëmption law merely declaratory of the custom or common law of the settlers."

It is safe to say that the legislation with regard to land, tariff, and internal improvements—the American system of the nationalizing Whig party—was conditioned on frontier ideas and needs. But it was not merely in legislative action that the frontier worked against the sectionalism of the coast. The economic and social characteristics of the frontier worked against sectionalism. The men of the frontier had closer resemblances to the Middle region than to either of the other sections. Pennsylvania had been the seed-plot of frontier emigration, and, although she passed on her settlers along the Great Valley into the west of Virginia and the Carolinas, yet the industrial society of these Southern frontiersmen was always more like that of the Middle region than like that of the tide-water portion of the South, which later came to spread its industrial type throughout the South.

The Middle region, entered by New York harbor, was an open door to all Europe. The tide-water part of the South represented typical Englishmen, modified by a warm climate and servile labor, and living in baronial fashion on great plantations; New England stood for a special English movement—Puritanism. The Middle region was less English than the other sections. It had a wide mixture of nationalities, a varied society, the mixed town and county system of local government, a varied economic life, many religious sects. In short, it was a region mediating between New England and the South, and the East and the West. It represented that composite nationality which the contemporary United States exhibits, that juxtaposition of non-English groups, occupying a valley or a little settlement, and presenting reflections of the map of Europe in their variety. It was democratic and nonsectional, if not national; "easy, tolerant, and contented;" rooted strongly in material prosperity. It was typical of the modern United States. It was least sectional, not only because it lay between North and South, but also because with no barriers to shut out its frontiers from its settled region, and with a system of connecting waterways, the Middle region mediated between East and West as well as between North and South. Thus it became the typically American region. Even the New Englander, who was shut out from the frontier by the Middle region, tarrying in New York or Pennsylvania on his westward march, lost the acuteness of his sectionalism on the way.

The spread of cotton culture into the interior of the South finally broke down the contrast between the "tide-water" region and the rest of the State, and based Southern interests on slavery. Before this process revealed its results the western portion of the South, which was akin to Pennsylvania in stock, society, and industry, showed tendencies to fall away from the faith of the fathers into internal improvement legislation and nationalism. In the Virginia convention of 1829-30, called to revise the constitution, Mr. Leigh, of Chesterfield, one of the tide-water counties, declared:

One of the main causes of discontent which led to this convention, that which had

the strongest influence in overcoming our veneration for the work of our fathers, which taught us to contemn the sentiments of Henry and Mason and Pendleton, which weaned us from our reverence for the constituted authorities of the State, was an overweening passion for internal improvement. I say this with perfect knowledge, for it has been avowed to me by gentlemen from the West over and over again. And let me tell the gentleman from Albemarle (Mr. Gordon) that it has been another principal object of those who set this ball of revolution in motion, to overturn the doctrine of State rights, of which Virginia has been the very pillar, and to remove the barrier she has interposed to the interference of the Federal Government in that same work of internal improvement, by so reorganizing the legislature that Virginia, too, may be hitched to the Federal car.

It was this nationalizing tendency of the West that transformed the democracy of Jefferson into the national republicanism of Monroe and the democracy of Andrew Jackson. The West of the War of 1812, the West of Clay, and Benton and Harrison, and Andrew Jackson, shut off by the Middle States and the mountains from the coast sections, had a solidarity of its own with national tendencies. On the tide of the Father of Waters, North and South met and mingled into a nation. Interstate migration went steadily on—a process of cross-fertilization of ideas and institutions. The fierce struggle of the sections over slavery on the western frontier does not diminish the truth of this statement; it proves the truth of it. Slavery was a sectional trait that would not down, but in the West it could not remain sectional. It was the greatest of frontiersmen who declared: "I believe this Government can not endure permanently half slave and half free. It will become all of one thing or all of the other." Nothing works for nationalism like intercourse within the nation. Mobility of population is death to localism, and the western frontier worked irresistibly in unsettling population. The effect reached back from the frontier and affected profoundly the Atlantic coast and even the Old World.

But the most important effect of the frontier has been in the promotion of democracy here and in Europe. As has been indicated, the frontier is productive of individualism. Complex society is precipitated by the wilderness into a kind of primitive organization based on the family. The tendency is anti-social. It produces antipathy to control, and particularly to any direct control. The tax-gatherer is viewed as a representative of oppression. Prof. Osgood, in an able article, has pointed out that the frontier conditions prevalent in the colonies are important factors in the explanation of the American Revolution, where individual liberty was sometimes confused with absence of all effective government. The same conditions aid in explaining the difficulty of instituting a strong government in the period of the confederacy. The frontier individualism has from the beginning promoted democracy.

The frontier States that came into the Union in the first quarter of a century of its existence came in with democratic suffrage provisions, and had reactive effects of the highest importance upon the older States whose peoples were being attracted there. An extension of the franchise became essential. It was *western* New York that forced an extension of suffrage in the constitutional convention of that State in 1821; and it was *western* Virginia that compelled the tide-water region to put a more liberal suffrage provision in the constitution framed in 1830, and to give to the frontier region a more nearly proportionate representation with the tide-water aristocracy. The rise of democracy as an effective force in the nation came in with western preponderance under Jackson and William Henry Harrison, and it meant the triumph of the frontier—with all of its good and with all of its evil elements. An interesting illustration of the tone of frontier democracy in 1830 comes from the same debates in the Virginia convention already referred to. A representative from western Virginia declared:

But, sir, it is not the increase of population in the West which this gentleman ought to fear. It is the energy which the mountain breeze and western habits impart to those emigrants. They are regenerated, politically I mean, sir. They soon become *working politicians*; and the difference, sir, between a *talking* and a *working* politician is immense. The Old Dominion has long been celebrated for producing great orators; the ablest metaphysicians in policy; men that can split hairs in all abstruse questions of political economy. But at home, or when they return from Congress, they have negroes to fan them asleep. But a Pennsylvania, a New York, an Ohio, or a western Virginia statesman, though far inferior in logic, metaphysics, and rhetoric to an old Virginia statesman, has this advantage, that when he returns home he takes off his coat and takes hold of the plow. This gives him bone and muscle, sir, and preserves his republican principles pure and uncontaminated.

So long as free land exists, the opportunity for a competency exists, and economic power secures political power. But the democracy born of free land, strong in selfishness and individualism, intolerant of administrative experience and education, and pressing individual liberty beyond its proper bounds, has its dangers as well as its benefits. Individualism in America has allowed a laxity in regard to governmental affairs which has rendered possible the spoils system and all the manifest evils that follow from the lack of a highly developed civic spirit. In this connection may be noted also the influence of frontier conditions in permitting lax business honor, inflated paper currency and wild-cat banking. The colonial and revolutionary frontier was the region whence emanated many of the worst forms of an evil currency. The West in the War of 1812 repeated the phenomenon on the frontier of that day, while the speculation and wild-cat banking of the period of the crisis of 1837 occurred on the new frontier belt of the next tier of States. Thus each one of the periods of lax financial integrity coincides with periods when a new set of frontier communities had arisen, and coincides in area with these successive frontiers, for the most part. The recent Populist agitation is a case in point. Many a State that now declines any connection with the tenets of the Populists, itself adhered to such ideas in an earlier stage of the development of the State. A primitive society can hardly be expected to show the intelligent appreciation of the complexity of business interests in a developed society. The continual recurrence of these areas of paper-money agitation is another evidence that the frontier can be isolated and studied as a factor in American history of the highest importance.

The East has always feared the result of an unregulated advance of the frontier, and has tried to check and guide it. The English authorities would have checked settlement at the headwaters of the Atlantic tributaries and allowed the "savages to enjoy their deserts in quiet lest the peltry trade should decrease." This called out Burke's splendid protest:

If you stopped your grants, what would be the consequence? The people would occupy without grants. They have already so occupied in many places. You can not station garrisons in every part of these deserts. If you drive the people from one place, they will carry on their annual tillage and remove with their flocks and herds to another. Many of the people in the back settlements are already little attached to particular situations. Already they have topped the Appalachian Mountains. From thence they behold before them an immense plain, one vast, rich, level meadow; a square of five hundred miles. Over this they would wander without a possibility of restraint; they would change their manners with their habits of life; would soon forget a government by which they were disowned; would become hordes of English Tartars; and, pouring down upon your unfortified frontiers a fierce and irresistible cavalry, become masters of your governors and your counselers, your collectors and comptrollers, and of all the slaves that adhered to them. Such would, and in no long time must, be the effect of attempting to forbid as a crime and to suppress as an evil the command and blessing of Providence, "Increase and multiply." Such would be the happy result of an endeavor to keep as a lair of wild beasts that earth which God, by an express charter, has given to the children of men.

But the English Government was not alone in its desire to limit the advance of the frontier and guide its destinies. Tidewater Virginia and South Carolina gerrymandered those colonies to insure the dominance of the coast in their legislatures. Washington desired to settle a State at a time in the Northwest; Jefferson would reserve from settlement the territory of his Louisiana Purchase north of the thirty-second parallel, in order to offer it to the Indians in exchange for their settlements east of the Mississippi. "When we shall be full on this side," he writes, "we may lay off a range of States on the western bank from the head to the mouth, and so range after range, advancing compactly as we multiply." Madison went so far as to argue to the French minister that the United States had no interest in seeing population extend itself on the right bank of the Mississippi, but should rather fear it. When the Oregon question was under debate, in 1824, Smyth, of Virginia, would draw an unchangeable line for the limits of the United States at the outer limit of two tiers of States beyond the Mississippi, complaining that the seaboard States were being drained of the flower of their population by the bringing of too much land into market. Even Thomas Benton, the man of widest views of the destiny of the West, at this stage of his career declared that along the ridge of the Rocky mountains "the western limits of the Republic should be drawn, and the statue of the fabled god Terminus should be raised upon its highest peak, never to be thrown down." But the attempts to limit the boundaries, to restrict land sales and settlement, and to deprive the West of its share of political power were all in vain. Steadily the frontier of settlement advanced and carried with it individualism, democracy, and nationalism, and powerfully affected the East and the Old World.

The most effective efforts of the East to regulate the frontier came through its educational and religious activity, exerted by interstate migration and by organized societies. Speaking in 1835, Dr. Lyman Beecher declared: "It is equally plain that the religious and political destiny of our nation is to be decided in the West," and he pointed out that the population of the West "is assembled from all the States of the Union and from all the nations of Europe, and is rushing in like the waters of the flood, demanding for its moral pres-

ervation the immediate and universal action of those institutions which discipline the mind and arm the conscience and the heart. And so various are the opinions and habits, and so recent and imperfect is the acquaintance, and so sparse are the settlements of the West, that no homogeneous public sentiment can be formed to legislate immediately into being the requisite institutions. And yet they are all needed immediately in their utmost perfection and power. A nation is being 'born in a day.' ... But what will become of the West if her prosperity rushes up to such a majesty of power, while those great institutions linger which are necessary to form the mind and the conscience and the heart of that vast world. It must not be permitted. ... Let no man at the East quiet himself and dream of liberty, whatever may become of the West. . . . Her destiny is our destiny."

With the appeal to the conscience of New England, he adds appeals to her fears lest other religious sects anticipate her own. The New England preacher and school-teacher left their mark on the West. The dread of Western emancipation from New England's political and economic control was paralleled by her fears lest the West cut loose from her religion. Commenting in 1850 on reports that settlement was rapidly extending northward in Wisconsin, the editor of the *Home Missionary* writes: "We scarcely know whether to rejoice or mourn over this extension of our settlements. While we sympathize in whatever tends to increase the physical resources and prosperity of our country, we can not forget that with all these dispersions into remote and still remoter corners of the land the supply of the means of grace is becoming relatively less and less." Acting in accordance with such ideas, home missions were established and Western colleges were erected. As seaboard cities like Philadelphia, New York, and Baltimore strove for the mastery of Western trade, so the various denominations strove for the possession of the West. Thus an intellectual stream from New England sources fertilized the West. Other sections sent their missionaries; but the real struggle was between sects. The contest for power and the expansive tendency furnished to the various sects by the existence of a moving frontier must have had important results on the character of religious organization in the United States. The multiplication of rival churches in the little frontier towns had deep and lasting social effects. The religious aspects of the frontier make a chapter in our history which needs study.

From the conditions of frontier life came intellectual traits of profound importance. The works of travelers along each frontier from colonial days onward describe certain common traits, and these traits have, while softening down, still persisted as survivals in the place of their origin, even when a higher social organization succeeded. The result is that to the frontier the American intellect owes its striking characteristics. That coarseness and strength combined with acuteness and inquisitiveness; that practical, inventive turn of mind, quick to find expedients; that masterful grasp of material things, lacking in the artistic but powerful to effect great ends; that restless, nervous energy; that dominant individualism, working for good and for evil, and withal that buoyancy and exuberance which comes with freedom—these are traits of the frontier, or traits called out elsewhere because of the existence of the frontier.

Since the days when the fleet of Columbus sailed into the waters of the New World, America has been another name for opportunity, and the people of the United States have taken their tone from the incessant expansion which has not only been open but has even been forced upon them. He would be a rash prophet who should assert that the expansive character of American life has now entirely ceased. Movement has been its dominant fact, and, unless this training has no effect upon a people, the American energy will continually demand a wider field for its exercise. But never again will such gifts of free land offer themselves. For a moment, at the frontier, the bonds of custom are broken and unrestraint is triumphant. There is not *tabula rasa*. The stubborn American environment is there with its imperious summons to accept its conditions; the inherited ways of doing things are also there; and yet, in spite of environment, and in spite of custom, each frontier did indeed furnish a new field of opportunity, a gate of escape from the bondage of the past; and freshness, and confidence, and scorn of older society, impatience of its restraints and its ideas, and indifference to its lessons, have accompanied the frontier. What the Mediterranean Sea was to the Greeks, breaking the bond of custom, offering new experiences, calling out new institutions and activities, that, and more, the ever retreating frontier has been to the United States directly, and to the nations of Europe more remotely. And now, four centuries from the discovery of America, at the end of a hundred years of life under the Constitution, the frontier has gone, and with its going has closed the first period of American history.

Richard Hofstadter, "Turner and the Frontier Myth", *The American Scholar,* vol. XVIII, (1949), pp. 433, 435-443. Reprinted from THE AMERICAN SCHOLAR, Volume 18, Number 4, Autumn 1949, by permission of the Publisher and the Author.

The Frontier Thesis Under Attack

American historical writing in the past century has produced two major theories or models of understanding, the economic interpretation of politics associated with Charles A. Beard, and the frontier interpretation of American development identified with Frederick Jackson Turner. Both views have had a pervasive influence upon American thinking, but Beard himself felt that Turner's original essay on the frontier had "a more profound influence on thought about American history than any other essay or volume ever written on the subject." It is the frontier thesis that has embodied the predominant American view of the American past. . . .

. . . the strength of Turner's thesis, which had an influence extending far beyond the historical profession, rested upon the appeal of the frontier to the American imagination. Some of its initial impetus no doubt came from the Western agrarian revolt of the nineties; before long, however, it lost its vague Populist edge and became identified with a complacent nationalist

romanticism, as congenial to the Eastern mind as to the Western. The notion of an aggressive pioneering national spirit nurtured by repeated exposure to primitive conditions became a means to national self-glorification. Appealing to the common desire to root native history in native soil, the Turner thesis sanctioned the tendency to shrink from comparative reference to the experience of other peoples. It also satisfied the desire, common in the age of Progressivism and muckraking, to have a "materialistic" interpretation of history that did not risk the ideological pitfalls of the class struggle idea. Happily it was vague enough to be used in different, often opposite ways. Conservatives could point to the value of the hardihood and rugged individualism allegedly derived from the frontier heritage. Those who wanted to justify a "progressive" departure could answer that the frontier period, after all, *was* over. As late as 1932, in his memorable Commonwealth Club address, Franklin D. Roosevelt utilized the Turnerian inheritance as the historical rationale of the New Deal: "Our last frontier has long since been reached, and there is practically no more free land . . . . There is no safety valve in the form of a western prairie to which those thrown out of work by the Eastern machines can go for a new start."

Again, the frontier myth has been accepted even by critics of American culture who have repudiated its provincial nationalism and isolationism, and espoused antithetical values. During the 1920's, when the dominant mood of American intellectuals was one of estrangement from their country, the frontier was assigned a prominent place—along with puritanism, pragmatism and the commercial spirit — among the forces that had corrupted American culture. In Van Wyck Brook's biography of Mark Twain, for example, the frontier became an almost demonic force that had barbarized, cramped and distorted Twain's genius.

The Great Depression of the thirties brought a revaluation of the frontier myth. Obviously, the depression was world-wide, and the central problems confronting the United States were those of the world at large. The feeling that the Republic was not what it used to be led to the suspicion that it never had been. Re-examination of old clichés was encouraged by the new popularity of Marxism, with its emphasis upon classes rather than sections or areas. It was also encouraged by a rising interest in the history of ideas: no one who focused upon ideas and their influence in American history could hold very long to the notion that the main stream of American ideas and habits of behavior moved from West to East. During the last fifteen years, more and more historians have become circumspect about the frontier process, and critical writing on the Turner thesis has become a prominent feature of professional periodicals. The Turner thesis is increasingly viewed as an inadequate concept with which to "explain" American development, and by some even as a positive hindrance to sound inquiry into the American past.

The initial plausibility of the Turner thesis lies in the patent fact that no nation could spend more than a century developing an immense continental empire without being deeply affected by it. Few critics question the great importance of the inland empire, or that Turner originally performed a service for historical writing by directing attention to it. Many accept Turner's emphasis on the frontier as one of several valid but limited perspectives on American history. But it has been forcefully denied that the frontier deserves any

special pre-eminence among several major factors in "explaining" American development. The question has also been raised (and frequently answered in the negative) whether Turner analyzed the frontier process itself clearly or correctly.

It became plain, as new thought and research was brought to bear upon the problem, that the frontier theory, as an analytic device, was a blunt instrument. The terms with which the Turnerians dealt —the frontier, the West, individualism, the American character—were vague at the outset, and as the Turnerian exposition developed, they did not receive increasingly sharp definition. Precisely because Turner defined the frontier so loosely ("the term," he said, "is an elastic one"), he could claim so much for it. At times he referred to the frontier literally as the edge of the settled territory having a population density of two to the square mile. But frequently he identified "the frontier" and "the West," so that areas actually being settled could be referred to as frontier. At times he spoke of both the "frontier" and the "west" not as places or areas, but as a social process: "The West, at bottom, is a form of society rather than an area." When this definition is followed to its logical conclusion, the development of American society is "explained" by a "form of society"—certainly a barren tautology. Again, at times Turner assimilated such natural resources as coal, oil, timber, to the idea of "the West"; in this way the truism that natural wealth has an important bearing upon a nation's development and characteristics was subtly absorbed into the mystique of the frontier and took on the guise of a major insight.

However, the central weakness of Turner's thesis was in its intellectual isolationism. Having committed himself to an initial overemphasis on the uniqueness of

given to unprincipled political agitation

the historical development of the United States, Turner compounded the error by overemphasizing the frontier as a factor in this development. The obsession with uniqueness, the subtly demagogic stress on "the truly American part of our history," diverted the attention of historical scholarship from the possibilities of comparative social history; it offered no opportunity to explain why so many features of American development—for example, the rise of democracy in the nineteenth century—were parallel to changes in countries that did not have a contiguous frontier. Historians were encouraged to omit a host of basic influences common to both American and Western European development—the influence of Protestantism and the Protestant ethic, the inheritance from English republicanism, the growth of industrialism and urbanism. More than this, factors outside the frontier process that contributed to the singularity of American history were skipped over: the peculiar American federal structure, the slave system and the Southern caste complex, immigration and ethnic heterogeneity, the unusually capitalistic and speculative character of American agriculture, the American inheritance of *laissez faire*. The interpretation seems particularly weak for the corporate-industrial phase of American history that followed the Civil War. Indeed, if the historian's range of vision had to be limited to one explanatory idea, as it fortunately does not, one could easily argue that the business corporation was the dominant factor in American development during this period.

As a form of geographical determinism, the frontier interpretation is vulnerable on still another ground. If the frontier alone was a self-sufficient source of democracy and individualism, whatever the institutions and ideas the frontiersmen brought with them, frontiers elsewhere ought to have had a similar effect. The early frontier of seignorial French Canada, the South American frontier, and the Siberian frontier should have fostered democracy and individualism. The frontier should have forged the same kind of democracy when planters came to Mississippi as when yeomen farmers came to Illinois. Turner's dictum, "American democracy came out of the American forest," proved to be a questionable improvement upon the notion of his predecessors that it came out of the German forest. Plainly the whole complex of institutions, habits and ideas that men brought to the frontier was left out of his formula, and it was these things, not bare geography, that had been decisive. Turner's analysis, as George Warren Pierson aptly put it, hung too much on real estate, not enough on a state of mind.

If American democracy originated on the frontier or in the West, it ought to be possible to trace successive waves of democratic sentiment and practice from West to East. But when the periods of democratic advance are examined, no such process can be found. After almost two centuries of life under frontier conditions in colonial America, democracy had made little headway; society was still highly stratified and the suffrage was restricted. The American Revolution gave a considerable impetus to democratic developments, but it is not easy to assign any priority in the Revolution to the Western or frontier population. Eastern merchants took a notable part in the pre-Revolutionary agitation—as did urban mobs and eastern farmers, who also contributed much to the fighting. The ideas that were used to justify the Revolution and later adapted to the democratic cause were not generated in the wilds around Kaskaskia, but derived from the English republicanism of the seventeenth century—notably, of course, from Locke.

Both great periods of the upsurge of democracy in nineteenth century America, the Jeffersonian and the Jacksonian, are far more intelligible in terms of social classes than of the East or the West, if only because both had so much strength in Eastern and urban areas. Jeffersonianism, which was strong among seaboard slaveholders and in many of the towns, is somewhat more comprehensible as a movement of agrarians against capitalists, than as a movement of the frontier against the East. The age of Jackson has been held up more than any other as an example of the democratic spirit of the frontier in action. Yet Arthur M. Schlesinger, Jr.'s recent study of that era does not employ the frontier thesis, and it is highly successful in asserting the crucial role of Eastern Jacksonians. With the exception of a few scattered local areas, many of which were in the West, Jackson swept the country when he was elected in 1828, and Jacksonian democracy can best be understood as a nationwide movement, supported by parts of the planting, farming, laboring and entrepreneurial classes.

It may be conceded to the Turnerians that the West occasionally gave democratic ideas an especially favorable area for operation—but it should be conceded in return that these ideas were generated in the Eastern United States and in Western civilization as a whole. By and large, Western settlers appear to have been more imitative than original in their political institutions. The case for the West as a special source of individualism is similarly mixed. It is possible to point to a fairly strong stream of Western demands for governmental interference of one kind or another from the days of internal improvements to the age of railroad regulation, parity and price supports.

One of the most criticized aspects of Turner's conception of American history, the so-called safety-valve thesis, maintains that the availability of free land as a refuge for the oppressed and discontented has alleviated American social conflicts, minimized industrial strife, and contributed to the backwardness of the American labor movement. As Turner expressed it, the American worker was never compelled to accept inferior wages because he could "with a slight effort" reach free country and set up in farming. "Whenever social conditions tended to crystallize in the East, whenever capital tended to impede the freedom of the mass, there was this gate of escape to the free conditions of the frontier," where "free lands promoted individualism, economic equality, freedom to rise, democracy."

The expression "free land" is itself misleading. Land was relatively cheap in the United States during the nineteenth century, but the difference between free land and cheap land was crucial. Up to 1820 the basic price of land was $2.00 an acre, and for forty years afterward it was $1.25. Slight as it may seem, this represented a large sum to the Eastern worker, whose wage was generally about $1.00 per day. Economic historians have estimated that during the 1850's, $1,000 represented a fairly typical cost for setting up a farm on virgin prairie land, or buying an established one; and the cost of transporting a worker's family from, say, Massachusetts or New York to Illinois or Iowa was a serious additional burden. Farming, moreover, is no enterprise for an amateur, nor one at which he has a good chance of success. The value of "free land" in alleviating distress has been challenged by several writers who have pointed out that periods of depression were the very periods when it was most difficult for the Eastern worker to move. Scattered instances of working-class migration to the West can be pointed to, but detailed studies of the origins of migrants have failed to substantiate the Turner thesis.

The Homestead Act of 1862, which was designed to give family-size farms (up to 160 acres) to bona fide settlers, does not seem to have changed the picture drastically. It suggests an era of great bounty, which turns out upon examination to be illusory. By 1890, after a generation of hectic national growth, only about 372,000 farms had been entered and kept under the Homestead Act. In the meantime, about 180,000,000 acres had been given by state and federal governments to the railroad companies, who held some of it and disposed of much of it at a considerable markup. Much of the best land was also withheld for sale by the government—and it usually went at prices well above the minimum of $2.50 an acre. Out of every six or seven acres that the government had given up by 1900, only one had gone to homesteaders. Unfortunately, the showing of the homesteaders was poorer than this figure indicates, for not all of them were legitimate. The administration of the Homestead Act was so hopelessly bad that scores upon scores of speculators, using dummies to masquerade their entries, secured parcels of land often running into tens of thousands of acres, and these lands passed into the hands of farmers only after the speculators had taken their cut. As Roy M. Robbins remarks in his study of *Our Landed Heritage*, the period was one in which "the corporate and capitalistic forces had gained complete ascendancy over the settler as the pioneering agent."

By 1900, 35.5 per cent of the farms in this nation of "free land" were operated by tenants.

In spite of these criticisms, something has been salvaged from the safety-valve thesis. Although the West was not filled up by workers moving in time of depression, the evidence indicates that it was filled up by farmers moving in times of prosperity. In this way the presence of available land is generally conceded to have played an important part in relieving *rural* discontent—the dominant form of discontent in nineteenth-century America. And it presumably had a roundabout effect on the urban situation. In Europe the city was the characteristic haven of the surplus farm population. Insofar as the comparable surplus population of the United States took another choice, migration further West, instead of swelling the ranks of the urban working class, there may have been an indirect operation of the safety valve. Its magnitude and importance are uncertain.

But the safety-valve principle also operated in reverse, and it is a signal weakness of the Turner version that it concentrates attention on the less significant of the two population movements. The dominant tide of migration from 1860 to 1900 was not from East to West, but from the farm to the city. In forty years the farm population grew by about nine million, while the non-farm population grew by almost thirty-six million. It was the cities that received not only the bulk of the immigration from abroad, but also the bulk of the surplus farm population. This flow of the farm surplus to the cities may have been intermittent, broken and partially reversed during depression periods, but its net size is undeniable. Fred A. Shannon has estimated that "at least twenty farmers moved to town for each industrial laborer who moved to the land, and ten sons of farmers went to the city for each one who became the owner of a new farm anywhere in the nation." It is possible that the acuteness of the agrarian unrest of the 1890's can be traced in some part to the fact that the pace of city growth had slackened off, and that this safety valve for the farmers was beginning to fail. At any rate, to follow the Turner emphasis upon "free land" as a primary outlet, and to ignore the migration to the cities, is to perpetuate a major distortion of American history.

Finally, Turner acknowledged but failed to see the full importance for his thesis of the fact that the United States not only had a frontier but was a frontier —a major outlet for the countries of Western Europe during the nineteenth century. From 1820 to 1929, the total European emigration to the United States was more than 37,500,000—a number only a million short of the entire population of the United States in 1870. In one decade alone, 1901-1910, 8,795,000 people came from Europe. If Europe shared to such a major extent in this safety-valve economy, its uniqueness for American development must be considerably modified. The mingling of peoples

that took place in the United States must be placed alongside the presence of "free land" in explaining American development; the closure of the American gates after the First World War becomes an historical event of broader significance than the disappearance of the frontier line in 1890. And the facts of immigration probably provide a better key to the character of the American labor movement than any speculation about the effects of "free land" upon workers who could not reach it.

It should be added, in justice to Turner, that his historical writing was better than his frontier thesis, and not least because he regularly made use in practice of historical factors which were not accounted for in his theory. Although he often stated his ideas with the vigor of a propagandist, his was not a doctrinaire mind, and he was willing, as time went on, to add new concepts to his analysis. In 1925 he went so far as to admit the need of "an urban reinterpretation of our history." "I hope," he frequently said, "to propogate inquiry, not to produce disciples." In fact he did both, but he propogated less inquiry among his disciples than among his critics.

Fred Landon, *Western Ontario and the American Frontier,* Carleton Library No. 34, (Toronto, McClelland and Stewart Limited, 1967), pp. xiii-xx. Reprinted by permission of The Canadian Publishers, McClelland and Stewart Limited and the Author's Estate.

The History of Upper Canada in Frontier Perspective

This is not a history of Western Ontario but is, as its title suggests, a study of the influences exerted upon this particular area of old Upper Canada (Ontario) by neighbouring American communities. In general, it is the period preceding Confederation which has been examined since, by the time the British North American provinces had achieved a partial federation, the American frontier was a thousand miles farther to the West. Comparisons or contrasts with the earlier American frontier were no longer valid. . . .

In the decade of the 1850's when John A. Macdonald spoke of the voters in the Western Ontario of his day as "Yankees and Covenanters, the most yeasty and unsafe of populations" he was not the first, and certainly not the last, to express such a political judgment. Western Ontario was then, and continued to be, an area marked by political uneasiness and an uncertainty as to where its support would go in any particular political situation. . . .

When Macdonald used the term "Yankees and Covenanters" he was incidentally recalling the racial origin of the earlier settlers in this area: Loyalists, driven from their homes in New York State by their support of the English cause during the Revolution; the land-hungry American immigrants who entered Upper Canada at the invitation of Governor John Graves Simcoe; and Scottish immigrants who arrived soon after the close of the War of 1812 and occupied land in the western townships.

The characteristics of these elements have been retained by their descendants. The American strain in the population is still alert to any business opportunity, while the Scottish element has shown remarkable tenacity in holding on to its land. Even today many farms, in Elgin County for example, remain in the hands of descendants of the original owners. Moreover, these Scottish Canadians have preserved their racial habits and way of life to a remarkable degree. . . . However, both American and Scottish elements had one common characteristic in Macdonald's day, namely, their leaning toward Reform principles. It was their adoption of "Clear Grit" ideas in the fifties that stirred Macdonald's ire. Their demand for a widely extended suffrage, the secret ballot and a broad extension of the elective principle indicated their belief that the United States represented the ultimate form of democracy. One man was as good as another. This phase of Canadian politics corresponded to Jacksonian democracy or the later Lincoln republicanism. This challenge to Macdonald's political views came from a characteristically agrarian community. Geography and the historical background combined to explain its uneasy, restless disposition.

Colonel John Graves Simcoe, the first governor of Upper Canada, was an admirer of monarchy, aristocracy and the established Church of England. He aimed to set up in the Canadian wilderness a replica of these three institutions which he regarded as the most perfect that man's mind had ever conceived. Their acceptance and adoption might, he believed, lead to the reunion of the separated states with the mother country. To this end he welcomed settlers from the republic and granted them land on their taking the oath of allegiance. The writings of British travellers who visited the province before the War of 1812 abound with references to the "Yankee" character of the common people and the prevalence of "Yankee" manners and habits of speech, even among those of other than American origin.

Governor Simcoe might dislike the "Yankee" twang and the crude manners of his American settlers but he must have known and appreciated the fact that they were experienced North American farmers. To some observers their methods seemed inefficient and shiftless but their energy and practical ability were quite as noticeable. The American settler knew how to clear the heavily wooded land, build himself a log house and barn, harness any nearby watercourse and provide for himself and neighbours a sawmill or a grist-mill. He was so adept at making satisfactory tools that American scythes had a distinct superiority over those brought from abroad.

Simcoe must also have realized that the American immigrants, whether Loyalist or non-Loyalist, had recently passed through a great social, economic and political revolution which they had heard discussed in its every aspect. Whether they approved or disapproved of the outcome, they had been subjected to such unsettling ideas as the equality of men, freedom of religion and hostility to any special privi-

lege. These liberalizing concepts, North American in character, permeated the thinking of the Upper Canadian community and contributed to the unrest and desire for change which affected the province during its first half-century.

Simcoe's admiration for monarchy did not greatly trouble the American immigrants, many of whom had earlier lived under King George III. Nor was the concept of a republic as yet deeply rooted in their minds. With the prospect of ownership of good land it mattered little to them whether they were under a royal governor or under the appointed representative of the republic. As for aristocracy, they were fortunately spared its creation. Simcoe could not find enough "gentlemen" in the province to set up an elite class on the British model.

Much more dangerous for the future peace of the province was the claim, accepted by Simcoe and his successors, that the Church of England was "established" in Upper Canada just as it was in England. Establishment meant financial support, a close connection with government and a primacy over other church bodies. This conflicted with American ideas of freedom of religion and special privilege. It became one of the basic grievances of the Rebellion era and continued to bedevil provincial politics even beyond that date.

For more than a generation after its official entry into Upper Canada the Church of England was a stranger to the scattered settlers. Its growth in numbers and influence was retarded by the pioneer's dislike of ritual and by its claims to be established. On the other hand, the missionaries sent in by American Protestant bodies, Methodist, Presbyterian and Baptist, more truly met the religious needs of the province. Moving about on horseback, they reached the population as no settled ministry could have done. American settlers also had a broad concept of what was meant by freedom of religion— not merely the right of believers to worship in their own manner without interference of any kind but also the right of the individual to change from one church body to another for any reason that might appear good in his eyes. This American freedom of church affiliation contrasted sharply with the lifelong adherence to one belief commonly observed in older lands. Travellers in Upper Canada frequently noted this early version of modern ecumenicism.

When war came in 1812, disturbing the hitherto peaceful relations between Upper Canada and the United States, it was inevitable that the province would be the chief battleground. With a population of little more than 100,000, four-fifths of whom were Americans, the government had reason for worry and the American settlers were themselves placed in a difficult situation. Some left the province and went back to the United States, others were expelled by the authorities, and a few were openly traitorous. There was disloyalty even in the Assembly and two members were formally expelled in 1814. Three years of war left deep feelings of resentment against the United States in the minds of Upper Canadians and the process of Americanization received a severe check.

The reaction to peace when the Treaty of Ghent was signed differed as between the antagonists. In the United States it did much to dispel the lingering colonial complex and uncertainty in foreign affairs. Freed from external entanglements, the republic now turned to the opening up and development of its West. Six new states entered the Union in the first seven years after the war, five of them carved from frontier territory. By 1820 the new West had 27 per cent of the country's total population. Upper Canada, on the other hand, suffering considerable material damage in a war for which it could see no reason and which it had certainly not itself provoked, was now in a mood to demand reform of abuses under which it had been suffering. Political groups began to emerge. Further immigration from the United States had been forbidden at the end of the war and Canadian businessmen were aggrieved over the drying up of land sales. Of the great trek to the American West only a trickle came into Upper Canada though this trickle was of a superior type, including as it did men with capital and technical skills, also professional men such as doctors who had hitherto been few in number. The majority of the physicians entering Upper Canada at this time had received their training at the Fairfield Medical School in Herkimer County, New York State.

The outbreak of political violence in 1837-38 registered the pent-up feelings of a considerable element among the common people. It was really an epoch in the struggle between the democratic forces of the Upper Canada frontier and the official effort to impose a class society and a privileged established church. Unfortunately, the American people in their own land largely mistook the character of the uprising, regarding it as a definite struggle for independence. This mistaken idea led to the rise of "Patriot" movements in the mid-western states which by invasions and raids along the border sought to free the "enslaved Canadians." Frequent alarms, necessitating the rousing of the militia and other defensive measures, disquieted the province for more than a year.

The background for the widespread unrest in the province lay in the abuses of the Family Compact at the capital and lesser local compacts elsewhere, and in the claims of the state-supported church. Permeating all was the democracy introduced by the early settlers. These factors acting together produced a Reform party after the War of 1812 which battled for its claims in the Assembly and on the hustings at election times. What is not always realized is that there was no general uprising in Upper Canada. Though eastern districts were subjected to "Patriot" invasion they themselves had little part in the attempt to overthrow the provincial government at York. In the London District there was a secondary uprising under Dr. Charles Duncombe while elsewhere unrest showed itself in forms ranging from plain fist fighting to the passing of mere resolutions or refusals even to protest. Lesser known features of the uprising were the arrests and imprisonment of hundreds of persons against most of whom no charge could be proven, senseless militia raids on Quaker settlements and the use of Indians in tracking down Duncombe's scattered contingent. Canadian-American relations were much worsened by the uprisings in the British provinces, partly because of the widespread suspicion that the Washington administration condoned the "Patriot" threats and invasions. The inheritance of anti-American prejudice from the War of 1812 was added to and strengthened by the events of 1837-38. On the other hand Upper Canada gained a large accession of British population during the twenties and early thirties when the British government was able to release the masses of people carefully conserved for "cannon fodder" during the Napoleonic Wars. The province took on a more British colouring as the American tinge faded. . . .

Closely related to the American religious ideas and practices which entered Upper Canada in its pioneer era was a later contagion of interest in the humanitarian and moral reform movements which agitated the republic from the thirties. In the northern states almost every department of life was being examined and given a new evaluation. The old Puritan theology was fading away and in its place there was a rising interest in such matters as temperance, prison reform, care of the insane, labour conditions, education and anti-slavery. National societies interested in such fields were increasing their memberships by thousands yearly.

Temperance was one of the first of such moral issues to enter Upper Canada and received enthusiastic Methodist support. In the early thirties there were twenty such societies with a membership of ten thousand. Better treatment of the insane and prisoners in jails had been proposed as early as 1836 by Dr. Charles Duncombe after a visit to New York State but not until 1850 were his recommendations carried out. His ideas on prison reform received attention earlier when an experienced American prison administrator was appointed to supervise the first provincial prison established at Kingston.

The anti-slavery movement in the United States was of particular interest for Western Ontario because, ever since the War of 1812, fugitives from the Southern slave states had been making their way to freedom in the province. When Congress passed the infamous Fugitive Slave Act in 1850 the Negro migration to Upper Canada became a torrent and friends of the fugitives at once organized the Anti-slavery Society of Canada. This body functioned until the Civil War ended and slavery in the republic disappeared.

Public education, so important for the welfare of any people, made little advance before the period of the rebellion. Governor Simcoe had dreamed of a university but thought little of the education of the children of common folk. Nor did the Assembly produce any worthwhile measures. As for the Church of England, it continued to seek full control of education. No real advance came until 1844 when the Rev. Egerton Ryerson, Methodist leader and educator, was appointed Superintendent of Education for Upper Canada. Ryerson, who was well acquainted with United States educational practices, made his investigations chiefly in the British Isles and in European countries. His findings were embodied in the Common School Act of 1846. From the United States was drawn the guiding principle that every child was entitled to an education provided by the state. This aim, Ryerson felt, could only be realized through the provision of well-qualified teachers, suitable buildings and equipment, regular inspection and uniform textbooks. Ryerson's inclusion in his system of various American ideas was questioned but when secondary education was also established in 1853 it was noticeably modelled on the American example. Ryerson's findings and methods continued to dominate the education of the province for the better part of the next century.

The fifties and early sixties saw the development of the movement earlier suggested by Lord Durham of a union of all the British provinces in North America. Canadian historians have at times seemed reluctant to admit that the United States could have had anything to do with bringing about Confederation. Today, however, it is generally recognized that fear of the course the United States might follow at the end of its civil struggle was probably one of the greatest influences in bringing the British provinces together in a new nation, the Dominion of Canada.

Canadian Historians Debate the Turner Thesis

A.R.M. Lower, "Some Neglected Aspects of Canadian History", *Canadian Historical Association Annual Report,* (1929), pp. 65-68. Reprinted by permission of the Author.

Much has been written about the picturesque side of pioneer days. Everyone knows that the settler, leaving wife and children in a rude log cabin, was accustomed to trudge through the almost pathless woods for many miles with a heavy sack of wheat upon his back, and so on. But the general principles which underlay the whole process have not as yet been much canvassed. Has there been a frontier psychology in Canada as there was in the United States? Was the attack on the wilderness methodical despite its seeming confusion? Did certain classes of persons take upon themselves certain classes of work? Maria Chapdelaine's father with his self-appointed task of clearing a farm and then moving on again to the wilderness to do the same thing

over again represented a type whose existence was well-defined on the American frontier. Did it exist in Canada? Hémon's novel is one bit of evidence showing that it did. There are doubtless others which would establish the point. Did the newly arrived person push on out to the frontier or did the biologic law of dispersion hold good, that law which teaches that it is the edge which moves and the old ground that is occupied by later comers?

In the United States, the innate genius of the Anglo-Saxon for self-government was illustrated over and over again as the frontier rolled westward by innumerable duplications of the Mayflower compact. Did anything of the sort occur in Canada or did government tread so closely on the heels of the settler that local arrangements were not necessary? If so, what has been the effect on our population of the orderliness of our development? Has it robbed us of some initiative? Or is our cautiousness a racial trait, to hazard a guess, Scottish in origin?

Both in Canada and the United States, democracy has been a condition, not a theory. It has been the spontaneous product of the frontier and the forest. In both countries it has had its battle to fight with the representatives of an older order of things. In the United States it had to contend with the propertied classes of the east and in Canada with propertied and privileged family compacts. Of the two survivals of aristocracy, the Canadian version was probably the more invidious and certainly the more petty. Not long after Andrew Jackson scored his ringing victory of 1828, Mackenzie led his guerilla raid against a foe akin to his. While other champions of the new order duly appeared, its victory in Canada was not as complete as in the United States and as a result there has always been an aristocratic tinge to our politics—or at least to our political system—not observable in those of the republic. Even if we would—which God forbid!—we could not have a party convention such as the Democrats held in 1924.

Leadership and direction, the "tone" of life, have in Canada, tended to come from above, that is, directly or indirectly from English aristocratic tradition, the Americans, on the other hand, while not exactly getting these things from below, have at least made them up as they went along. The result is a fairly considerable difference in the political and social atmosphere of the two countries, a difference which has been reflected in laws and institutions. In Canada, for example, democratic theory has never gone to such extreme limits as to bring about universal municipal suffrage and to-day, in most provinces, only ratepayers may vote on money by-laws. In the United States, the elected council reigns supreme. [Again] . . .

. . . it has been much easier to "close" a profession in Canada than in the United States, which land in these matters has acted consistently on its principles of equality. Here is a field, the nice balance between the natural tendencies of a new community and its inherited influences, which could be richly worked.

*   *   *

John L. McDougall, "The Frontier School and Canadian History", *Canadian Historical Association Annual Report,* (1929), pp. 121-125.

No early settlement in North America was more thoroughly exposed to all the influences of the frontier than that of the French Canadians in the St. Lawrence Valley. All the frontier influences beat upon them with unparalleled force. Their trade routes to the west by way of the St. Lawrence and the Ottawa, to the north by way of the Saint Maurice and the Saguenay, and to the south by the Richelieu, were infinitely better than those open to the English speaking colonists to the south, and they showed very early how ready they were to make use of them. The early explorations of Etienne Brulé, Champlain, Jean Nicolet, and others, provide an enviable record, and they were only the first fore-runners of a long line of great discoveries culminating in the great work of La Verendrye who may himself have merely consolidated the achievements of earlier and unknown traders. By the support given to the Huron and Algonquin tribes they won for themselves the enmity of the Iroquois and were periodically under attack for nearly a century. It was not until the treaty of Montreal (1701) that the peak of danger was passed. Until that time the colony was exposed to and suffered cruelly from all the horrors of Indian warfare. Easy communications work both ways and time after time the Iroquois carried war into the very heart of the colony. In defence and in retaliation the French adopted Indian methods of warfare and became highly expert in them. Their capacity for canoe travel is traditional. Under such conditions the more adventurous spirits gravitate to the frontier, so sheltering the more sedentary and peaceful. That tendency was in part counteracted by the corvée which acted as a form of conscription. As the great scheme of hemming in the English east of the Ohio and the Mississippi developed, with its incessant need for men, this corvée pressed more and more heavily upon Quebec and the chances of escaping its action grew ever slimmer. It can never be said, therefore, that Quebec escaped that baptism into frontier ways which, we are told, so strongly affected America. It was no mere sprinkling but a total and prolonged immersion. Yet despite it all, they created an excessively stable, un-adventurous society. All of it, with the exception of three seigneuries, lay below the first rapids. They recreated upon the banks of the St. Lawrence a replica of the French society which they had left. Nor can it be urged that this was solely, or even primarily, the influence of the form of government. It is perfectly true that government from Versailles lay like a dead hand over every activity of the colony. But that ended in 1763 without making any serious change in the social situation of Quebec. After the Cession, the Scots merchants of Montreal built up their great fur trade with the west but in that activity only one or two French merchant families took part, although the whole trade rested upon an adequate supply of French-Canadian voyageurs. Nor were the voyageurs themselves affected very much by their experiences. Those who came back, melted into the general community.

As time went on, Ontario and the Eastern Townships of Quebec were settled by folk of British stock. The French population grew without spreading beyond the original area until the pressure of population created a serious problem on many seigneuries. In 1829 the Special Committee on Roads and Other Internal Communications reported that "The necessity of forming new settlements becomes more and more pressing for there are parishes in which fathers of families live on mere building lots; — this is a most alarming circumstance because it tends to the rapid introduction of poverty among the agricultural classes." In the 1830's a movement of casual harvest labour to the New Eng-

land States began, but no competent observer ever looked upon this redundant population as forming a reserve of colonizing material. Only those of British stock, it was believed, were ready to face the hardships inevitable in the first years of pioneering. Perhaps the best testimony upon this point is that of C. F. Fournier, the Surveyor. Fournier had been engaged on the request of the Post Office authorities to see if a practicable road could be cut from the Rivière Ouelle to the mouth of the Madawaska. The old Temiscouata portage had never been properly maintained because settlers could not be induced to live along it. He reported in favor of the new route "d'autant plus qu'il est probable qu'un certain Nombre d'emigrés s'y établiraient aussi, qui, comme on est forcé de l'avouer, s'entendent mieux que nos cultivateurs dans les commencemens d'un défrichement d'une terre et sont plus industrieux." . . .

Up to this point, examples have been drawn from the history of French Canada. Before bringing this section to a close I would like to notice two other instances of importance to the point at issue, namely, the history of British Columbia in the decade after 1858 and that of the Yukon after 1898. The great majority of the miners who came in the Fraser River and Cariboo gold rushes were either Americans by birth or had worked in California or in the Inland Empire. The lawlessness in the two latter areas is as much a matter of common knowledge as the relative peace of British Columbia, yet all three areas were raw frontiers, and as if to make the lesson clearer most of the miners who were successful in British Columbia went back to California each winter. The same comparison holds between Alaska and the Yukon after 1898. In view of these facts is it not proper to ask whether the external environment, the frontier, really was the dominant creative force which moulded American life? Would it not be more proper to describe it as a catalyst which set free elements in the American character not present in the same degree in other civilizations? . . .

That is the line of attack which gives the best returns. The distinguishing mark of French Canada is the degree of social cohesion which it possesses. The fur-trader with his word of good lands farther on was dynamite to the American society of his time, he was an alien curiosity in Quebec. To the French-Canadian, living well meant living in community. The Coureurs des Bois were men who had surrendered that right and were more to be pitied for spiritual blindness than to be envied for their greater economic opportunities. The present colonizing activities in Northern Ontario and Quebec, so markedly at variance with the first seventy years of the last century, merely witness to that cohesion. The whole movement was begun by the Church and is carried on by it. It began as a relief movement to the older areas and as a counter-attraction to the mill-towns of New England. Nothing could be farther from the American experience—what is aimed at is not a haphazard response to the call of free land, but a carefully pre-arranged building of new communities. The raw frontier is not something whose passing is regretted as it has been in the United States. It is to be wiped out as soon as possible. Success is attained when the village spire is within the view of every settler and the angelus marks the beginning and the ending of his day.

Certain criticisms of a wider nature must also be urged. What is a frontier? What are natural resources? A moving frontier is in its essence the reverse side of a developing technique of production and transportation. Before one can understand the frontier one must have a working knowledge of the industrial order which created it, its trend and its rate of growth. Natural resources are the creation of this advancing technique and for their development call for enormous supplies of capital. It is immaterial whether that capital is supplied in the form of long-term commercial credits to the early planters and fur-traders or, as in the later period, through loans to the individual states for the building of canals and railways. To draw upon current history, the whole of the gold mining industry in Canada rests on the cyanide process, a product of the last fifty years, while the present activity in prospecting for base metals is the fruit of developments of the last two decades in metallurgical extraction methods and in the aeroplane. And incidentally is not a great deal of the prospecting for copper now going on inside the Arctic circle a reflex of the rise of copper to 18 cents per pound. If, as now seems probable, that metal is to remain above 16 cents for the next five years the frontier is automatically advanced hundreds of miles. It is impossible to take one particular aspect of a broad movement of this kind to the neglect of all others and still hope to give an adequate picture of its causation or of its results.

It may have been fortunate that Professor Turner dismissed French Canada in his original essay in some thirteen lines by saying that it was dominated by its trading frontier while the English colonies were dominated by their farming frontier. One might even go farther and say that it is one of the most fortunate of errors for all concerned. Had he grasped the full significance of the facts which he dismissed so lightly, his essay might have gained in insight but would have lost that priceless certainty which has given to all the workers in the field freedom to devote their whole energies to working up the factual detail without a glimpse of that paralyzing doubt which comes when the adequacy of the basic thesis upon which the whole effort rests is in question. But such a wholesale disregard of pertinent facts cannot be fruitful of sound opinion. And whatever justification there may be for

Professor Turner's thesis as an explanation of American history it could be little short of a calamity if Canadian historians were to attempt to deform the story of our own development to fit the Procustes bed of the frontier theory. One has heard England described as a land where bad German philosophies go when they die. One may at least hope that Canada will not stand in a similar relation to the United States.

A Long View of Canadian History, text of two half-hour programs by Professors Donald Creighton and Paul Fox, CBC Television, June 16th and 30th, 1959, (Toronto, CBC Publications Branch, 1959), pp. 3-6. Reprinted by permission of the Authors.

Alternatives to the Frontier Thesis: Paul Fox Interviews Donald Creighton

FOX: Has the fact that we've had a western frontier in Canada tended to clash with these ideas that we've imported from Europe?

CREIGHTON: I don't think it clashes because I don't think the frontier has been that important in Canadian history. I think the Americans had a frontier. I think they made an enormous amount of it. They have even created an historical theory on it which they call 'The Frontier Thesis' and by that historical theory they ascribe to the frontier the greatest formative influence in American history. I don't think the frontier in Canada has played any such part and I think that however useful the concept may be in the United States, and they are beginning to be a little doubtful about that now there too, it has only a very limited relevance to Canada.

FOX: Would you say, then, that this is another major difference between Canada and the United States?

CREIGHTON: I think it is, yes.

FOX: In other words the frontier has been important in American history but not in Canadian history?

CREIGHTON: I think it has not been as important in Canadian history.

FOX: Just what is this frontier theory?

CREIGHTON: The hither edge of the free land, the constantly expanding frontier of settlement moving into unoccupied regions in a continuous movement from the original hearth of settlement on the Atlantic seaboard.

FOX: And that this provides the dynamism?

CREIGHTON: This provides the dynamism.

FOX: And the democratic ideas?

CREIGHTON: The democratic ideas: equalitarianism, courage, intrepidity, all the rest of it. The whole American epic, almost, derived from the frontier.

FOX: Well, I can think of some intrepid ideas that have come out of our Canadian West.

CREIGHTON: Well, of course the West has been a democratic and dynamic influence in Canadian politics and that is true of the distant past as well as of the present. I mean I think it's true for example, of Upper Canada as well as it is of the Prairie West.

FOX: You mean that at one time Upper Canada was a frontier?

CREIGHTON: Yes. The West, and Canada West, the present Ontario, was *the* West. It created the Clear Grit party and similarly, of course in the Prairie West, western agrarianism has created the Progressive party and also, of course, Social Credit. But I think it's got to be remembered that there are qualifications to this in both cases. I think in the first place that the East had a part to play in the development of several of those movements and I think also they derive some nourishment from ideas imported from overseas; from Chartism, for example, the British radical movement of the 1840's in the nineteenth century, and from the Labour Party in the twentieth century. And, finally, another thing seems important in judging the weight of the significance of the West in Canadian history, and that is to remember that some of these movements have been very short-lived. Or, if they've not been short-lived they have ended in a conservative if not in a reactionary fashion.

FOX: And this, you would say, proves that they haven't a vitality of their own, a long vitality?

CREIGHTON: They have a vitality and they've contributed much. I think they have contributed a great deal but it is simply one more illustration of the fact that the frontier, the periphery, the boundary, is not the main source of inspiration—or not necessarily the main source of inspiration—for action or any kind of creative activity.

FOX: Professor Creighton, were the Riel and Northwest rebellions typical frontier rebellions?

CREIGHTON: No, I don't think they were typical frontier rebellions. It seems to me that this is one example of the failure of the frontier thesis to explain the facts of Canadian history.

FOX: What were these rebellions?

CREIGHTON: These rebellions took place in 1885 on the Saskatchewan—Riel and a few bands of Indians, in other words French-speaking half-breeds and a few small bands of Indians—and in 1869 and '70 at the Red River, again Riel, no Indians this time, but with the tacit support of a good deal of the white population of the region. It's more difficult, certainly, to generalize about the 1869-70 rebellion; but it's easier, I think, about the Northwest, and it's easier about the still earlier rebellion, the rebellion of 1837. In

1837 the part that rebelled was right here in the County of York; in other words, one of the oldest settled districts in the province. The Loyalists, the people who wanted to support the government, were in the meantime making their difficult way down to York to defend it against the rebels who were close to it up here in Montgomery's Tavern. And similarly out West. It's true that at Red River Riel did secure the support of other white and English-speaking members of the population. But the core of the resistance was the Métis resistance. French-speaking half-breeds; and out West in 1885 the core of the resistance was again French-speaking Métis half-breeds. The white settlers who had been irritated enough by what they took to be the mismanagement of the federal government in the West were ready to talk and argue but they didn't want to fight. Riel was left with his Indians. In other words, the rebellions, the hard core of rebellion, in each case, was made up not of typical frontiersmen at all but of people who represented the old West—the West which was to be destroyed by the new frontier. They didn't exemplify the modern frontier, the ever-creeping edge of free land. They exemplified the resistance to the onward progress of that movement.

FOX: What would you say has been the main source in Canada if it wasn't the frontier?

CREIGHTON: Well, I think it's been a moving of the entire thing. I simply don't want to have the frontier given the prominence which it has been given in the American theory, and I don't think that their history exemplifies that prominence in any way at all.

FOX: The opposite theory to the frontier would be what?

CREIGHTON: The opposite theory is the theory of metropolitanism: the idea that culture, capital investment, political ideas, social organization—the whole thing—expands out from the main centre of cultivation into the interior.

FOX: And you feel this is a much more relevant theory?

CREIGHTON: For Canada, I think it is a much more relevant theory, and it's particularly relevant because of this enormous transcontinental transport system —the St. Lawrence, the Saskatchewan— which has made it possible for us to focus our lives, our activities, in a way that wouldn't have been possible otherwise.

FOX: What would the metropolitan centre be here? Are you thinking of London, Montreal, or Toronto?

CREIGHTON: Well, in earlier days it was London, or it was Paris, or it was the Channel ports; it was in Europe. Then by degrees it did find root in North America. It became Montreal, Toronto. Out from these focal points, these influences radiated. In the meantime, of course, other metropolitan centres are built up. The country becomes bigger, more complex, more varied. The old simple metropolitan centres are no longer as unopposed as they were.

FOX: On this point of transcontinentalism I'd like to read you a quote from one of your books. You said: 'Transcontinentalism, the westward drive of corporations, encouraged and followed by the super-corporation of the state, is the major theme in Canadian political life.' Do you still hold that view?

CREIGHTON: Well, I might perhaps express it with a little less enthusiasm than I did a good many years ago.

FOX: Why, because you're older or what?

CREIGHTON: Well, perhaps because I've become . . .

FOX: Wiser?

CREIGHTON: Wiser with discretion, perhaps,—I don't know. But I think on the whole these are rather magnificent terms I used there. Super-corporation of the state, for example, and corporation. When you think of the Northwest Company as it was, a loose co-partnership of people. You think of Mackenzie reaching the Pacific in 1793 with about twelve to fifteen men with him and this was all; and a tattered and battered canoe. The idea of a giant corporation—this big mouth-filling word certainly seems extremely inappropriate doesn't it?

FOX: Maybe you were thinking about the building of the C.P.R. and the Canadian Dominion following the rails westward?

CREIGHTON: I was thinking of that, certainly. Though there again, of course, for the first ten years the C.P.R. was nearer to bankruptcy at least twice than was any other major corporation in Canadian history.

FOX: You also said in that book that the instinct of both politicians and businessmen was toward unity and centralization. Is that still true?

CREIGHTON: I was speaking of a period at the middle of the last century. I was speaking of people living on the St. Lawrence River who wanted to make the St. Lawrence River a great highway for the transport outward of goods from North America and the transport inward of materials from Europe. Their whole conception of Canadian life, which was the commercial conception, was based upon the river. And I do think that they transferred a good deal of that view to the politicians who, after all, were just as fascinated by the river and its possibilities as they were. You can see this awfully early in Canadian history. Even Frenchmen—Colbert, Talon—Talon comes out to Canada filled with the idea of making this a typical little France, a new France, a real new France in the new New World. And then he yields to the seduction, to the compulsion of the river. He begins dreaming grandiose dreams of what an enormous continental empire you could create in the centre of the continent. The same thing happens with the politicians. This river was first of all to be the basis of an international commercial system which stretched right into the international West, both American and Canadian. It was only later on, when those first dreams were falsified by the triumphs of New York and the other Atlantic ports in the United States, that we substituted a variant of it which was our own Canadian Northwest, as the hinterland for the river. But we had two alternatives before us. We have tried to play them both. We are trying to play them still. The St. Lawrence Seaway is an illustration of this.

FOX: I want to ask you about that. Is the St. Lawrence Seaway the modern version of the Canadian obsession with the great river?

CREIGHTON: I think it is, yes.

FOX: Is it worth the money we've put into it?

CREIGHTON: Of course it is. This is something on which our lives depend and something upon which our future is centred. We must not let this opportunity go. All that I regret is that we made the agreement with the Americans that we did, and did not keep the canal on our side, and did not keep its control, as it always has been, wholly in our hands.

FOX: Could we have gone it alone?

CREIGHTON: I think so.

FOX: And should we?

CREIGHTON: My feeling is we should have.

FOX: Would you agree with me that Canadians are a curious mixture of socialist and individualist? That they seem to want a large measure of government protection, and at the same time they are fiercely individualistic at times?

CREIGHTON: I think we've had to have a large measure of government intervention. There are always things too big in this country for any individual to do. We've been forced to attempt to do things together simply because to survive in this continent, to try and make our own life, to win our own autonomy, secure our own independence, this needs collective effort and collective effort is the only thing that will preserve that for us.

FOX: This means that we are socialists whether we like it or not really?

CREIGHTON: We are socialists really, I think, whether we like it or not.

FOX: And on the other hand, then, this means that we cannot ever have the amount of free enterprise that they have in the States, or that they believe they have in the States?

CREIGHTON: They believe they have in the United States. I think that we shall always be somewhat limited by the necessities of our collective existence.

FOX: Do we pay a price for this? In other words, does a large percentage of our taxes go to the continuance of a collective entity in Canada spread out over a wide geographical area?

CREIGHTON: The whole thing is a heavy burden for a small people to bear; but it's a burden which gives us at the same time a very rich and satisfying life, and above all it is our own life.

Part II

French Canada and the Frontier

As J. L. McDougall gleefully pointed out in his essay reprinted in Part I, the French Canadians have caused some difficulty for frontierist historians. How did a people who even at the Conquest lived in a frontier province emerge from their brush with the North American environment so apparently unaffected by the experience? The characteristics Turner described as resulting from frontier life—individualism, ambition, acquisitiveness, commitment to democracy—hardly typified the Lower Canadian peasant. Did French Canada, as McDougall believed, prove the fallacies of the Turner thesis?

Historians like E. R. Adair, Mason Wade, Walter Sage and A. L. Burt have discussed the society of New France in terms of the frontier hypothesis or some near variant. If their analysis is correct, the question becomes not why the frontier did not influence French Canada, but why that influence was neutralized in later years. The obvious answer, to *nationaliste* historians in Quebec, would be the British Conquest, which, they would argue, deformed French Canadian society and prevented its growth in natural directions. The twin questions of the nature of society in New France and the impact of the Conquest on that Society are, to say the least, contentious ones among historians; dealing with them is something like wading through oatmeal porridge (or perhaps pea soup). Since Professor Nish's volume in this series, *The French Canadians 1759-1766*, has coped with these problems, we can thankfully avoid them except to emphasize how they complicate any assessment of the influence of the frontier on the French Canadians.

Given the paucity of appropriate literature, this section makes no attempt to invent artificial controversies. The selections cover a wide time-span from the period of the Conquest to the era of Confederation. The first is taken from a recent book by Raymond

Douville, a high-ranking Quebec civil servant, and Jacques-Donat Casanova, a French scholar. Theirs is a strongly environmentalist interpretation of French Canadian society. It is the climate of New France that they see as particularly important in bringing forth a new society and a new people among the French of Canada. While not following an orthodox frontierist line, Douville and Casanova ascribe to the environment many of the same results as did Turner, and look on its influence with the same moral favour. The healthy and unique society which the North American environment had created along the St. Lawrence was, in their view, damaged but not destroyed by the Conquest. The tone of the discussion of the beginning of British rule makes it clear that the book is as much a document of the Quebec nationalist mind as it as a history of New French society.

The second selection gives two contemporary views of Lower Canadian life in the early nineteenth century. Joseph Bouchette, author of the volume from which the passage is taken, was surveyor general of Lower Canada and a close associate of the ruling groups in the province. Much of the material, however, was quoted from another study, *A Political and Historical Account of Lower Canada*, published in 1830 by a man of very different political and social views, the reformer Pierre de Sales Laterrière. Despite their differences, however, both men agree in an interpretation of French Canadian society which falls somewhere between the positions of, say, McDougall and of Douville and Casanova. While stressing the greater conservatism of the *habitant* as compared to the American pioneer, they indicate how far the French Canadian had moved away from his European peasant

roots and towards the North American pattern. This movement is not explained in Turnerian terms. Rather, they point to a different kind of frontier influence. It is abundance, the sheer wealth of the New World, not the environment *per se*, which is the crucial factor in transforming the peasant of France into the vigorous French Canadian.

An 1850's report by T. Boutillier and a recent article by Arthur Silver both deal with the problem of French Canadian migration. By the late 1840's population pressure in the seigneurial lands of Lower Canada was focussing attention on the need to expand the area of French Canada. Boutillier was sanguine about the possibilities of new settlements being established in the wilderness areas of the province. His discussion might have been written in the United States, it bubbled with frontier optimism—except for the vital, and typical, reservation that the migrations Boutillier referred to were not movements of individual pioneers, as in the United States, but of groups, under the leadership of Catholic clergy. The Silver article is less convinced that Boutillier's "vigorous race of French Canadians" were really very vigorous. He pictures them turning their back on the great West opening to Canada at Confederation; he pictures them as a cautious and defeated people. In the process, he expresses some interesting views on the frontier thesis itself. Silver contends that ambitious, pioneering people are not created by the frontier, but by the societies from which they spring. He is turning frontierism on its head: pioneers create frontier conditions, not vice versa. Could Turner have absorbed this into his thesis? A. R. M. Lower in his essay in Part I surely could have.

Raymond Douville and Jacques Casanova, *Daily Life in Early Canada*, translated by Carola Congreve, (New York, The Macmillian Company, 1968), pp. 44-45, 101-102, 104, 215-217, 219-220. Reprinted by permission of The Macmillan Company. © Hachette Paris, 1964, © George Allen & Unwin, Ltd, 1967.

The North American Environment and the French Canadians: a *Nationaliste* Interpretation

One of the greatest achievements of the first colonists, missionaries, *coureurs de bois* and explorers was the way in which they overcame the cold; what is more they made friends with it and learned control over it. With its help they were to found in less than one century an entire new nation. Because the white man tried to understand and tolerate it, the Canadian winter in its turn inspired him to seek out the best means of housing, to dress and feed himself, and, while the long winter months held him captive, the time to reflect upon his new destiny. . . .

Winter was an important factor in the determining of the social entity into which the settler of Canada evolved. Little by little he became civilized, more shrewd, and more conscious of his worth. His existence was composed of his family life, his leisure, the sensible manner in which he performed his everyday domestic duties. Even the animals became tamer, since they were visited, cared for and fed three times a day in their stalls, where they were likewise confined until the com-

ing of the summer days. When these tasks had been attended to, and when he was not obliged, as he was on stormy days, to clear the snow in order to avoid being cut off from his neighbours, the settler lived in the bosom of his family. He sat before his hearth, busying himself with little tasks which required a degree of skill, intelligence and thought. Sometimes he would develop his natural artistic talents in the making of furniture for his house; winter saw the fashioning of tables, chests, chairs, beds, cradles and toys for the children. In this sort of household, where the settler was all the time developing a new outlook, his wife had an important part to play. If she were educated she would teach not only her children but her husband as well to read and write, for a colonist who was able at least to sign his own name had climbed a rung of a social ladder in the parish hierarchy. The woman of the house was also in charge of the daily devotions. She set an example for hard work by weaving, sewing and cutting out all the clothes and dresses for her family as well as the bedcovers and the carpets. She showed great ingenuity in cooking meals which had to be at once varied, substantial and appetizing, since a good table was one of the most important assets in these months of apparent inactivity. . . .

The Canadian learnt at an early stage to live philosophically, content with small rewards, relying only upon his own ingenuity, organizing his existence to achieve some degree of comfort. Economic conditions were such that he was not able to save any money. The few sales he did succeed in making were paid for in kind. He allowed himself no luxury, save that of being free. La Hontan observed with accuracy that the settler paid neither salt nor poll tax, that is to say board nor lodging, that he was free to hunt and fish.

In a word he was rich. His farm belonged to him. It had cost him nothing but his labour and now it was his most precious possession, and an inalienable right. 'The Canadian is proud,' remarked Bougainville disdainfully during the last years of the rule of France. Others before him had stigmatized him as being 'undisciplined, full of his own importance.' He was merely independent of character. Circumstances had ensured that he could depend on no one but himself, and now he only wished to live far away from any complicated problem. . . .

A great proportion of the purest strength of the soil of France was rooted here in this newly established nation. Here too was mingled a deep religious feeling which helped to straiten its growth. The mysticism felt by the first founders was added to the constant feeling of danger during the years of terror, and it wrought a spirit which was both practical and elevated. Most of the Governors and Intendants were to endorse Hocquart's observation: 'Religion means much to them all.' The traveller Kalm observed that the colonists of New France devoted much more time to their prayers and outside devotions than did the English and Dutch in the British colonies. He was struck by the way in which the soldiers at Fort Saint-Frédéric met together for morning and evening prayers.

And so native instincts purified by spiritual and religious feeling found their way into the minds of this nation, which gradually discarded its racial origins. In 1700, when the first generation born in Canada was at the height of its powers, observers were already attempting to analyse the stages of its extraordinary and rapid development. This physiological phenomenon intrigued Bacqueville de la Potherie, Lebeau, d'Aleyrac, and more especially Charlevoix who lingered over his description in which he examined it in great depth. Apart from the language—in which these people retained a classic purity—Charlevoix observed other signs; the carefree spirit, the 'gentle and polite manners which everyone seems to possess. Boorish behaviour in speech as well as in manners is never contemplated, even in the most distant parts of the countryside'. His comparison with the Saxons who had colonized the coast in the South [was] by no means unfavourable: 'Anyone who attempted to judge these two colonies by their mode of life, or by their behaviour and the speech of their people would not hesitate in concluding that the balance is in our favour: ours is the most flourishing.' The writer goes on to delineate the essential features: the air one breathed in this enormous continent never ceased to strengthen a spirit of independence and an aversion to routine hard work, which was accentuated by the example of and contact with those native inhabitants, the Indians, 'who are happy in freedom and independence', and this was more than enough to mould and crystallize this characteristic. Every other serious observer over the years, Kalm, for instance, La Hontan, and Bougainville, summed up the people of Canada, using the same sort of words as Charlevoix and reaching very much the same conclusions. Bougainville, a witty cultivated man, who was a member of many scientific bodies, and who was so harsh in his judgment of Canadian officers, yet had nothing but praise for the people themselves. He wrote half a century after La Hontan: 'They are undoubtedly of better material, they have more spirit and a better education than the people of France.' As to the explanation of this: 'Their spirit of independence derives from the fact that they pay no taxes, and that they are able to hunt and fish.'

All these features contributed to the fashioning of a nation, which, but for the events of 1760, was preparing to present France with a whole new continent. . . .

. . . we have tried to summarize the development and, so to speak, the transformation of a nation of pure French origin, which took root in a strange land 2,500 miles from the mother country. By virtue of the prevailing conditions, above all the climate, the immensity of the area, and the proximity of the Indians who surrounded them, this population evolved a new culture. But in two essential ways it remained French: in its language and religion. And now suddenly the chance of a war's ending placed them under the protection of a country which was alien in both. . . . England was to keep Canada.

A superficial politeness hid the real intention, which was to dominate, and in the end stifle, Canada. In Quebec, Canon Briand, who administered the diocese during the absence of the Bishop (Mgr de Pontbriand died in 1759) received orders to pray during the Sunday service henceforth, 'for the King George III, the Queen and for all the Royal family, according to the usual form of prayer, and declaring each one by name'. This order was accompanied by another obliging all settlers save the Captains of militia, to surrender their arms to the General in charge of the administration of their Government, and to swear the oath of allegiance.

The broader understanding shown by certain Swiss attached to the Army of occupation, such as Haldimand and the secretary Bruyère, who were Protestants, yet French-speakers, did much to soften the blows which fell during this period of transition.

A Frenchman by birth, Canon

Briand obeyed official orders because he had experienced so much of the changes and chances of war and of the vagaries of treaties. But when these proud and independent settlers heard from the pulpit the foreign names of those for whom they were supposed to beg Divine protection, they scowled, shrugged their shoulders, and shut their eyes in silent protest. When they were safely out of the Church, they cursed their predicament: 'Nobody is going to stop me speaking French to my horse when I am in the fields,' one obstinate settler was heard to remark. Here were the seeds of passive resistance sown to last for a very long time, and to prove obstinate and invincible.

With rage in their hearts, the Canadians laid down their arms and took the oath of allegiance to a country they had fought against for as long as they could remember. They no longer possessed anything: no animals, no harvests, no hope. Almost everywhere throughout the countryside their farm buildings had been burnt down. Sons from almost every family had been killed in the war. The authorities who had been in the colony returned to France with the able-bodied forces of the Army. The settlers were alone, finally, alone, with the priests who were part of their ranks; these had not forsaken them.

After the first shock of bewilderment had passed by, they set themselves once more to work. And here the whole strength of the seigneurial system, set up throughout the country, came into its own. These people who had lost everything, at least still possessed their own land, and which was wholly theirs. Like the first colonists, their ancestors, they took heart once more after years of trial, and swore to survive and to group themselves within the seigneuries of their three Governments. These 60,000 settlers of

French descent dug themselves into this little corner of the American continent which already contained more than a million English. Nobody would be able to dislodge them.

This nation, as it had under French rule, wished to preserve its freedom and the way of life it had created for itself.

Joseph Bouchette, *The British Dominions in North America*, I, (London, 1832), pp. 403-405, 411-413, 416.

Contemporaries Explain the Frontier in Terms of Free Land

In a work professing to describe topography and statistics a description of manners and customs will not probably be expected, nor indeed had we contemplated the consideration of a subject more strictly within the province of a different class of writers. It happens, however, that we have been recently anticipated in this task in a book under the title of "A Political and Historical Account of Lower Canada, by A CANADIAN;" and although we are far from coinciding in the politics of the author, and concurring in the views which he sometimes takes of his subject, we cannot withhold the cordial expression of our testimony to the graphical truth with which he has so admirably depicted the habits, usages, and character of the Canadian peasant. An attempt to improve upon so lucid and faithful a description would, perhaps, be worse than idle, and we shall therefore take the liberty of extracting largely from the 4th chapter of the work in question, and confine ourselves to occasional remarks as we proceed.

"Of the various circumstances connected with the habits and manners of a people, the most important are, *first*, the degree of difficulty experienced by them in obtaining the means of subsistence; *secondly*, the proportions in which these means of subsistence are spread over the whole mass of the population; and, *thirdly*, the quantum of the means of comfort which the people at large deem requisite to their happiness. Where the obtaining of subsistence is not a matter of overwhelming or exceeding difficulty, where the wealth of the country is spread in nearly even portions over the whole of the inhabitants, and where the standard of enjoyment is a high one, happiness must of necessity be the lot of that people. Such is the situation of my countrymen; and, from the experience which my travels in various parts of the globe have given me, I well know that their comfort and happiness, excepting, perhaps, in the United States of America, can find no equal; and that the unfortunate peasant of Europe, apparently degraded in mind and worn out in body, exhibits a picture of wretchedness, which to the poorest *habitant* on the banks of the St. Lawrence would appear almost utterly inconceivable, and upon which his imagination could not dwell without surprise and disgust.

"The people, with hardly an exception, are proprietors of land, and live by the produce of their own labour from their own property. By the law of the country the property is equally divided among all the children; and from the small quantity of capital yet accumulated in individual hands, the divisions of land have become somewhat minute. Among the people of the United States there exists a roving disposition, that leads them in multitudes to make new settlements in the wild lands, and thus rapidly to spread civilization over the immense unreclaimed territories which they possess. This feeling exists not in Canada: the inhabitants, generally, are far from adventurous; they cling with pertinacity to the spot which gave them birth, and cultivate with contentedness the little piece of land which, in the division of the family property, has fallen to their share. One great reason for this sedentary disposition is their peculiar situation as regards religion. In Canada, as in all catholic countries, many of the people's enjoyments are connected with their religious ceremonies; the Sunday is to them their day of gaiety; there is then an assemblage of friends and relations; the parish church collects together all whom they know, with whom they have relations of business or pleasure; the young and old, men and women, clad in their best garments, riding their best horses, driving in their gayest *calèches,* meet there for the purposes of business, love, and pleasure. The young *habitant,* decked out in his most splendid finery, makes his court to the maiden he has singled out as the object of his affections; the maiden, exhibiting in her adornment every colour of the rainbow, there hopes to meet *son chevalier:* the bold rider descants upon, and gives evidence of, the merits of his unrivaled pacer; and in winter the power of the various horses are tried in sleigh or cariole racing: in short, Sunday is the grand fête—it forms the most pleasurable part of the *habitant's* life; rob them of their Sunday, you rob them of what, in their eyes, renders life most worthy of possession. Moreover, the people are a pious people, and set an extraordinary value upon the *rites* of their religion. Take them where they may be unable to participate in these observances, and you render them fearful and unhappy.

The consequence of all these circumstances is, that the Canadian will never go out singly to settle in a wild territory, neither will he go where his own religious brethren are not. . . .

"From what I have already stated, it is almost needless for me to say, that the situation of the people, such as I have described it, is not merely the situation of a part but of the whole. Wealth and comfort are not confined to a few individuals, but the whole mass of the population have almost an equal share in the good things of the world. The division of property, by law, has, of itself, rendered this almost necessary; the ease with which the means of subsistence are obtained has also contributed to the same desirable state. Whatever may be believed to be the cause, the fact of the great approximation to equality in property is indisputable.

"From the various circumstances I have mentioned, it will not be difficult to form something like a correct conception of the character of the people.

"Free from the pressure of want, and unexposed to the temptations created by surrounding affluence, they are free from the vices which poverty and temptation engender; property is perfectly safe, both from petty pilfering and open attacks. In the country, the doors of the houses are never fastened, and all sorts of property are openly and carelessly exposed. In the social relations also, the same circumstance of ease induces, to a great degree, honesty in dealing. It is to be remarked, however, that, in a country like England, where great transactions are daily carried on, great faith is often absolutely required; this faith becomes extended to less important dealings, and a general feeling of honesty is introduced into the intercourse of the people.

"In the kindlier affections, they, like

all happy people, are eminently conspicuous; though, from being less rich, they are perhaps less remarkable in this particular than the people of the United States. Except in those portions overrun by the Irish and Scotch settlers, the traveller never meets with a refusal to give him assistance; and, in all parts, the distress of the neighbour is promptly and, I may say, generously relieved. No party feelings, no feelings of religion, no religious or political watch-words or signs, here break in upon the gentle tendencies of the people. The same intolerance of opposite sects is not to be found here as in Europe; I have myself known the most perfect cordiality to exist between the priest of the parish and his jewish neighbour; and have heard a sentimental deist openly avow his unbelief before the same clergyman, discuss the propriety of his opinion, and he on the most perfect terms of intimacy and good feeling. This tolerance has hitherto led to no evil results, the people being one of the most pious and decorous to be found on the face of the globe; their piety at the same time being free from austerity and bigotry, and their decorum from hypocrisy.

"A bold spirit of independence, moreover, reigns throughout the conduct of the whole population; happily they are yet undebased by the dominion of a rich oligarchy; they live not in fear of any man's power or influence; upon themselves only—on their own industry, do they depend for subsistence; and thus they have not, hitherto, learned to make distinctions between the welfare of the poor and the rich; to bow down with abject servility before the powerful, and in their turn to exact a wretched prostration from those still weaker than themselves: courteous in their manners, polite in their address, they offend not by rude and rough familiarity, or indifference to the comfort of others; neither do they forget their own dignity, even though they be poor; they cringe not, they fawn not, nor are they, like slaves, cruel and oppressive; they preserve an even simplicity and honest straightforwardness of manner; alike free from servility on one hand and bluntness on the other. In this circumstance again they differ widely from the people of the United States. The Americans, from a desire to mark their independence, their freedom from all the pernicious restraints of European despotisms, too often forget the common courtesies of life. To insult a man they sometimes consider an effective method of informing him that they are free from his control; just as by cheating him, they believe that they save themselves from being over-reached. The Canadian, on the contrary, while acting with independence, is polite; while guarding himself from becoming a dupe, is honest. . . .

The people of the townships form a distinct class of themselves, and are strikingly contrasted with the French-Canadian peasantry of the province. The tenure of their lands, their language, and their habits, are essentially, their laws partially, different from those of the seigneurial population, and assimilate in many respects with those of the neighbouring settlements of the United States. The origin of the similitude may be traced to the early stages of the colonization of the eastern townships, when the settlers were almost exclusively, if not altogether, natives of the adjacent country, and emigrants from the New York, Vermont, and New England States. The numerous class of British and Irish emigrants that subsequently took up crown lands in the townships, strangers in general to the mode of clearing and cultivating new lands, were naturally prone to imitate those who had preceded them in these important operations, and the American settlers, proverbially dexterous and active in removing forests with the axe, thus became the model of the European emigrant. This imitation was not long confined to the mode of converting a wilderness into corn fields, but soon extended to the plan of building their houses, dividing and tilling their farms, &c. The domestic economy of the establishment and the usages of the new settlers thus gradually approximated to those of the old, and although there are now some exceptions, the manners and customs of the people of the townships, generally, bear a close analogy to the manners and customs of the Americans.

Province of Canada, Legislative Assembly *Journals,* 1854-1855, Appendix M.M., Report on sums expended . . . towards aiding the settlement of the vacant lands of the Crown in Lower Canada . . . , by T. Boutillier, Inspector of Agencies.

The Communal Nature of the French Canadian Frontier

The Eastern Townships

The Eastern Townships are bounded by the seigniories which lie on the south of the St. Lawrence, by those which are situated east of the River Richelieu, by the River Chaudière, and by the Province Line. Their population amounts to 94,275 souls. They comprise the six counties of Drummond, Megantic, Missisquoi, Shefford, Sherbrooke and Stanstead.

Within a few years, the Eastern Townships have made rapid and important progress. Arthabaska, Stanfold and Somerset, which ten years ago were unbroken forest, now support a number of cultivators of their soil in comfort, and contain villages with houses that would be ornamental in those of the Seigniories. Stanfold which recently beheld its pious Missionary perish a few arpents from his chapel, in a swamp, over which passed the only road in the place, has now not only excellent means of intercommunication, but also with Arthabaska and Somerset, &c., a railway.

A number of other Townships into which our vigorous race of French Cana-

dians have thrown themselves, are making rapid strides to overtake their predecessors, and will soon be in no way inferior to them, if the Government continues its work of benevolence and justice towards the inhabitants of the Eastern Townships.

The sum of £ 7275 was appropriated for the Eastern Townships, but such is the extent of the land, and such the necessities of the population crowding thither from so many different quarters, that that sum is far from sufficient. In the distribution of any future grant, I think that it will be of great importance to take into account the influx of Settlers into these Townships, and that the opening of roads in such circumstances, should keep pace with the tide of immigration, in order that the settler may not lose courage at the outset. . . .

The Saguenay

. . . In order . . . to complete and render practicable these two roads only, that is to say that from St. Urbain to *Grande Baie,* and that from the *Rapides des Roches* to Lake St. John, and to build the Bridges thereon, the sum required is £ 11,731.

If this sum cannot be obtained from the Legislature, the colonization of the Saguenay will have gained nothing or next to nothing by the expenditure of the sum of £ 4,250 appropriated as before mentioned.

If the work be not complete, its failure will be nearly so, and the settlers, whom a confiding hope and trustfulness in external aid may have led to penetrate into the depths of the forests of the Saguenay, must either abandon the settlement or resign themselves to live there cut off from the rest of mankind. . . .

I cannot close these reflexions on the Saguenay, without making mention of the great services rendered to the cause of

colonization by Mr. Hébert, Curé of Kamouraska, and Mr. Boucher, Curé of St.
Ambroise, both of whom had the courage to place themselves at the head of the
settlers who first began to colonize the
Upper Saguenay.

Messire Hébert even passed a considerable time amongst the settlers in
order to encourage and advise them in
their labors, and at my entreaty consented,
for the benefit of the new colony, to
undertake the superintendence of the new
road from Lake St. John to the *Portage*
des Roches.

In his management of the affairs of
the Colonization Society of L'Islet and
Kamouraska he has shown administrative
talents of the highest order.

His settlement has now attained a
degree of prosperity which augurs well for
the future, but we must not forget that if
it has been led into the forests of the
Upper Saguenay by the impulse of courage, it is induced to remain there by the
sentiment of hope.

A. I. Silver, "French Canada and the Prairie Frontier, 1870-1890", *Canadian Historical Review,* vol. L, No. 1, (1969), pp. 27-32, 34, 36. Reprinted by permission of the Author and of the Publisher, University of Toronto Press.

The French Canadians and the Pioneering Instinct

In the quarter-century after the Manitoba Act, . . . when English Canada was looking to the prairies as the land of promise, the key to Canada's future, and when thousands of Ontarians were pouring onto the plains, three main trends of opinion tended to keep French Canadians away from the region: a disbelief in the material value of prairie land; a fear that to go there was to expose oneself and one's national identity to danger; and a conviction that Quebec alone was the French-Canadian *patrie* so that to go west was to expatriate oneself. The letters of Taché's agents, reporting on their contacts in Quebec, seem to indicate that the first of these reasons was most important with farmers, the actual potential settlers, while the educated, the community leaders, were most concerned with the problem of expatriation and depopulation of Quebec.

Running through all these attitudes is a strain of pessimism, defeatism, or demoralization. One *fears* bankruptcy, harassment, loss of identity, or exile.

This frame of mind differs markedly from what has been typically represented as the frontier mentality. The frontiersman is supposed to be fearless, optimistic, independent, expansive. His boundless enthusiasm and self-confidence impel him to enterprise, often recklessly. Essential to the frontier hypothesis is the idea that these characteristics are "forest-born," are the result of the impact of the physical environment in changing the personality of the man who comes to the frontier. In this, the frontier hypothesis may well be psychologically questionable, for psychologists appear agreed that personality is established with virtual permanence by the time adulthood is reached. Far from being created by the frontier, the frontiersman was probably the kind of man whom his home society could create, and who was attracted by the frontier because he already was (at least latently) a frontiersman. Thus, J. B. Bickersteth, a young Protestant missionary on the north-west frontier, noted that "an entirely English [European] settlement is seldom very progressive. The presence of a few bustling Americans or Canadians creates an atmosphere of push." . . . One has to be born, or at least brought up, in the right kind of society to become a frontiersman—the kind of society that will mould a man's character so that he will be attracted by, and be able to survive at, the frontier.

Societies which have produced frontiersmen or colonizers seem always to have been characterized by a certain mobility or dislocation of their parts. The North American *Aufmarschgebiet* was a semi-settled area whose inhabitants moved around within it and moved out when more stable elements moved in. Nor was this frontier society created in a generation. Anglo-American colonists spent a century and a half in the Atlantic coastal area, gradually adapting to new conditions, still tied to Europe's lengthening apron string while facing the frontier, developing the society that would produce Turner's westerners. And even the first colonizers who came from Britain in the seventeenth century were already unsettled men, products of a century of enclosures, of an economic revolution that threw them out of their homes and set them wandering around England, gaining in generations on the road the experience necessary for colonizing.

Again and again we see that great colonizing movements are preceded by a period of mobilization—a period, moreover, in which some obstacle, whether military or economic, is met and surmounted. The Israelites spent forty years in the desert before they could settle Canaan—long enough for the slave generation to die off and a new breed of desert-born strong men to take over. The colonizing activities of the ancient Greeks followed a similar period of migratory wandering. So it was with mediaeval colonizers. The Vikings spent centuries in their Scandinavian homelands, forced into lives of mobility by the scarcity of arable land, before beginning their great settling movement. Norway was an *Aufmarschgebiet* that prepared the settlement of Vikings in Ireland. Ireland prepared the settlement of Iceland, and Iceland that of Greenland.

French Canada in 1870 was far from the condition of any of the great colonizing societies. It was not a society in movement and, rather than having overcome some obstacle, it considered itself conquered, had failed in 1837-8 to liberate itself, and had finally settled for a compromise with the conquerors, politically in Confederation, economically by a withdrawal from competition with the English.

Not movement, but stasis, enforced by the very nature of the task of "survival," was the keynote of French-Canadian society. The conquest cut off prospects of French-Canadian growth by immigration, giving both conquerors and conquered the idea that the *Canadien* population was fully formed. So too, the Proclamation of 1763, by drawing the boundaries of the province close in around the limits of the seigneuries, created the impression that the province, if not already settled, was not so unsettled that the heirs of the present population would not fill it. Indeed, by 1824, the Montreal *Gazette* was reporting that land "in situations fit for cultivation is now nearly all taken up." This encouraged French Canadians to consider the country as already settled rather than being settled. Lord Durham noted the attitude: "The English population . . . looked on the American Provinces as a vast field for settlement and speculation. . . .

"[The French Canadians] looked on the Province as the patrimony of their own race; they viewed it not as a country to be settled, but as one already settled; and instead of legislating in the American spirit, and first providing for the future population of the Province, their primary care was, in the spirit of the legislation which prevails in the old world, to guard the interests and feelings of the present race of inhabitants . . . ." This attitude involved a rejection of mobility. Durham himself described French Canada as a "stationary society," and his chief investigator, Stewart Derbishire, was more emphatic, quoting Papineau as saying that French Canadians "never want to go beyond the sound of their own Church Bells." . . .

. . . colonization appeared not as a way of creating a new world but of preserving an old one. The church especially, concerned for the souls of its children, saw in colonization a way to maintain the old, parish-centred society of peasant farmers. This society seemed ideal not only because it promoted the Catholic virtues but because it conformed to the agricultural romanticism which Quebec's priests, like the lay intellectuals, had picked up in the classical colleges. Thus, colonization propaganda was largely priest-written, and church-sponsored societies raised money to help young farmers get started on new lands. An un-frontiersman-like attitude was natural here. Settlement was not a new start, but a way of preserving the old society of the St. Lawrence Valley. While the frontiersman went off to start a new, materially better life, French-Canadian colonizers saw in settlement very different goals: "Prévenir l'émigration de nos compatriotes; ramener dans le sein de la patrie ceux dont la Foi est exposée à l'étranger; fixer notre peuple au sol; le détourner du luxe, de l'oisiveté, de l'ivrognerie, du blasphème; lui faire aimer la vie simple et paisable des champs . . . ."

French-Canadian attempts at colonization had, therefore, a very special form. The organization of the new parish had to be set up; in particular, a church had to be built and a priest brought in. Then, "à son arrivée, le colon trouvera toutes choses bien chères à son coeur: le prêtre, l'église et l'école pour ses enfants." This scheme for a frontier settlement, aimed at making the move to the frontier as smooth as possible, at minimizing the differences between home and frontier, and therefore, tailored to the needs of a stable, home society, differed greatly from the typical frontiersman community. "Everyone in the West," wrote Bickersteth, "is out to make every red cent they [sic] can, and the preacher is almost always considered to be on the same quest."

At the frontier, he continued, material ambition rules, and "religion (if it stands in the way) must necessarily, like everything else, go to the wall." English-language colonization propaganda played on material motives. A typical pamphlet on the North-West promised that "a farmer in this vicinity SHOULD MAKE A FORTUNE in two or three years . . . ." How irrelevant, in contrast, seems the attitude of the great French-Canadian colonizer: "Le Canadien . . . sait que l'homme ne vit pas seulement de pain, que s'il est pauvre sur la terre, il est riche dans le ciel et, si la mort se présente à lui, à sa femme, à ses enfants, avec son triste cortège, le médecin des âmes est là pour lui ouvrir les portes de la Jérusalem céleste. Peut-on reprocher à un chrétien de préférer le ciel à la terre?" Indeed, if the real frontier spirit was materialistic, the French Canadians must take special care not to appeal to material motives in their colonization propaganda. Thus a typical pamphlet begins with the warning: "Le Manitoba et le Nord-Ouest Canadien ne sont ni bons ni avantageux pour le jeune monsieur qui voudrait vivre . . . sans ne jamais ôter son habit et sans ne jamais transpirer . . . ." . . .

. . . there may well have been reason to expect a worse performance from French Canadians at the frontier than from, say, Ontarians. The lamentations of the directors of the Ste-Anne-de-la-Pocatière agricultural school indicate the inability or unwillingness of French-Canadian farmers to adapt to new conditions even in Quebec. On the prairies they still applied the old methods. Failure to adopt more progressive techniques—the same problem faced at Ste-Anne-de-la Pocatière —led to the displacement of French-Canadian settlers into marginal lands by new waves of English immigrants. . . .

Conquest had probably taught French Canadians to curb their own ambition. One does not expect to rise so high under a foreign rule as under a familiar régime. Decades of exclusion from governmental, military, and other offices led to a habit of self-restriction: "Tandis qu'il faudrait toute une population de gens hardis jusqu'à la témérité, actifs jusqu'à la frénésie, vous recontrez à chaque pas des imbéciles qui [répètent] un tas de sornettes sur l'incapacité, sur l'ignorance, sur la jalousie, sur l'inertie, sur la *malchance* . . . sur la fatalité, qui empêchent leurs compatriotes de réussir . . . ." This discouragement—so far from the optimism of the frontiersman—became, in fact, an acceptance of defeat in certain areas, a turning to restricted domains. It became the sort of attitude lauded by Curé Labelle when he claimed that the French Canadian knew "que s'il est pauvre sur la terre, il est riche dans le ciel . . . ." When the Queen's 1879 birthday honours list contained the names of six Canadians, only one of them French Canadian, *L'Evénement* commented characteristically that

titles and honours were not necessarily a sign of the real worth of a society. This was the sort of self-consoling attitude that accepted English control of the West perhaps a little too quickly, that found the inferior "terres incultes de la province de Qúebec" more worth developing and settling with French Canadians.

This demoralization, this lack of self-confidence, bolstered a conservatism whose virtues were not the independent, erratic ones of the frontier but the steady sober ones of the meek labourer. When in 1884 a French Canadian was named auditor-general of a Manitoba district, Montreal's *L'Etendard* pointed him out as "un exemple de ce que peuvent le travail, la régularité, l'amour du devoir, unis à une conduite irreprochable." Whatever these virtues might accomplish in the way of getting a subservient auditor promoted, they were hardly the characteristics of a people that would undertake the mighty imperialistic enterprise of stamping its image in a land like the Canadian North-West.

Part III

The Process of Frontier Settlement

Despite a good deal of scholarly writing, and a vast outpouring of antiquarian literature, the actual process of the movement of population out to the frontier remains largely unknown. There has been much romanticizing about the lonely frontier farm, the self-sufficient farmer, his ingenuity and versatility—the typical Turnerian picture. But this reconstruction of backwoods life has usually been developed from little, and dubious, evidence. And the crucial first step has not been taken, the investigation of the migration process itself. Did settlers usually come to the frontier individually or in groups? This is a vital question, for the frontierist model is based upon individual family settlements, not larger groups in which the individual might be more sheltered from the influence of the frontier environment. What was the role of the government in the population movement? What kind of services did it provide for the pioneers, how obvious was the government presence in the settlements? Again this is important, because the government could also act as a shield against the effect of the frontier. What is needed, clearly, is systematic investigation of the migrations to many areas, with such questions firmly in mind. Then the nature of frontier life can be investigated more intelligently.

The selections here obviously cannot solve the problem. But they can offer some conflicting views on these matters, views mostly from contemporaries of the pioneer period. First among them are some selections from the Coventry Transcripts. George Coventry, in the late 1850's, determined to rescue from oblivion the memory of the Loyalist migration to Upper Canada, while some of the pioneers were still alive. He collected reminiscences from all early Loyalists he could contact, and added to them copies of items relevant to pioneer life from early Upper Canadian newspapers. This extremely valuable collection is now in the Public Archives of Canada in Ottawa. The first passage is from Coventry's introduction to the transcripts, in which he draws a typically romantic portrayal of pioneer life. Turner would have approved of his description of the settlers as existing "in a state of nature." Next is the rambling account of Capt. James Dittrick, a Loyalist settler in the Niagara district. There is a good deal here of the old man's foggy remembrance of the "good old days." But it is interesting as evidence from a contempary which supports the views of Coventry: Dittrick emphasizes the isolation of the settlers, and the way in which they were forced to rely on their own initiative; and he stresses the breakdown of traditional class lines in the frontier environment. This is a view which is not entirely shared by John Kilburn of Brockville, Mrs. White of the Cobourg area, or the article from the *Upper Canada Gazette* of 1799. All three of these sources discuss the communal, rather than individualistic, nature of pioneer life. Mrs. White points to the role of government in the early settlements, with her deep regard for the pioneers' protector, "our faithful Governor." The *Gazette* article offers the useful reminder that many areas had men of capital, who ameliorated conditions for their neighbours as well as for themselves by employing their capital to open communications to the outside world and to provide employment in their districts. Kilburn's reminiscences, like Dittrick's, make it clear that some caution is necessary before accepting these accounts in their en-.irety. Again there is much here of the rosy colouring of the days of his youth, when even the weather was better. The final selection from the Coventry Transcripts, a passage from the *Upper Canada Gazette* of 1801, indicates that even in the period of "frontier simplicity", the pretensions of would-be aristocrats, and their importation of Old World customs, was to be found.

Many of the early settlers in the Canadas came in groups, rather than as individuals or single families. The Highlanders who were brought in clan groups to Glengarry County in Upper Canada; the Loyalist regiments who settled along the western St. Lawrence; the military settlers placed in Carleton and Lanark Counties, Upper Canada, after 1818; the Irish paupers settled in Lanark and in the Peterborough area by Peter Russell: these were some examples of group settlement. Also active in large-scale, organized settlements, in the 1820's and 1830's, were two large private land companies, the Canada Company, with its huge tract of land in western Upper Canada, and Lower Canada's British American Land Company, with holdings in the Eastern Townships. Two selections from the papers of the British American Land Company have interesting implications for frontierist interpretations. The first shows how such group approaches to settlement neutralized to some degree the effect of the frontier, for the trappings of civilization were provided before any immigrants were introduced to the new frontier. The second despatch not only demonstrates some of the problems such companies faced, but also implies that the character of the settlers who came to the frontier was at least as important as the environment in determining their success or failure as pioneers. The lazy will remain lazy, rather than be transformed by the North American landscape. This is the same theme which appears in the letter by Lord Dalhousie, Governor General of British North America from 1819 to 1828.

The next two items, both from the 1850's when a new pioneering age was opening in the Shield area of Upper Canada, return us to the basic difference of interpretation. William Spragge, a veteran member of the Crown Land Department of Upper Canada, insisted to a select committee of the Legislature that the government must take it upon itself to encourage the expansion of the agricultural population. This should be done by establishing large group settlements, for Spragge considered individual settlers virtually doomed to ignorance and to a bare subsistence existence. J. Sheridan Hogan, however, glorifies the individual pioneer, who has tamed the Upper Canadian wilderness. This essay, written to advertise Canada at an international exhibition in Paris, has a strongly frontierist tone.

The views of Hogan are balanced by those of a modern historian, J. M. S. Careless, in the last passage. This excerpt from his book *The Union of the Canadas* gives a very different picture of the society of Canada in the mid-nineteenth century. It is not a pioneer community of rugged individualists in his view, but a society growing sophisticated, a society with complicated interrelationships—economic, cultural, personal.

Careless

Land Companies
Canada Company (upper Canada)

The Frontier Experience of the Loyalists

isolated

individual pioneer

George Coventry Papers, 1793-1863, XI,
*Loyalists: Memoirs of Some of the Early
Settlers in Upper Canada,* Introduction by
George Coventry, Public Archives of
Canada, pp. 6-7. MG 24, K2.

Settlers in a Canadian Wilderness
had to bear the burthen and heat of the
day, had to exist by the sweat of their
brow—to undergo wonderful privations
and to pass through realities, which would
scarcely be credited in a work of fiction.
Still a Century had passed and proved
the truth of the Assertion of Macaulay,
that the British Colonies have become far
mightier and wealthier than the realms
which Cortez and Pizarro had added to
the dominions of Charles the fifth.

The history of the Country therefore
during the last Century is eminently the
history of physical, of Moral and of intellectual improvement.

The history of the settlers, the progress of agriculture [,] of Horticulture—
of the useful and ornamental—the change
in the habits and manners of the people
—the exchange of the Spinning Wheel
for imported finery—the daily luxury and
comforts of the inhabitants contrasted
with the privations of their Ancestors, will
all form subjects of Interesting Moments
in the results of our Enquiries.

The people having their daily duties
to perform with a constant succession of
work from sun rise to sun set were cut
off from all intercourse with the world and
for months together never saw a White
mans footsteps around their dwellings—a
solitary Indian occasionly crosses their
grounds, with whom they traded for skins
and Deer. They might almost literally be
said to have existed in a state of Nature—
Old associations were their thoughts and
the reflection, that they were laying the
foundations of prosperity for their children.

The Bible they carried with them
formed their principal Solace and Conso-
lation—and their endeavours were
blessed . The superstition, so characterised
to the Aborigines, seemed to form no part
of their existence—their minds were
constantly occupied with some useful
work, and as the shades of Evening drew
around them they retired and in such
sound sleep, that a Monarch would have
envied.

*   *   *

Coventry Papers, XI, Reminiscences of
Capt. James Dittrick, St. Catharines, District of Niagara, Upper Canada, February 7, 1860, pp. 101, 103, 105-106.

The whole Country was a forrest
a wilderness which had to be subdued by
the Axe and toil—
For a time we led a regular Robinson
Cruso life and with a few poles and
brushwood formed our tents in the Indian plan.

hardships but much group cooperation

As the clearances enlarged, we were supplied with some agricultural Implements, for we brought nothing with us but a few seeds prepared by the careful forethought of the Women—

My father who had naturally a mechanical turn, amused himself of an evening in making spinning Wheels, a loom, and a variety of useful things for farming purposes. Time passed on and having grown some flax and obtained some sheep my Mother set to work to prepare the same for some cloathes in which we were greatly in need of.

She had not any thread, so my father which doubtless he learned from the Indians, stripped off the Bass wood Bark, saturated it in Water like Flax, and obtained a fine strong and useful thread— Necessity has no law. — . . .

The most trying period of our lives, was the year 1788 called the year of scarcity —everything at that period seemed to conspire against the hardy and industrious settlers. All the crops failed, as the earth had temporarily ceased to yield its increase, either for Man or Beast—for several days we were without food, except the various roots that we procured and boiled down to nourish us. We noticed what roots the pigs eat, and by that means avoided anything that had any poisonous qualities. The officers in Command at the Military Stations did all in their power to mitigate the general distress, but the supplies were very limited, consequently only a small pittance was dealt out to each petitioner.

We obtained something and were on allowance until affairs assumed a more favourable aspect—our poor dog was killed to allay the pangs of hunger, the very idea brought on sickness to some but others devoured the flesh quite ravenous — . . .

There was then no distinction, as is the case now a days—All were on an equality and ready to do any kind acts and services for one another. The happy meetings we often had, I look back to with much pleasure. I am decidedly of opinion that true happiness, as far as human nature has the privilege of enjoying it, was far more abundant then than the present frivolities of the age.

Dress was the last thing thought of. The women all wore their linsey woolsey gowns, and the men and lads homespun cloathes, far more suitable to the rude log houses and rough Country, than those of a finer material. Marriages were celebrated by Magistrates, thinly scattered around the Country. I think David Secord performed more ceremonials and united more happy young people than any one else. I really believe when those events took place, they were the happiest people in the world. There were seldom any quarrels or bickerings—they pulled together, and their sole aim appeared to be, to contribute to each others comfort, and to improve their farm for the benefit of their children.

The present appearance of the farms, thriving homesteads, well shew, what can be accomplished by perseverance and Industry.

The owners are the bone and sinew of the Country, and when the War of 1812 was declared, they were loyal, and ready to stand forward in defence of their property, and to keep the British Flag untarnished.

No period of History furnishes a brighter record, than the Loyalty and devotedness of the settlers, who rose in mass, when they found their Country invaded by a neighbouring nation and the war cruelly carried on by a party for mercenary motives.

The same spirit still exists, and al-

though a few dissatisfied paltry dema-
gogues who have no landed property at
stake, may attempt to shake the Loyalty
of the old settlers, yet I am confident they
will never succeed.

*   *   *

George Coventry Papers, XI, Reminiscences of John Kilburn Esqr. born at
Brockville. U.C.—1794—(date Sept. 8,
1862), p. 219.

At this early period, the State of
Society however humble, was in many
respects I think superior to the present.
All parties then, were more or less de-
pendant on each other for favours and
occasional assistance, and all felt more or
less interested in each others condition
and prosperity, and as far as acquaintance
extended, which was for thirty or forty
miles around, all were acquainted, and all
were neighbours and friends, entirely unlike our present position.—
    The seasons were then, I think, ma-
terially different from the present. We
had deeper snows, the winters were regular, commonly lasting until the first of
April, when the snows would disappear,
and be succeeded by warm Showers and
Sunshine until early in May, when farming would Commence, and Continue until
Autumn, without the late and early frosts
so Common in late years.

*   *   *

George Coventry Papers, XI, Reminiscences of Mrs. White of Whites Mills
near Cobourg Upper Canada. Formerly
Miss Katherine Chrysler of Sydney—
near Belleville. (Aged 79). p. 123.

The Bay of Quinté was covered with
Ducks of which we could obtain any

quantity from the Indians—As to fish
they could be had by fishing with a
scoup I have often speared large Salmon
with a pitchfork—, Now and then provisions ran very scant, but there being
plenty of Bull frogs we fared sumptuous-
ly This was the time of the famine I
think in 1788, we were obliged did [dig]
up our potatoes after planting them to
eat We never thought of these privations but were always happy and cheerful
—No unsettled minds no political strife
about Church Government or Squabbling
Municipal Councils,
We left everything to our faithful Governor, I have often heard My father
and Mother say, that they had no cause
of complaint in any shape, and were always thankful to the Government for
their kind assistance in the hour of need.

*   *   *

George Coventry Papers, IX, Transcripts
from the *Upper Canada Gazette,* 1799,
pp. 419-421.

The settlements from the head of
the Lake began about four years ago, excepting the Mohawk village; in this
period several Townships have so far
encreased in population and cultivation,
that there are several neighbourhoods at
convenient distances until we come to the
mouth of the Le trenche or Thames, and
supplied with more than a sufficiency of
produce of their own raising, for the residents: Oxford has this year one thousand
bushels of grain more than will be con-
sumed within itself. The settlements in
these Townships were commenced at a
period when the undertakers and followers were under every possible discouragement common to a new country.
    Among these were Mr. Thomas In-

new ¶ capital to employed it reads open communication

gersoll an enterprising man of consider-able property, and who held the minutes of the Council for Oxford; . . . Mr. Ingersoll, in particular, being already in the country, with a numerous family pursued his plan of improving the Township, by removing thither and many other families at his expence, and pursuading others to remain who had entered in it. They were all confirmed by Government in the small tracts they had begun on, as well as the actual settlers in the other Towns. These settlers being aware of the importance of roads in raising the value of property, early set about to open and extend them; and notwithstanding the numerous discouragements, and the immediate necessities of their families, they in one year, at the expence of Mr. Ingersoll cut and Bridged a road from Burford to Le Trenche, through a wilderness of 25 or 30 miles. This was done previous to the escheating of the Townships. Mr. Elisha Putnam of that Town (Oxford) by subscription has since continued the road from thence thirty miles to Allen's (Delaware) township. Here is a Villa and a Church raised and now finishing by Mr. E. Allan, after the model of that of the Mohawk Village. The subscription being inadequate to completely finishing the work, it was left in an unfinished state, but passable for sleighs. He has been by no means discouraged but issues a subscription to cut a road from Allans to the Moravians grant, a further distance as it must run, of fifty miles, to be ten feet wide, and the logs laying crosswise to be cut out 12 feet long. Without waiting the issue of the subscription, and relying on the patriotism of his neighbours, and

Gentlemen in other parts of the Province who hold lands upon that river, he began, and has already opened half the distance, and promises, if the liberality of his friends be equal to it, that he shall immediately complete the whole. The Moravians will extend it seven miles when it shall form a junction with the old road, from whence there will be a good waggon road forty miles to the mouth of the River. Thus we shall have by the ensuing winter a land communication with Detroit and not a days ride without settlements, such is the enterprise of our Western inhabitants, that one hundred and fifty miles of road is made without the least allowance from Government.

* * *

George Coventry Papers, IX, transcripts from the *Upper Canada Gazette*, 1801, pp. 628-629.

Hoicks! Hoicks! Hoicks!

On Thursday last, William Jarvis Esq. entertained the inhabitants of this place with a diversion new in itself to many and in some of its circumstances to all. About noon he caused a fox of full-growth to be unbagged, near the center of a fine sheet of ice which now covers the Bay, and when at a suitable distance turned loose the hounds upon it.

As previous notice had been circulated, the chace was followed by a number of gentlemen on horse back, and a concourse of the beau-monde of both sexes in carioles and sleigh.—Poor Reynard was probably the first of his species concluded in this manner to his fate.

Land Companies as Agents of Frontier Settlement

trapping of civilization provided before came to settlers frontier

British American Land Company, 1830-1936, II, *Correspondence,* 1835-1859, J. B. Forsyth and R. H. Gairdner, Commissioners of the Quebec and Megantic Land Company, to Andrew Russell, surveyor, August 10, 1838, pp. 225-228 PAC, MG 24, 154.

His Excellency the Governor General having sanctioned the expenditure of £1500 by us on surveys & improvements on the block of lands in the County of Megantic lying to the north-east of the St. Francis Territory, we have thought fit to employ you to perform this service, and subjoin the following Instructions for your guidance. . . .

You will proceed in the first place, to select the most proper site for a Village, on or near the shore of Lake St. Francis; paying due regards to the vicinity of water power and other circumstances which would tend to accellrate the prosperity of the Village. Having chosen this site, you will contract for the building of a log house on it, (to serve as a depôt for provisions), and the clearing of 20 acres,

to be ready for cropping next spring. You will then, after careful examination and exploration, determine on the most proper location for a road from the site for the Village to the old settlements on the river Chaudiere, or to Craigs road; by which a good communication could be established between the city of Quebec and the block of land. . . .

You will then proceed to survey and subdivide the land into townships, ranges and lots.

The precise manner of this survey cannot, at present, be pointed out, as it will depend on the actual features of the country and kind & quality of the soil; you are therefore left to exercise your judgment in laying off the lots in the most convenient forms for farming, so as to contain about 120 acres. You will however attend to the following general directions. Survey a range of lots on each side of the road from the old settlements to the site for the Village. Then survey the lands round the Lake St. Francis, the first range of lots fronting on the Lake, and ther range lines as nearly parrallel to the general course of the lake and of the County line as the nature of the country will admit. . . .

In laying out the Townships we do not wish any Reserves made except a lot for a Glebe which should be in some central part of each Township & a small reservation of 25 acres should be made in the same place for a Church[,] School House &ct.

* * *

The British American Land Company, 1830-1936, I, *Early Transcripts,* extract from the dispatch of December 21, 1836, pp. 132-133, PAC, MG 24, 154.

The Directors cannot help being anx-

Character of settlers important factor in determining success)

ious in regard to the expenditure which has taken place with a view to assist the poorer classes, and which, under existing circumstances may still be called for. Although they are sensible that you feel the importance of limiting as much as possible, the disbursements which have in consequence, devolved upon the Company, they must request you to impress upon Mr. Webster [the company attorney in Canada] the necessity of discouraging the Emigrants from relying too much upon the assistance for support by urging them to depend on their own exertions whenever practicable.

The Directors are induced to offer these suggestions from a conviction, that the class of persons who are most likely to be burdensome, will make no effort to serve themselves, if they find a facility in obtaining relief by application to the Agents of the Company, and that Mr. Websters position may sometimes embarrass him, unless he is armed with the authority of the Court and yourselves to confine his assistance to *imperative* cases.

Dalhousie Papers, 1816-1833, VIII, Lord Dalhousie to Alex MacLean, October 25, 1821, PAC, MG 24 A12.

subject too long to touch at present, it ought to discourage emigration, if anything can stop that unfortunate disposition. The industrious do very well but the 9/10 ths that come out are people who have not been industrious at home (to say the best of them) and cannot well be expected to change morals and manners and habits by a passage across the Atlantic.

A Governor's Discouraging View of Settlement

Pray advise your countrymen against the folly of coming to this country—such fellows as that Cameron on board the Earl of D. are mere crimps and cheats— it is shocking to hear the report made to me of his conduct to these people—he has got all the money he can out of them, and I have no doubt the far greater part will be beggars this winter either at Montreal, or wherever he has led them higher up.

Capt. Scott of the Vessel is a most honest, and civil creature as I have ever met with. The truth is, the country here is too full of people, and as neither the Crown, nor the Province, allow me to use any funds to survey and lay out lands *in preparation* for the 10, or 12,000 Emigrants that arrive annually, I find it impossible to satisfy the demand. They are sent to wander about, and enquire; and after all if they find a lot they have to pay for the survey of it, besides monstrous fees of Office. I never in my life have seen so much general distress and poverty as is daily exhibited here—but that is a

Province of Canada, *Journals,* 1854-1855, Appendix M.M., Report of the Select Committee appointed to examine and report upon the present system of management of the public Lands . . . , letter from William Spragge, Crown Land Department, March 28, 1854.

The Necessity of Government Involvement in Frontier Settlement: A Civil Servant's View

An experience of now upwards of twenty-five years in the Land Departments, during which I have aided in remedying many errors in system and practice, which I found to exist, has convinced me, and enabled me to convince others, that the sanctioning or tolerating speculatiion in the public lands, and the accomplishing their actual settlement, are incompatible the one with the other; and that if Government must make sales to individuals who have [not] immediate intention of settling, separate tracts are the only localities in which special privileges of that nature be exercised; of late years, the main consideration seems to have been the creation of a Land Revenue. But without sacrificing highly important interests, this can be attained only to a limited extent, and should be viewed as of secondary moment, and as not to be placed in competition with the great object at which we ought to aim; the increasing the Agricultural productions of Canada, and the adding to the numbers, of that best and most valuable of all our

Agriculturalists [independent small farmers]. They add more than any other to the material wealth of the Colony; mainly contribute towards realizing that which our financial indebtedness is rendering more pressingly important; the balance of trade. And as the most moral, as well as superior, physically, to the other classes, are the source whence those other classes can be best reunited.

To promote Agriculture, and encourage such as will embark in that pursuit, I would suggest the offering the public lands upon such terms, and accompanied by such inducements, as will be calculated to cause all who have it in their power to do so, to select this road to independence. . . .

A desultory manner of settling the public lands, is to be carefully avoided. The aid and encouragement which a united and compact body of settlers furnish to each other, is productive of the best consequences, and a few remarks on the advantage of placing them on lands with that object in view, may not be out of place. The moral, social and religious condition, is, I believe almost universally found to become depreciated among those people, whether in the United States or Canada, who, debarred by their isolated situation from the privileges of educational and religious instruction, have, as regards those of mature years become insensible of the restraints which they impose, while the younger members of families, never having enjoyed the opportunity necessary for the inculcation of the principles which they teach, exhibit the melancholy spectacle of responsible beings ignorant of the obligations and duties due them to God, and to man.

The better class of settlers, it is true, will endeavor to avoid those localities, where there is little prospect of education and religious instruction being attainable;

while the lawless and profane who must need both the influence and example of persons of orderly habits, and well regulated minds, are indifferent as to the localities they select, because they cannot value the privileges and advantages which they are not capable of comprehending: on every account therefore, whether as respects the better class of settlers, or those who have not yet learnt to estimate aright the objects which they so highly prize, it behoves the Government, in devising a mode for extending the interior settlements, to offer facilities for the introduction of education and religious instruction. It is manifest, that a scattered population cannot adequately maintain either those who disseminate the one, or promulgate the other; and no preliminary step in that direction can be more effectual, when throwing open a new section of country, than in peopling it in the first instance, as densely and compactly as circumstances will admit of, with industrious settlers, not entirely devoid of pecuniary resources; and by providing them with a means of direct communication, by opening out the roads laid off at the period of survey.

NB

gov't - encourage expansion
↑ agricultural expansion
– establish large group
  settlements

J. Sheridan Hogan, *Canada. An Essay: To Which Was Awarded the First Prize by the Paris Exhibition Committee of Canada*, Montreal, John Lovell, 1855, pp. 9-11, 24-30, 108-109.

Upper Canada as a Frontier Utopia: A Contemporary Judgment

In 1829, the population of Western Canada . . . had but one hundred and ninety-six thousand inhabitants. Its assessable property, being the real and personal estate of its people, was estimated, and I think with sufficient liberality, at £2,500,000. Its population in 1854 had increased to 1,237,600; and its assessed and assessable property, not including its public lands, the timber on them, or its minerals, is set down, in round numbers, at fifty million pounds. . . .

Thus then the remaining inhabitants of 1829, and the descendants of those who have died, together with the settlers who have come into the Province since, divide between them fifty million pounds worth of property, being £200 4s. 2d. to each family of five, and £40 0s. 2d. to each man, woman and child,—a degree of prosperity it would be difficult to credit, were it not established by proofs wholly incontrovertible.

And who and what are the people who divide among them this magnificent property? And how have they acquired it?

Did they come in as conquerors, and appropriate to themselves the wealth of others?—They came in but to subdue a wilderness, and have reversed the laws of conquest; for plenty, good neighbourhood, and civilization mark their footsteps. Or did capitalists accompany them, to reproduce their wealth by applying it to the enterprises and improvements of a new country? No;—for capitalists wait till their pioneer, industry, first makes his report, and it is but now that they are studying the interesting one from Canada. Or did the generosity of European Princes, or European wealth or benevolence provide them with such outfits as secured their success? On the contrary, the wrongs of Princes, and the poverty of Nations, have been the chief causes of the settlement of America. Her prosperity is the offspring of European hopelessness. Her high position in the world is the result of the sublime efforts of despair. And he who would learn who they are who divide among them the splendid property created in Canada has but to go to the quays of Liverpool, of Dublin, of Glasgow, and of Hamburg, and see the emigrants there embarking, who knew neither progress nor hopes where they were born, to satisfy himself to the fullest. . . .

Great as has been the prosperity of America, and of the settlements which mark the magnificent country just described, yet nature has not been wooed in them without trials, nor have her treasures been won without a struggle worthy of their worth. Those who have been in the habit of passing *early clearings* in Upper Canada must have been struck with the cheerless and lonely, even desolate appearance of the first settler's little log hut. In the midst of a dense forest, and with a "patch of clearing" scarcely large enough to let the sun shine in upon him, he looks not unlike a person struggling for existence on a single plank in the middle of an ocean. For weeks, often for months, he sees not the face of a stranger. The same still, and wild, and boundless forest every morning rises up to his view; and his only hope against its shutting him in for life rests in the axe upon his shoulder. A few blades of corn, peeping up between stumps whose very roots interlace, they are so close together, are his sole safeguards against want; whilst the few potatoe plants, in little far-between "hills," and which struggle for existence against the briar bush and luxuriant underwood, are to form the seeds of his future plenty. Tall pine trees, girdled and blackened by the fires, stand out as grim monuments of the prevailing loneliness, whilst the forest itself, like an immense wall around a forest, seems to say to the settler,—"how can poverty ever expect to escape from such a prison house."

Yet there is, happily, a poetry in every man's nature; and there is no scene in life, how cheerless soever it may seem, where that poetry may not spring up; where it may not gild desolation itself, and cause a few to hope where all the world besides might despair. That little clearing—for I describe a reality—which to others might afford such slender guarantee for bare subsistence, was nevertheless a source of bright and cheering dreams to that lonely settler. He looked at it, and instead of thinking of its littleness, it was the foundation of great hopes of a large farm and rich corn fields to him. And this very dream, or poetry, or what you will, cheered him at his lonely toil, and made him contented with his rude fire-side. The blades of corn, which you might regard as conveying but a tantalizing idea of human comforts, were associated by him with large stacks and full granaries; and

the very thought nerved his arm, and made him happy. His little lonely hut, into which I saw shrink out of sight his timid children—for they rarely if ever saw a stranger,—was coupled by him, not with the notion of privations and hardships you might naturally attach to it, but with the proud and manly idea, that *it* should be the place where he should achieve the respectability and independence of those children. But, besides this, he knew the history of hundreds, nay, thousands of others in Canada, who had gained prosperity against similar odds, and he said in his manliness, that he should go and do likewise.

Seven years afterwards I passed that same settler's cottage—it was in the valley of the Grand River in Upper Canada, not far from the present Village of Caledonia. The little log hut was used as a back kitchen to a neat two story frame house, painted white. A large barn stood near by, with stock of every description in its yard. The stumps, round which the blades of corn, when I last saw the place, had so much difficulty in springing up, had nearly all disappeared. Luxuriant Indian corn had sole possession of the place where the potatoes had so hard a struggle against the briar bushes and the under-wood. The forest—dense, impenetrable though it seemed—had been pushed far back by the energetic arm of man. A garden, bright with flowers, and enclosed in a neat picket fence, fronted the house; a young orchard, spread out in rear. I met a farmer, as I was quitting the scene, returning from church with his wife and family. It was on a Sunday, and there was nothing in their appearance, save perhaps a healthy brown colour in their faces, to distinguish them from persons of wealth in cities. The waggon they were in, their horses, harness, dresses, everything about them, in short, indicated comfort and easy circumstances. I enquired of the man who was the owner of the property I have just been describing? "It is mine, sir," he replied; "I settled on it nine years ago, and have, thank God, had tolerable success."

Such was an early settler of Upper Canada. Such were his hardships, his fortitude, and his success. His history is but that of thousands in the same Province. . . .

To persons not practically acquainted with Upper Canada, these evidences, not only of comfort but of considerable refinement may appear extraordinary, because mere rude husbandry, just emerging from a wilderness, could hardly be expected to produce such results. Wealth in agriculture, like wealth in every other occupation, is usually the offspring of skill and judgment, as well as of labour and perseverance. But it is a remarkable fact that the farmers of Upper Canada have opportunities of improvement, and of enlarging and correcting their views, beyond what are enjoyed by many of their class even in England. And this arises from the circumstance of the population being made up of so many varieties. The same neighbourhood has not unfrequently a representative of the best farming skill of Yorkshire; of the judicious management and agricultural experiences of the Lothians, and of the patient industry and perseverance of Flanders. In a country so peopled the benefits of travel are gained without the necessity of going away from home. Other countries, in fact, send their people to teach Canadians, instead of Canadians having to go to other countries to learn. A thousand experiences are brought to their doors, instead of their having to visit a thousand doors to acquire them. Nor is the advantage of this happy admixture of population altogether on the side of the Canadian; for whilst he gleans from the old countryman his skill and his science, he teaches him, in return, how to rely upon himself in emergencies and difficulties inseparable from a new country,—how to be a carpenter when a storm blows down a door, and there is no carpenter to be had; and how to be an undismayed wheelright when a waggon breaks down in the midst of the forest, and there is no one either to instruct or to assist him. The one, in short, imparts to a comparatively rude people the knowledge and skill of an old and highly civilized country: the other teaches skilled labour how to live in a new land. The consequence is, the old countryman of tact becomes, in all that relates to self-reliance and enterprise, a capital Canadian in a few years; whilst the Canadian, in all that pertains to skillful industry, becomes an excellent Englishman. As a natural result of this, there is scarcely an improvement effected in English farming which does not find its way into Canada soon after; nor is there an agricultural implement of value, which can be adapted to Canadian soil, that is not immediately copied or imported. And Agricultural Societies have sprung up and prospered in the country, to an extent hardly paralleled in any other part of the world. The result is that Durham cattle may be seen at the very verge of civilization in Western Canada; that there is scarcely a neighbourhood where may not be found the descendants of Berkshire pigs, nor a village that has not horses which exhibit all the fine peculiarities of the best breeds of England and Scotland. That a country so circumstanced, with a fine climate, and with abundance of land for those who had the energy to clear and cultivate it, should have enjoyed great prosperity, is really not so much a wonder as it would be a matter of surprise if it had not had such success.

The same causes which have produced these results upon agriculture have also had an eminently beneficial effect upon society. The settler who nobly pushes back the giant wilderness, and hews out for himself a home upon the conquered territory, has necessarily but a bony hand and a rough visage to present to advancing civilization. His children, too, are timid, and wild, and uncouth. But a stranger comes in; buys the little improvement on the next lot to him; has children who are educated, and a wife with refined tastes,—for such people mark, in greater or lesser numbers, every settlement in Upper Canada. The necessities of the new comer soon bring about an acquaintance with the old pioneer. Their families meet—timid and awkward enough at first perhaps; but children know not the conventionalities of society, and, happily, are governed by their innocence in their friendships. So they play together, go to school in company; and thus, imperceptibly to themselves, are the tastes and manners of the educated imparted to the rude, and the energy and fortitude of the latter are infused into their more effeminate companions. Manly but ill-tutored success is thus taught how to enjoy its gains, whilst respectable poverty is instructed how to better its condition. That pride occasionally puts itself to inconvenience to prevent these pleasant results, my experience of Canada forces me to admit; and that the jealousy and vanity of mere success sometimes views with unkindness the manner and habit of reduced respectability—never perhaps more exacting than when it is poorest—I must also acknowledge. But that the great law of progress, and the influence of free institutions, break down these exceptional feelings and prejudices, is patent to every close observer of Cana-

dian society. Where the educated and refined undergo the changes incident to laborious occupations—for the constant use of the axe and the plough alters men's feelings as well as their appearances,—and where rude industry is also changed by the success which gives it the benefit of education, it is impossible for the two classes not to meet. As the one goes down —at least in its occupations,—it meets the other coming up by reason of its successes, and both eventually occupy the same pedestal. I have seen this social problem worked out over and over again in Upper Canada, and have never known the result different. Pride, in America, must "stoop to conquer;" rude industry rises always. . . .

The people, I may say, of all North America—I mean the descendants of the British race, and emigrants from Britain —are, perhaps, of all others the best trained to understand and to enjoy the benefits of representative institutions. Their habits of self-reliance and the necessity for combination to effect the simple purposes of existence—to build the log hut far in the woods; to "log" the first acres of ground cleared; to throw a bridge over a stream, or to clear a road into the forest,—naturally lead them to respect skill, and to put themselves under the guidance of talent. The leading spirit of a *"logging bee,"* and the genius who presides over the construction of a barn, what more natural than that they should be elected, at the annual meeting of the neighbourhood, to oversee the construction of bridges, and to judge of, and inspect, the proper height of fences? And this is the first legislation such a people have to do. The useful individual, too, in a settlement, who draws deeds and wills, and settles disputes without law, and gives good advice without cost, what more natural, also, than that he should be selected by the people he benefits by his education and his kindness, to make their laws, and to guard their interests? The Canadian people, too, have no tenant rights, nor "trades unions" to secure higher wages, or to prevent too many hours of work. Their necessities are their orators. Their ways and means of living, and taking the best care of what their labour brings them, are the principles by which they are governed. Their democracy begins at the right end; for, instead of weaving theories to control the property of others, they think of but the best means of taking care of their own. Need it be wondered at, then, that a people so edu-cated—and such has been the universal education of North America—should know how to govern themselves; should gradually rise from the consideration of the affairs of a neighbourhood to those of a county and a country; that they should have sufficient conservatism to guard the fruits of their industry, and sufficient democracy to insist upon the right to do so. And such is a true picture of the Canadian people. Their municipal system is but a small remove from the leader of the "*logging bee*" being elected builder of the bridge, and their parliament is but a higher class in the same school of practical self-government.

Strong frontierist tone.

J. M. S. Careless, *The Union of the Canadas: The Growth of Canadian Institutions, 1841-1857,* (Toronto, McClelland and Stewart Limited, 1967), pp. 20-21, 28-29, 35-36. Reprinted by permission of The Canadian Publishers, McClelland and Stewart Limited.

Upper Canada in a Metropolitan Context: A Historian's Analysis

Well over a million people lived in the Province of Canada in 1841: 670,000 in the Lower Canadian half, now denominated Canada East; 480,000 in the Upper Canadian half, now Canada West. And the St. Lawrence-Great Lakes waterway linked them not only to each other but to the transatlantic British metropolis at one end and the core of the great republic at the other. The Canadian hinterland was supplied and shaped by both: British trade, immigration and political structure expressed the transatlantic connection; American-style enterprise, ways of life and social outlook, the influence of the continent. Remote as the world of Canada might seem, rimmed as it was by interminable forests and the timeless emptiness of the north, its people were still in decisive contact with the far wider worlds of Britain and the United States. . . .

Canada West generally was so full of recent immigrants, and so much in the stage of extensive rather than intensive growth, that its social structure was naturally ill-defined. Nevertheless, in the towns one could distinguish an upper class of officials, often sizable landholders (who were in close social contact with the officers of the British garrison, where that existed); a middle class of merchants, shopkeepers and skilled craftsmen, whose wealthy upper ranks might certainly be allied with the office-holders; and a lower class of wage labourers composed largely of immigrants, without the resources yet to farm. Many would never acquire them. Already Toronto and other towns were evincing the presence of the permanent poor, raising local problems of bad housing, sanitation, and winter relief, even in a society presumably characterized by the robust, self-reliant pioneer. There was also brawling and family suffering caused by the "liquor evil," which was endemic in this hard-drinking frontier society but was concentrated in the inns, bars, and squalid dram-shops of towns. In response, a temperance movement was developing. Toronto's temperance society, founded in 1839, had 1,300 members by 1841. Similar societies were being established in Lower Canada, where Roman Catholic *curés* sponsored them for the parish poor.

The upper and lower strata of society were less in evidence in the Upper Canada countryside than in the towns. Small proprietors working their own farms constituted a broad agrarian middle class; though there were, of course, hired men on one hand, and on the other, an element of gentry in the government-appointed magistrates and British half-pay officers who managed to maintain themselves on the land. Moreover, there were differences within the middle class itself, between increasingly prosperous commercial farmers in more advanced districts and settlers in the still primitive backwoods, clearing land for their limited crops and lacking good roads out to market. Yet

strong, united, solid

both groups produced for sale, and were dependent on purchased, imported goods, whether or not barter was the immediate means of exchange at the local mill or general store. The self-sufficient pioneer was largely a creature of myth. Almost from the start the Upper Canadian farmer had been part of a cash economy, specializing in wheat production for outside markets. To this the backwoodsman could add valuable potash from the trees he cleared and burned, while the more developed farmer had hides, meat and other produce to offer from his broader fields. However, those fields were not necessarily well-treated, too much being attempted with too little labour available. Canadian-born farmers and those from the States were frequently the worst land-butchers. Some, indeed, were professional pioneers who made their profit in clearing and selling farms rather than in working them. Lowland Scots or English made better "improving farmers" and the Irish often poor ones. . . .

Thanks to improving provisions for education, some of the crudities and cultural limitations of a half-fledged frontier society began to pass away. But the frontier age in any case was passing as a more thickly settled, better defined community took shape. In Canada East, good land in the Townships was rapidly disappearing, and other new areas looked too remote and rugged to invite ready expansion. Though much fertile wild land remained to be occupied in Canada West, that section, too, was rapidly approaching its limits of good arable soil, as settlement spread along the shores of Lake Huron towards the limestone Bruce Peninsula, or probed inland towards the inexorable rock barriers of the huge Precambrian Shield. The end of the open agricultural frontier would soon have to come. And while this

still lay in the future, signs of a maturing, consolidating community were already apparent in Canada by the early 1840's. The constant rise in rural population, the improvement of rough, stump-filled clearings into well-cultivated fields, the transition in many localities from log shanties to farm buildings of sawn lumber—these were all aspects of a spreading social transformation. So were the rise of populated hamlets around sawmill and gristmill sites, and the emergence of flourishing urban communities where once there had only been "four corners" with mill, tavern, general store, and smithy. And throughout the developing western countryside, organized churches with substantial buildings were replacing the periodic meetings held by itinerant missionaries in taverns or barns.

Furthermore, despite the continuing problem of bad roads—mud pits in spring and fall, rutted tracks in summer—internal communications were steadily being developed to knit the community together. Yonge Street had been macadamized (graded with interlocked stone and gravel) nearly to Lake Simcoe by 1841. Governor Sydenham, by ordinance, had sought to improve the winter "snow roads" of Canada East. Wooden plank roads, which could be built for half the cost of macadamized ways, were increasingly being laid down. Traffic moved freely by steamboat or lake schooner along main water routes in open season, while canals would soon be building anew on the St. Lawrence. It only remained for the coming of the railway to provide sure, year-round heavy transport and lift the remaining burdens of inland isolation. Already lines were being talked of, charters sought; and a rail route from Toronto north to Georgian Bay had tentatively been surveyed.

Accordingly, the world of the united province was a world in process of vital change as it moved away from pioneering simplicity. The process, of course, would take years still to work itself out, but essentially the province of Canada was passing from a phase of extensive growth to one of intensive development. Ahead lay a different world, of the railway, steam-powered machinery, and the rising city; and a rural community with its own municipal life, well-developed commercial villages, and increasingly diversified agriculture. With the increase in wealth and population, class lines became more marked as advancing capitalism and the spread of wage-earning affected either end of the social scale. Old officialdom, backwoods egalitarianism in the West, French-Canadian agrarianism in the East, all gave ground before the growing power of middle-class business interests. This mounting bourgeois influence displayed itself in the politics of the union, in the parties of both sections, reform as well as tory. Under Baldwin and Hincks, for example, Upper Canadian reform soon lost its earlier suspicions of banks and large-scale business enterprise. And in Lower Canada, LaFontaine and his associates would successfully mediate between the French rural masses and the English commercial classes of the towns.

Part IV

The Frontier Challenge to Institutions

One major difference between frontierism and other forms of environmentalism is that frontierists have seen the environment not as a force shackling man, forcing him into a particular mould, but as a liberating force. The frontier frees man from the traditional institutions of the Old World, which wither and die in the free air of North America. The pioneer, then, is at liberty to create new institutions, ones suited to his new environment and his new society. So it is that oligarchical forms of government give way to democracy, established churches to evangelical sects, class distinction to social mobility. It is this role of the frontier in destroying imported institutions which is perhaps crucial in creating a new society in North America. And it is on this ground that critics should contend with the frontierists. One aspect, that of political institutions, has been debated at some length, as Part V will show. But the general question of institutions and their adjustment to frontier conditions has received little attention from historians. The selections here hope only to indicate some of the lines of inquiry which might be undertaken.

Two problems are dealt with in this section: the adjustment of religious institutions to the frontier; and the question of frontier violence, how traditional concepts of law and order, and traditional means of keeping the peace, fared on the frontier. It is probably in the area of religion that the frontier thesis has gained its greatest acceptance in Canada. Most historians have agreed with the view that Old World religious forms had a very hard time of it in frontier Canada, losing out to the evangelical sects in the struggle for the allegiance of the pioneers. The imported churches, and especially the Church of England, were unsuited for the frontier environment, so the argument runs, because of their emphasis on a trained clergy unavailable in Canada, because of their ritual which required the kind of religious instruction unavailable to pioneers, because of their practice of establishing churches and expecting isolated settlers to come to them. In contrast, the evangelical sects from the United States were suitable for frontier areas, because of their willingness to employ poorly educated and poorly trained preachers, because of the simplicity of their services and their theology, because of their use of circuit-riding preachers who took religion to the people.

These arguments have a plausibility which has convinced most Canadian historians. And one can find evidence in the sources to support this approach. The problem of dealing with frontier settlements was much on the mind of Upper Canada's first Catholic bishop, Alexander Macdonell, for instance. In 1835 he wrote to one of his priests concerning the riotous outpost of Bytown: "Bytown being a frontier town . . . I consider the honor & credit of Our Holy Religion more exposed there than in any other Mission in the Diocese." But a number of pressing questions remained unanswered, and necessitate some caution before accepting the conventional wisdom. There is very little hard data on the membership of the various churches and sects. And there is even less on how many settlers were converted from one denomination to another. We are left with uncertain speculation. If, as historians have believed, the sects held the allegiance of a majority of pioneers, did they do so by conversion of erstwhile Anglicans and Presbyterians? Or does the apparent success of the Methodists and others merely indicate that most of the Americans who entered Upper Canada in the early frontier period were evangelicals when they migrated? In fact, was there any significant number of permanent conversions?

This is not the only area in which there is reason for caution. Despite the traditional view, the Anglican Church did have circuit riding clergy, like the Methodists. Did these itinerants have measurably greater success than their settled colleagues? As yet, we simply do not know. What would have been the success of the established churches if they had moved out on to the frontier in force, with large numbers of trained clergymen? Was their apparent failure due to frontier conditions, or to the poor support offered them by their mother churches in Britain? Bishop Macdonell was certain that the biggest problem faced by the Catholic Church in Upper Canada was not the adjustment to a new environment but the poor quality and small number of clergy supplied by the British church. In contrast, the Methodists in the early period were backed by the resources of the Methodist Church in the United States. Viewed in this light, the religious situation in Upper Canada becomes a contest between two rival metropolitan systems. And, finally, there is the question of how successful *any* of the religious denominations were in reaching the pioneers. Michael Smith, an American Baptist who published an excellent account of the province in 1813, estimated that one-half of the people in western Upper Canada professed no religion at all.

Three items have been chosen to illustrate the religious issue. Few historians have given more than passing reference to the social side of religion, most have been concerned with the politico-religious questions of the period, such as clergy reserves, the marriage question and the university question. An exception is S. D. Clark. This passage from his book, *Church and Sect in Canada*, gives a broad spectrum approach, relating the conflict of the established churches and the evangelical sects to the nature of the frontier society, and linking it to other challenges to traditional institutions —

particularly the rejection of the British class system, and the frontier reaction against undemocratic forms of government. In discussing what he considers the failure of the traditional churches to provide the social leadership needed by a frontier society, to develop "a more inclusive social philosophy", Clark seems to come down squarely as a supporter of the evangelicals and their democratic approaches. As with the orthodox frontierists, then, there is a strong moral content to his history.

The next selection is from a book published in 1824 by William Bell, a Presbyterian minister in the military settlement at Perth, Upper Canada. Bell agrees about the problem faced by the British churches, but he sees it as one challenging all denominations, not just the established ones. And his analysis of the causes of this religious crisis is very different from Clark's. For Bell, it seems, the troubles of the churches were imported with the settlers, not found in the frontier landscape.

Finally, there is a curious document written by an ex-minister, G. B. Bucher, to the Chief Superintendent of Education in Upper Canada, Egerton Ryerson. As well as for the peculiarities of Bucher's florid writing style, and his brutal frankness in detailing the reasons for leaving the ministry, his letter is interesting for the light it casts on the problems of institutions like the churches and schools in a frontier area such as the wilderness around Pembroke in the upper Ottawa Valley. Bucher creeps close to Clark in emphasizing economic conditions, and adds the traditional frontierist explanation of the isolation of the settlers.

The second problem dealt with in this section is that of law and order. We come closer now to the Hollywood frontier with its shoot-em-ups. Certainly social disorder was characteristic of the Canadian frontier, and especially of the timber frontier from which

these documents have been chosen. Along the Ottawa, the premier timberland of Canada, the forces of law and order often seemed powerless against the forces of disorder. This was especially true in the 1830's when a gang of Irish desperadoes, the Shiners, terrorized the whole valley. This was a dramatic example of the violence and lawlessness which was often epidemic in pre-Confederation Canada. Political rioting, like that in Montreal in 1832 and in Montreal, Bytown, and other centres in 1849; the bloody clashes of the Protestant Orangemen and Irish Catholics that tore scores of communities throughout the 1840's and 1850's; the rioting of canal and railway workers; the everyday head-breaking which was taken for granted: the extent of violence and of disregard for public order is clear.

What is less clear is the cause. Or rather causes. Undoubtedly a variety of factors contributed to such a widespread phenomenon. Again the investigation of this area of social history has barely begun, so there hardly can be said to be a consensus in interpretations. Frontierists would argue that the environment liberated pioneers from authority, and created a situation in which traditional mores did not operate. Violence flourished until new, more suitable codes were created. Several of the documents in this section might point to the highly competitive nature of frontier economy and the violence generated in this competition. Other writers have preferred the antithesis of the frontier approach, insisting Canada fell prey to imported animosities of race and religion, carried over from Britain. These all help to account for some kinds of social disorder, but do not offer any comprehensive solution. Perhaps a more satisfactory general answer might lie in a theme touched on by all of these selections. The common denominator is the weakness of the police power, the failure of the colonial authorities to provide police or militia or troops sufficient to enforce the laws. Most communities in Upper Canada, until the 1850's, had no police, relying for law enforcement on part-time magistrates, men chosen for their positions as community leaders, rather than for their courage or their physical strength. They often did not make very impressive or very effective law officers. Was the crucial factor, then, not the influence of the frontier in weakening traditional institutions but rather the weakness of those institutions when they were established on the frontier?

The first of this group of selections is from the 1835 report made by a Select Committee of the British Commons on timber duties. Many witnesses argued that the duties encouraging the Canadian timber trade should be abolished because of the deplorable conditions on the timbering frontier. It would be a great service to Canada, they insisted, if the timber trade were allowed to die. Samuel Revans, a Montreal merchant, was typical in his disgust at the disorder and immorality found among the Ottawa timberers. Typical, too, was his explanation that this disorder sprang from the lack of compact settlements, and from the timberers' isolation from ordered society for much of the year. The second document is a letter, also from 1835, written by a large timber operator on the lower Ottawa, George Hamilton, to the lieutenant governor's secretary. Hamilton is describing the early stages of the so-called "Shiners War," the worst period of organized violence on the Ottawa. Next is a letter written twelve years later, but describing the same absence of authority, the same conflicts over timber tracts, of which Hamilton had complained. The author, William Rogerson, was a timberer on a tributary of the Ottawa River, the recipient, James Stevenson, was the Crown Timber Agent at Bytown. Two excerpts from a contemporary newspaper, the *Brockville Recorder*, described the height of the Shiner terror, and return us to the familiar problem of absence of authority. The *Bytown Gazette*, although reluctant to discuss the troubles in the town, strikes the same note. And the difficulty of rectifying this failure is illustrated by a letter from G. W. Baker to the governor's secretary. Baker, a former soldier, attempted to raise a citizen force, the Bytown Rifles, to cope with the disorders caused by the Shiners. The combination of economic interest and inadequate jail facilities limited the effectiveness of his effort. Finally, a passage from an article by M. S. Cross attempts to give a general interpretation of social problems on the timbering frontier.

S. D. Clark, *Church and Sect in Canada*, University of Toronto Press, Toronto, 1948, pp. 107-109, 127-129, 144-147, 168-172. Reprinted by permission of University of Toronto Press. Copyright Canada 1948, University of Toronto Press.

The Sociology of Frontier Religion

Failure of the traditional institutions of religion to adapt to new social conditions accounted for the weakening of their influence within the Canadian community. The fundamental problem of religious organization in Canada was the problem of meeting the needs of a scattered backwoods population. Within the new backwoods settlements, the traditional attachments of the old world—ties of folk and class—broke down in face of powerful forces of individualization, and new attachments had to be established in terms of a new sense of social purpose. It was the failure of the traditional churches that they offered no effective support of forces of social reorganization in the Canadian backwoods society. The traditional organization of religion weakened with the weakening of the traditional social organization in general.

Weaknesses in the organization of the Church of England early became apparent in Canada. In spite of government support, and the advantage of being first in the field, the Church from the beginning was unable to provide with the services of religion more than a small proportion of the growing Canadian population. Unlike Nova Scotia, where most of the missionaries after 1783 were recruited from the old colonies, missionaries for Canada had to be supplied almost entirely from overseas; it was not for some time that the Protestant Episcopal Church in the United States recovered sufficiently from the shock of the War of Independence to interest itself in foreign missions. Difficulties of transportation and communication provided obstacles to the recruitment of clergymen from overseas which were not readily overcome by a church lacking a strong missionary spirit. Missionary work in Canada was looked upon as that of providing for an outpost of empire, of assuring the supremacy of the established church within the imperial system, and the rank and file of the clergy in England shared in this lack of any real interest in spreading religious teachings. Considerations of a comfortable livelihood and of social prestige, and an emphasis upon the ministry as a career, discouraged emigration to a frontier area which held out little in the way of material reward.

Realization of the difficulty of securing clergy from overseas early led to proposals favouring a greater reliance upon local recruits for the ministry. "Few men of ability," Strachan pointed out in a report to the Chief Justice on the state of religion in Upper Canada, March 1, 1815, "will be found willing to leave England for so distant a Colony—much dependence ought not therefore to be placed on this source of supply." There was lacking within the colony, however, any large local reservoir of supply from which to call up workers; the recruiting methods and training programme of the Church were too rigid to permit the ordination of those whose only qualification was their desire to preach the gospel. "Of the persons born in the country," the Bishop of Quebec had written in 1800, "I need not inform your Grace that few indeed have been so educated as to give them any decent pretension to instruct others, and among the persons who come to settle here, there is less probability of finding proper subjects. Your Grace, I am sure would be very far from recommending it to me to open the Sacred Profession for the reception of such adventurers, as disappointed speculations may have disposed to enter it." Institutional impediments to safeguard the ministerial profession might have broken down if a greater number of the local inhabitants had insisted upon organizing Church of England congregations with local, untrained preachers in charge, but the membership of the Church in the colony was confined to the "respectable" portions of the population, and there was lacking favourable soil for the breeding of the religious prophet. Orthodoxy in clerical qualifications was maintained at the price of failing to secure a sufficient supply of ministers.

The result was that new settlements grew up and no clergymen were available to provide religious services. The Bishop of Quebec wrote in 1794 on the completion of a visitation of his diocese:

With respect to Religious instruction the state of these settlers is for the most part truly deplorable. From Montreal to Kingston, a distance of 200 miles, there is not one Clergyman of the Church of England: nor any house of religious worship except one small Chapel belonging to the Lutherans, & one, or perhaps two, belonging to the Presbyterians. The public worship of God is entirely suspended, or performed in a manner which can neither tend to improve the people in Religious Truth, nor to render them useful members of society. The Presbyterian and the Lutheran Clergymen are, I believe, men of good character, but their influence is necessarily limited to their own little congregations. The great bulk of the people have, and can have no instruction, but such as they receive occasionally from itinerant & mendicant Methodists: a set of ignorant enthusiasts whose preaching is calculated only to perplex the understanding, & corrupt the morals; to relax the nerves of industry, & dissolve the bonds of society. . . .

The emphasis upon class distinctions within the Church led inevitably to the weakening of the support of those who had no pretensions to upper class status. The frontier destroyed status relationships, and emphasized values of individual worth and equality, and where the frontier influence was strong, as a result, the social foundations of the Church disintegrated. In becoming the church of the colonial upper class, the Church weakened its influence among the large rural population. "To give the preponderance to the Church of England establishment," Strickland wrote, "that church in Canada, which at present is only that of a rising aristocracy, must become also the church of the poor." The failure of the Church to liberalize its social appeal resulted largely from its failure to adopt a more democratic principle in the selection of candidates for clerical orders.

Reared in an English upper class setting, sharp cultural differences set the Church of England clergy off from the backwoods farmers, particularly the backwoods farmers of American origin. Such a clergy could have little appreciation of the manner of life and peculiar problems of a pioneer farm population, and, as a result often looked with distaste upon forms of behaviour which were an inevitable feature of pioneer society. The rural population, on its part, had equally little appreciation of the manners and training of the Anglican clergy and often disliked that which was in the old world society an acceptable form of clerical behaviour. Thus differences in the cultural background of the clergy and population became exaggerated into issues of moral worth; the feeling of mutual distrust and antagonism, based upon a failure to understand each other, created a situation unfavourable to the acceptance of the ministrations of the Church. "It seems to me," J. J. Bigsby wrote, "that the Episcopal clergy are taken from too high a class for colonial service. They are usually so dissimilar from their flocks in tastes, habits, and prejudices, that they might come from another planet. Their early nurture has been too nice, and their education too academic, to admit of that familiarity, combined with true respect on the part of the people, which gives such well-earned influence to the Roman Catholic clergy in certain parts of Europe, and to the Wesleyan in Britain." Not only in their social contacts, but in their work in the pulpit, the class prejudices of the Anglican clergymen handicapped them in winning the support of the rural population. "That missionary zeal can scarcely be," the Reverend James Beaven wrote in 1846, "whilst the clergy are only men educated as gentlemen; whilst their mental condition and ordinary habits keep them involuntarily from familiar intercourse with the lower classes; whilst the gradations of clergy extend themselves to all the upper classes of society, but do not ramify through the lower."

The identification of the Church with the colonial upper class inevitably became closely related to its identification with British imperial interests and, in the end, with the cause of ecclesiastical establishment. The Church remained English as well as upper class in outlook, and, while such a disposition strengthened its hold upon the population of overseas origin, it weakened its influence among those of American origin and among those coming increasingly to think of themselves as Canadian in attachment. Failure of the Episcopalian Church in the United States to take any lead in the work in Canada inevitably led to the dependence upon leadership from England and to the dependence upon clergymen of English origin, and such clergymen of an old world background could not win the sympathy of people with a new world, American background. In 1815 Strachan, aware of this weakness, had written respecting the advantages of training men for the Church within the colony itself. "If brought up and educated in this Province," he pointed out, "the Clergy will be more useful among the people, and more happy themselves; and care may be taken that they be equally Loyal, and attached to the Mother Country." Twenty-one years later the same view was urged by the author of the anonymous pamphlet urging reform within the Church. "Without depreciating in the least," he wrote, "the valuable services of the clergy from England and Ireland, to whom the church owes much of its improvement, within the last ten years, I think that all will acknowledge, that young men, educated in the country, habituated to the manners and customs of the people, endeared to the fatigues and privations attendant upon a missionary's life in new countries, and accustomed to the climate, from which many strangers suffer severely, are, *caerteris paribus*, better suited for supplying our wants than those educated in Europe." The problem of the Church was one, as the anonymous author went on to point out, of building up in the country institutions for the training of men for the ministry. Unlike the evangelical churches, the Church of England was unwilling to recruit men without such training and, indeed, without in addition a thorough scholastic education; the establishment of theological schools which would admit young men with scarcely any education and in six months or a year would equip them for the ministry was something which the Church was never prepared to undertake. The result was that the Church only very slowly built up a Canadian ministry in the country.

The Church of England failed to become a Canadian church because its interests in maintaining the privileges of Establishment made it dependent upon the imperial tie. Any move to introduce a greater measure of autonomy within the Church carried the threat of weakening the relationship of the Church to the state. The Church could not become a Canadian church without becoming a "free" church. Vested interests of ecclesiastical Establishment, therefore, led inevitably to the identification of the Church with the tory cause in the colony. Imperial interests, on their part, sought within a system of Church Establishment to build up a body of sentiment within the colony favourable to the perpetuation of the imperial relationship. The interests of state and the interests of church became closely allied in maintaining ecclesiastical privileges and in discouraging the development of nonconformist religious denominations. . . .

The stability of some of the smaller sects, and of the Roman Catholic Church, in face of movements of population re-sulting from frontier, backwoods settlement in Canada suggests that, given certain conditions, religious organization was able to adapt itself to changing social demands without such disruption as that evident in the rise of new religious movements. The reason for this lay largely in the fact that any expansion of community life involved the emergence of what might be called the "closed frontier" side by side with the "open frontier." Individuals, as individuals, pushed into new areas of social life; their movements were dictated solely by personal interests, such as the desire to secure cheap land, to move as far as possible beyond the reach of the law, or simply to enjoy freedom from all social restraints. Where such development took place, the problem of religious organization—as of social organization generally—was that of meeting, without much possibility of controlling, the kinds of demands for social fellowship which emerged. Where, however, it was not individuals but groups which moved into new areas of social life, the problem of social control was very different. Group settlement implied direction from the beginning, and, where such direction could be maintained, demands for social fellowship were canalized within existing systems of social organization. It was the weakness of the Society of Friends, that the control which had characterized early Quaker settlement in the country could not be maintained in face of the emergence of open frontier conditions. Among the Mennonites, on the other hand, ethnic differences supported the social isolation secured through the controls of the sect. In somewhat similar fashion, ethnic and doctrinal differences supported the isolation of the Roman Catholic population secured through the elaborate denominational controls of the Church. In sharp contrast to the Church of England which exercised little control over the movements of the Protestant population, the migration of Roman Catholics tended to be a migration into a closed frontier area; the Church moved with its following, and to some degree directed the whole process of population movement. Religious —and social—stability was maintained by maintaining the conditions of the inherited religious and social system.

It was in the open frontier that the most complete breakdown of the traditional organization of religion occurred. Conditions of backwoods settlement in Canada led generally to a very considerable emphasis upon individual enterprise in economic and social life. Religious interests weakened with the weakening of social interests generally. The frontier society represented a break away from traditional systems of thought and traditional means of control. Folk ties disintegrated in face of the unsettling effects of frontier life, and class ties broke down in face of powerful levelling forces in the frontier community. Folk and class gave way to the social masses.

Such tendencies made inevitable a weakening of the basis of religious organization, but they made almost equally inevitable the emergence of new religious forms within the frontier society. The break from a traditional religious order was accompanied by a break from a traditional social order in general. Individualization weakened a sense of collective life and made difficult the building up of new forms of social organization. In Canada, as in the Maritime Provinces, secular interests were not sufficiently strong to support a vigorous group consciousness, and support of such a consciousness had to come in the end from religious interests

deeply inbedded in the culture of the new frontier population.

The strength of religious interests among the population accounted for the strength of new religious movements. The traditional churches weakened not because they lacked the support of strong religious interests but because they failed to capitalize upon such support. Too strong religious interests endangered the denominational ties of the Church, and, as a result, it tended to discourage any strong manifestation of religious feelings. The evangelistic religious movement, on the other hand, grew directly out of the expression of such religious feelings. Its forms of organization and appeal were determined by the needs of the population it served. Its strength lay in the close identification with a frontier people which had no strong social ties and group attachments. The strengths of the evangelistic religious movement were particularly evident in the case of Methodism.

The rapid growth of Methodist influence was owing to the success with which it met the peculiar needs of the Canadian frontier society. Its growth was in terms of the support of those people who stood on the margin of the Canadian community, geographically and socially— the backwoods farmers. The American— and overseas—heritage of the Methodist movement was essentially a frontier heritage. The movement had developed in both countries out of a social situation resulting from the migration of population. It had grown up to meet the needs of marginal social groups within the community. However different the particular circumstances may have been, the problem of religious organization presented by frontier settlement in Canada was fundamentally the same problem of religious organization out of which had grown the

Methodist movements in England and the United States.

That problem, in the first place, was one of providing a population cut off from the traditional social organization of the community with the services of religion. With their American and British experience, the Methodists were familiar with the sort of techniques required in extending the teachings of religion to people who were beyond the reach of the ordinary means of carrying on religious services. The success with which the movement recruited preachers for the work in the rapidly growing Canadian settlements was in itself an important factor in the extension of its influence. The system of apprenticeship by which young men with a desire to preach the gospel started out as local exhorters or as class leaders and went on to assume more responsible tasks provided an easy means of recruiting—and training—a body of Methodist preachers. Qualifications were such as to encourage the enlistment of large numbers of zealous persons who seized upon a career of preaching when more inviting careers were lacking in a pioneer society or required greater training than that which such persons possessed. . . .

The task of extending the influence of religion into the new frontier settlements and of gaining the support of those large sections of the population which had stood outside the area of religious teaching was one performed largely by the evangelical religious movement. Growth of the evangelical movement in the country, it is true, resulted in part from the settlement of people who had previously been adherents—without such support the evangelical religious movement could hardly have taken its rise—but many of those who came to be included among the evangelical following were drawn from outside. The evangelical religious movement owed its claim to the title of evangelical, to its capacity to gain recruits from among those who previously lacked any strong interest in matters of religion. It grew through the growth in strength of the religious interest. Inevitably, as a result, the strengthening of the evangelical religious cause tended to a weakening of the traditional religious order. The traditional religious denominations depended upon a nice balance between religious and secular interests. In the frontier settlement, where secular interests broke down, with the emergence of the evangelical religious movement there was a growing tendency to think exclusively in terms of religious ends. The other-worldliness of the evangelical religious appeal had the effect of developing an intolerance towards religious institutions which had accommodated themselves to the demands of the secular world. The convert of the religious revival was one who denied himself the privilege of compromise. The result was that those who came under the influence of religious revivals tended to break completely from the traditional religious order and to seek fellowship within the evangelical sect.

A crude manifestation of religious feelings amounting at times to an exhibitionism distasteful to people of reserved manners inevitably characterized to some extent the religious appeal of the revivalist movement. If evangelical religious meetings in Canada escaped some of the excesses of such meetings in the United States, there was still much in their character which struck the person accustomed to the dignity and ritual beauty of the traditional religious service as ugly, uncouth, and, indeed, degrading to human nature. Evangelical religion, theologically reactionary, involved a reversion to a system of thought based upon elementary passions and primitive superstitions. It was this character of evangelical teaching, however, which constituted its great strength. If it was deplored by the liberal philosopher who looked upon it as directly opposed to rationalist teachings, it served nevertheless to meet a real need in the rural frontier society. The crudeness of the evangelical religious appeal reflected the crudeness of frontier life. There was in the backwoods community little to support the paraphernalia of a mature, highly developed social system. The social losses accompanying frontier settlement inevitably involved the emergence of a society considerably more backward than those societies with which it was originally connected, and this social retardation was reflected in the reversion to a lower form of religious life. "Here, without means of instruction, of social amusement, of healthy and innocent excitements," Mrs. Jameson wrote, "—can we wonder that whisky and camp-meetings assume their place, and 'season toil' which is unseasoned by anything better? Nothing, believe me, that you have heard or read of the frantic disorders of these Methodist love-feasts and camp-meetings in Upper Canada can exceed the truth; and yet it is no less a truth that the Methodists are in most parts the only religious teachers, and that without them the people were utterly abandoned." The evangelical religious movement rapidly spread at the expense of traditional religious systems, not only because its religious teachings were available, but because it offered something which could be comprehended by a backwoods population, largely illiterate and cut off from any stimulating contacts with the world of knowledge. The evangelical movement brought the religious message down to the level of intelligence of the population.

The evangelical religious appeal provided, in a way much more effectively than the traditional religious appeal, the backwoods population with a meaningful interpretation of its relationship to the larger social cosmos. The close identification of the aspirations of the convert with the idea of salvation took on a social significance within the more general religious context. The experience of faith resulting from conversion was very closely related to initiation into the social fraternity of believers. The religious interest took on meaning only to the extent that it was supported by the social interest. The conception of religion in those terms, of course, was farthest from the thoughts of those who undertook its propagation or of those who accepted its teachings; the evangelical appeal gained social significance by the very fact that it was divorced from worldly interests and wordly systems of thought. In this way, the evangelical group freed itself from the inhibitions and restraints of the traditional social order and developed a form of fellowship in which a population cut off from traditional ties could freely participate.

It was in those areas, and among those people most cut off from traditional ties that the evangelical movement gained its greatest strength. Thus it was not simply the fact that the early movements in Canada originated in the United States that accounted for their success chiefly among the settlers of American background. The heritage of the frontier had provided that population which crossed the border into Canada with few cultural ties to support efforts to erect a society within the new frontier environment. For the most part, it was a second-generation frontier people which came from the United States to Canada, and such a people, cut off from the social heritage of the first generation, had not yet developed a rich heritage of its own. An extreme individualization, as a result, tended to characterize the American settlers in the country, and the effects of such individualization, or emancipation from traditional controls, were evident in a weakened sense of group consciousness. Concern was largely with immediate interests —clearing the land, planting the crop, caring for the livestock, transporting produce to market, and seeking such means of relaxation as those provided by the cross-roads tavern or neighbourhood group. Few points of collective interest emerged which served to focus attention upon some definite purpose or goal lying outside the individual's immediate range of activity. The mobility of the frontier had destroyed among the American settlers any sense of being a distinctive "folk"; on the other hand, lack of means of communication checked the development of any sense of belonging to "a public." It would be expected, therefore, that the evangelical religious appeal, as an agent in social unification, would exert its greatest influence among the American settlers; they had, of the various groups within the Canadian rural community, the fewest materials out of which to develop a cultural system.

The evangelical religious movement, however, spread beyond the population of American origin and made a strong appeal to the economically impoverished overseas immigrants settling in Canada after 1815. To some extent, it is true, the richer cultural heritage of the British settlers made them less inclined to the support of an evangelical religion; letters from friends and relatives in Great Britain, the cherished hope of returning eventually to the homeland, and the strong patriotism of the Britisher living abroad served to maintain among the immigrants from overseas a feeling of belonging to something outside the range of the individual's immediate interests. Such forms of social identification, however, provided no sense of intimate fellowship or even any sense of relationship to vital needs. Cultural attachments of the overseas settlers which had any real meaning were broken through the movement into a strange environment. The character of the new environment made such a break with a cultural past inevitable. The overseas settlers found themselves isolated within the backwoods community. Bush farms provided the only means by which the poorer English, Scottish, and Irish immigrants could establish themselves on the land, and speculative prices and incompetency in management eventually drove many of those with capital into the backwoods as well. Tendencies towards individualization inherent in the conditions of frontier life were accentuated in the case of the overseas settlers by a cultural heritage which emphasized dependence upon secondary institutions rather than upon the family or neighbourhood group; failure readily to adjust to this situation where many of the tasks normally performed by agencies of the formal social order were performed by the family or by informal social groups left the individual with virtually no cultural supports. Inherited class distinctions which had little relationship to the needs of a frontier society checked further the development of means of social intercourse among the overseas settlers and intensified the isolation of the individual. A detachment from traditional systems of thought and patterns of conduct proceeded rapidly among such people who found within their cultural heritage few means of adjustment to the strange frontier environment, and alternative forms of social fellowship developed slowly without the aid of outside agencies. The extreme loneliness of the upper class overseas settler, resulting on occasion in personal disorganization, was indicative of a failure to secure enduring social attachments without breaking outside a traditional class system. Among the large mass of overseas immigrants, free of the inhibitions of a social class system, the sudden break from old world cultural systems was more often followed by a strong reaction against traditional restraints of all sorts and the acceptance of new social supports such as those offered within evangelical religion. The highly emotional experience of the evangelical religious revival served, among the overseas settlers, as a means of personal re-organization and, on the social plane, as a means of securing new cultural ties.

The importance of the evangelical religious appeal in developing among the backwoods population a sense of belonging to something, of being a part of a social entity reaching beyond the horizon of the individual's immediate world, suggests a close relationship between the teachings of the evangelical religious movement and the moral and cultural values of the community. While the evangelical religious appeal gained its social significance from within itself, more general social characteristics of the movement promoted the social influence of the religious appeal. Even more, on the other hand, the social characteristics of traditional religious institutions weakened their religious appeal as an instrument in the development of a group consciousness among the rural population. The religious institution inevitably was made up of people with certain social interests and with a certain social standing in the community; the character of the institution in this regard was closely related not only to its purely religious appeal but to its attitude towards such problems as morals, education, nationalist ideologies, and politics. The social teachings of the evangelical sect supported its religious teachings in strengthening its position of leadership within the Canadian frontier settlements. The frontier emphasized self-sufficiency within the family and neighbourhood groups, and specialized skills were of less value than the general capacity to provide for the basic human needs. Non-specialization was evident in the organization of social institutions as in the organization of the labour force, and the success of religious institutions depended largely upon the degree of their integration within the community or neighbourhood structure. Denominational, sectarian, or class divisions restricted greatly the effectiveness of religious organization, and those churches were most influential which appealed to all religious, cultural and political groups within the community. The doctrine of salvation by faith propounded by the evangelical preachers offered no obstacle to the inclusion of people with a wide variety of beliefs. Only the smaller pietistic sects which had succeeded in maintaining the geographical segregation of their following could afford the luxury of adhering to the distinctive beliefs of a particular social group. Such religious denominations as the Church of England and Presbyterian Church, by failing to develop a more inclusive social philosophy, became inevitably class churches or churches dependent upon the support of particular ethnic groups in the community. The task of organizing the masses in terms of the wider community relationship was one assumed very largely by the evangelical sect.

William Bell, *Hints to Emigrants, in a Series of Letters from Upper Canada.* (Edinburgh, Waugh and Innes, 1824.)

A Clergyman Complains of Frontier Irreligiosity

Letter XIII

New countries are generally settled by adventurers, with whom religion is not a primary consideration. Pious persons are seldom found willing to break off their former connexions, and forsake the land where both they and their fathers have worshipped God. Persons coming from a country where religious institutions are observed, into one where they are neglected, unless they have known something of the power of godliness, will feel themselves set free from restraints which were far from being pleasant. They will find the profanation of the Sabbath, and the neglect of religion, quite congenial to their unrenewed minds; and if this is the case when they first settle in the woods, what can we expect when they have lived a number of years without religious instruction? May we not expect that depraved passions will be indulged, that vices will be practiced with avidity, and that the future world will be neglected amidst the clamorous demands of the present? This we find to be actually the case in the backwoods of America. It is true, there are few new colonies in which some persons are not to be found who feel the power of religion, but even they discover how soon evil communications corrupt good manners. Professing Christians themselves, when they are placed where no Sabbaths are observed, and no religious ordanances administered, soon become lamentably deficient in the discharge of Christian duties.

Though religion in Canada is at a low ebb, it is evidently upon the advance; and when the want of faithful labourers in different parts of the country is supplied, by the blessing of God, we may expect a great reformation to take place. The people are not so destitute of speculative knowledge, as of moral habits and religious principle. I have met with some of the old settlers, who have lived from twenty to forty years in the country, and who could talk fluently, and even correctly, in praise of religion, and yet they would drink, swear, profane the Sabbath, and neglect the duties of religion as much as the most ignorant of their neighbors. Occasional instruction will not suffice, there must be line upon line, and precept upon precept, before we can expect to see vice wither and religion flourish. Professing Christians must be collected into congregations and superintended by pious, active, and faithful ministers. But how is this to be effected? The people are neither able nor willing to support ministers at their own expense, and there is no provision of a general nature made for them, either by public authority or private exertions . . . O that some of your missionary societies, that have done so much for the heathen, would do something for this country.

Ontario Archives, Education Department Records, Incoming General Correspondence, Chief Superintendent of Education, Canada West, G. B. Bucher, Pembroke, to Egerton Ryerson, September 20, 1849.

Frontier Materialism and Its Effect on Religion

Rev & Dear Sir,

Having been prevented by piles & prolapsis from continuing in the itinerant ministry I gladly embraced a Providential opening in this vicinity to engage in the education of youth & have now been employed here nearly two years. During this period I have been an attentive observer of the mental & moral condition of the more youthful portion of the community resident among the deplorably dark & demoralized lumberers of the Ottawa. The wish has often darted thro' my mind that I had the power to interest some of the wealthy & benevolent energies of my native country in behalf of an enterprizing but illiterate people. Judge then my dear sir the pleasure with which I perused the announcement, on the part of an affluent individual in England, of an intention to devote "a special sum" to "the opening of 500 schools in the interior, for a sound, religious & scientific education". In accordance then with the request made in the Journal of Education "to any person interested in the great object proposed",

I embrace the earliest opportunity of suggesting this locality as a place peculiarly appropriate for the exercise of such beneficence.

The Ottawa is settled for more than 50 miles both above & below this vicinity & for several miles both North & South by people whose choice has been determined more, by the facilities presented to the lumberman than to the agriculturalist, & hence vast numbers of children are fast rising to manhood in the sparse & scattered settlements of this wilderness without either mental or moral culture. The pine tree is indeed to all intents & purposes the god of this demoralized community. At the shrine of this idol, here so generally adored, men sacrifice everything of which they are possessed. Ease, health, comfort, piety, reputation, wife, children, heaven, God, Christ, are all deliberately offered, as an awful hecatomb, in the dark druidical groves of the Ottawa. Would to God, this picture was too highly colored! It is alas the sober truth. The above description is no hyperbole. Equally, in the timber grove, in the domestic circle, in the tavern & the store, on the week day & on the Sabbath, is the conversation about the "one thing needful" of the lumberers, the pine. The price, the quality, the locality & the possession of timber are the themes of all classes young & old male & female.

But before I close permit me to offer a few thoughts on the mode of meeting the case above stated. The situations in which common schools could be established & in which a sufficient number of children could be collected together are but few. Where this was at all practicable the attempt has been made but hundreds of children are precluded by intervening obstacles, such as lakes, rapids, swamps, pine barrens from resorting to established schools & what is worse the evil is not likely to be soon remedied by the removal of these obstacles. The barren quality of pine lands present no inducement to the farmer & hundreds of acres of stunted, burnt or blasted pines present no attraction to the lumberer. It appears to me that the best mode of meeting the case would be the establishment of a lumber's [lumberers'] literary institution where the rising generation, removed from the demoralizing influence of their friends, might enjoy indeed the benefit proposed, "a sound, religious & scientific education." . . .

> Yours Most Sincerely
> G B Bucher.

To Rev E Ryerson D.D.

P.S. The above is not of course intended for publication and therefore if published I wish my connection with it to be concealed for altho' nothing is overstated yet such is the natural blindness of the human heart that many to whom the description is perfectly applicable might either not perceive the likeness or else take umbrage at the writer for the faithfulness of his delineations. A word to the wise is sufficient.

> G.B.B.

Great Britain, House of Commons Sessional Papers, 1835, XIX, Report of the Select Committee on the Timber Duties, testimony of Samuel Revans, pp. 175, 178.

Frontier Isolation as a Cause of Social Disorder

[Question]

2440. What advantage do you suppose can be derived to the country from the substitution of [agricultural exports] for timber?—We should have a more moral population, as we should have a population which would be more completely subjected to the law and the social influences.

2441. How would the population be more moral in consequence of the alteration of the trade?—Because concentration attends the pursuit of agriculture, and a concentrated population is more amenable to law than a population very much scattered. . . .

2493. What proportion of the population are employed in that preparation of the timber during the winter?—On the Ottawa River they are quite a population of themselves: a good many of them are Irish. A gentleman who has, I believe, nearly the whole of his capital invested in the timber trade, and lives at By-town, expressed his disgust at the scene of depravity which that trade furnished upon the Ottawa River, and though so deeply interested in it as I have described, wished it was at an end.

2494. Will you explain further in what way that depravity was exhibited?—By drunkenness and brutality. The timber trade, by causing bodies of men to live in the woods in shantees, (a small temporary building), places them beyond the good social effects consequent upon being surrounded by women, and the responsibility of being subjected to the laws of the country.

have taken a dift. shape, these bravoes & ruffians have headed & led on the whole mass of Irish laborers, to drive the Canadian laborers from the lower province, off the river, so that they might themselves be enabled to fix a high Standard of Wages.

I am sorry to say, however contrary this may be to the interests of those who employ men, yet some of the Employers have actually headed these disorders, without considering the effect it would have on their own business, but merely looking forward to the immediate gratification of some jealousy or pique (originating about boundaries) against other employers having Canadian laborers, the whole thing is made worse by a number of lawless characters, settled squatters . . . on unsurveyed lands of the Crown, introducing liquor in large quantities on the River, which they sell without any Licence to do so.

Social Disorder and
the Lack of Police Power

*   *   *

Crown Land Papers, Upper Canada, Shelf 100, William Rogerson to James Stevenson, February 2, 1847, Ontario Archives.

Upper Canada Sundries, v.152, George Hamilton, Hawkesbury, to Lt. Col. Rowan, Toronto, June 1, 1835, PAC, RG 5, A1.

Sir
I am induced by the disturbed state of that part of His Excellency Sir John Colbornes Government, above the Rideau Canal & bordering on the River Ottawa to offer you a few remarks on the subject . . .

These disturbances commence by persons employing Men to cut timber on the Waste lands of the Crown getting into disputes as to their respective boundrys & there not being any person to appeal to for the settlement of such disputes, they have had recourse to hire bravoes & ruffians of the worst description, to intimidate the more peaceably disposed, this mode of proceeding has been carried on for about three years, which has been the means of introducing a number of the very worst of Characters (Irish) into that part of the Country—this year the disturbances

Sir
There is a person of the name of John McMillan trespassing upon my Limit on the Bonnechere River which I hold under licence No. 277. He has cut about four hundred pieces of Red pine Timber. I went personally to give this man notice of his trespass and that unless he desisted, and came to some arrangement I would at once take the necessary legal proceedings to secure the Timber. He merely laughed at me however, stating that he was perfectly aware that he was working upon my limit, but that he was aware of no law which would render my licence of any avail or enable me to take the proceedings I proposed against him.

Upon taking legal advice which I have done now and have done under other circumstances, before, I find strong doubts expressed by every lawyer I have consulted as to the practicability of obtaining legal redress.

The impression has in fact gone about among the people in the lumbering districts to such an extent that unless some steps are taken by the Crown, to have the matter set upon a proper footing, licence will become altogether valueless. In fact the only recognised principle at present seems to be physical force, to which however I am extremely reluctant to resort. Such a system although the only successful one I know—being directly at variance with the laws of the Country. There is also another man of the name of James MacGibbon who has made Timber in a similar manner a little higher up on my limit to the amount of one hundred and fifty pieces.

I have therefore to beg that you will submit these circumstances to the Honorable the Commissioner of Crown Lands, that he may suggest the necessary remedy. I would remark in conclusion that the ordinary remedy proposed by the Department of never granting licence to the trespasser hereafter is entirely useless in the present instance as the man McMillan told me that he has heard of such threats having been used, but merely laughed at it, as he said he never held or never expected to hold a licence.

Would you be pleased to request an early reply from the Commissioner that I may know whether I may depend upon any assistance from that quarter or not.

I am
Sir
with respect
your obt.
Wm. Rogerson.

Brockville Recorder, October 23, 1835 and February 23, 1837, quoted in S. D. Clark, *The Social Development of Canada,* (Toronto, University of Toronto Press, 1942), pp. 241-242.

A correspondent asks us, what we mean by "the blood thirsty scenes of Bytown," and we answer him. That in Bytown, there is band of desperadoes, who entirely swarm the place, a Canadian is not allowed to live there, if he is caught on the bridge, he is thrown into what is called the kettle, (a whirlpool,) and that terminates his miseries, but if caught in the woods or towns, these 150 Shiners, as they are denominated, beat and injure them so that few recover. If any of this band enter a shop, and demand any particular goods or ware, the shopkeeper dares not refuse, for should he his life is instantly sought, and failing to get which, his property is sure to be destroyed by fire. In fact the law is there a dead letter, and before so many of our journalists, exult in the continued riots in the States, and deprecate as severely as they do, the recourse to Lynch law, they should look nearer home and call the attention of the Government to these facts. If the arm of the civil authorities cannot restrain the scenes such as are daily reacted in Bytown, let the aid of the military be called in and let no more quarter, or mercy be shown to these demons in human shape than they have shown to them they have sacrificed. His Excellency Sir John Colborne, ought to be made acquainted with these circumstances without delay.

STATE OF SOCIETY AT BY-TOWN.—We learn by a gentleman who has recently visited By-town that outrages of a most brutal nature are of frequent occurrence in that place and its neighbourhood;—

the work of a set of men called "Shiners." A few weeks since a poor Indian was taken into a house and after being most inhumanely mutilated thrown out at a window—He was taken up by some humane individuals who endeavoured to preserve his life but it was useless, he expired in a few hours.

On Saturday week, a man named Scarf was dragged from his sleigh in Lower By-town, his shoulder dislocated, his head cut open in three places by a stake taken from his sleigh, and his body otherwise badly beaten. Another man named Hobbs, had his horses taken from him their ears and tails cut off, the side of one cut open, and his harness cut to pieces. Two others were attacked that afternoon; and a man named Isabell was the same evening robbed of Thirty dollars, within two miles of Richmond. Notwithstanding the frequent occurrence of such outrages on society, no means seem to be adopted to put the Laws in force. The men in authority either want the *power* or the will to discharge their duties. If the former, their hands should be strengthened, if the latter, dismissed from office. As matters appear to stand, the inhabitants in and about By-town must live in a wretched state of apprehension; which is likely to be much enhanced by the high prices of the necessaries of life.

*   *   *

Bytown Gazette, February 23, 1837.

REPORTED DISTURBANCES IN BYTOWN. This is a subject we approach with a good deal of reluctance; and shall endeavour to speak of matters as they are, "to nothing extenuate or set down aught in malice." Our more intelligent readers will doubtless perceive, that a subject of this nature will be viewed in so many different lights by different men, that no recital of occurrences will satisfy every one. We regret to say that occasional differences have occurred, as was to be expected from so heterogeneous a population as are in the habit of frequenting this place, and so limited means to keep them in order.—But it is no less true, that although these disturbances have been in general attributed to the Lumber-men, under the cognomen of Shiners, there have been instances in which our yeomanry have been the aggressors. Be this as it may, we find, and this is our urgent reason for these remarks, that the reports of disturbances in Bytown have been very much exaggerated at a distance; and whether these magnified reports resulted in the timidity of the reporters or in more mischievous intentions, to forward the views of speculators, they are equally prejudicial to the interests of the place and call equally loud for contradiction when untrue. . . .

. . . but as before mentioned we must admit, that many lawless characters have been going about, and many acts of wanton aggression have been committed. —Hence it becomes a subject well meriting attention to enquire into the cause of such outrages. There is no remissness in the conduct of our Magistrates in their endeavours to check these outrages, but from the want of a goal [jail] where delinquents could be confined; the want of this and the vicinity of Bytown to Lower Canada, allows frequent instances of escape from justice, which leads to complaints against the Magistrates and Constables, and sometimes leads those hardened in vice to the perpetration of crimes a wholesome dread of prompt punishment would deter them from committing. Much of the irregularities and disorders are also attributable to the great numbers of unlicenced Tippling Houses, which present opportunities of obtaining spirits, to many who abuse them.

*   *   *

Upper Canada Sundries, v. 173, 94641, G. W. Baker to J. Joseph, December 9, 1836, PAC, RG 5, A1.

Sir,

Referring to my letter of 9 t. June last in reply to Mr. James Johnstons address to His Excellency the Lieutenant Governor respecting my conduct in the formation of the Bytown Rifle Corps; and your reply of 20 t. June wherein you stated that you had not been able to bring the matter to His Excellencys notice.

I have the honor to request you will be pleased to submit it to His Excellency at your earliest convenience—the more especially as I am now unfortunately compelled to proceed by Indictment against Nine Persons who have refused or neglected to be sworn in as Constables to which office they were duly appointed at the General Quarter Sessions last March.

The general reluctance of the Inhabitants to act as Constables is so great, arising principally from their dependance in trade upon the Raftsmen, and the heavy expense attending the transit of Prisoners to the Gaol at Perth, for which they are not adequately remunerated; that it has been next to impossible to bring delinquents to Justice.

Michael S. Cross, "The Lumber Community of Upper Canada, 1815-1867," *Ontario History,* vol. LII, no. 4, (Autumn 1960), pp. 221, 226-231. Reprinted by permission of The Ontario Historical Society.

A General Interpretation of Social Disorder on the Timber Frontier

The lumberman of legend, mackinaw-clad, hobnail-shod, this was the lumberjack of the Ottawa; the Spartan life of the camboose, the giant drive, the roistering plague of Quebec, this was the lumber community of the Ottawa. Lumbering in the Ottawa [Valley] was unlike lumbering anywhere else in British North America. It was an almost completely professional trade, carried on by "a regular labour force which increasingly became differentiated from the rural population, and came to constitute rather a part of an urban proletariat".* The lumberer was that, nothing else. Perhaps Professor Clark should have coined a new phrase, "rural proletariat". Quebec suffered under the lumberer's celebrating for a few summer weeks, Bytown for a few more in the early autumn. But the woods and the river were his life. His contacts with the outside world were few and tenuous but his

* S. D. Clark, *The Social Development of Canada,* p. 210.

relations with the farm population were equally distant. The lumber community of the Ottawa Valley was a world unto itself, proud, vigorous, vicious, recognizing no law but its own. . . .

The lumberman, perhaps even more than the agriculturalist, was the true pioneer of British North America. He pushed on ahead of the government, ahead of the farmer, opening the hinterland of Canada. But, in doing so, he became introverted. The lumber trade was not one designed to produce the clean-cut, all-round, all-Canadian personality. The lumberman spent from September to June in the woods, cutting and hauling the logs. Late June and July were occupied with the drive to Quebec. His only contacts with the outside world were during a few weeks in Quebec, spent in a whirl of drinking and wenching. Then the routine started all over again.

Even those not directly concerned with the cutting of timber were isolated. Bytown was a city living almost exclusively for the lumber trade. It was an island in the forest, kept afloat with wooden moorings. Even the lumber merchant, the great entrepreneur of Montreal or Quebec, lived and thought only for the trade. He was constantly alert for any alteration of the routine, an alteration which could spell ruin. Isolated, delicately-balanced, the lumber community was ultra-conservative.

This insularity, rule of habit and routine, and highly sensitive economic balance, manifested itself in the politics of the Ottawa Valley. . . .

The lumber community of Upper Canada was more concerned with the mechanics of the trade than its political and financial ramifications. The politics of the lumber trade remained primarily those of Montreal. The Family Compact, unlike the Chateau Clique, was made up largely of landowners, not merchants. It was a social and political, rather than a commercial, alliance. But the incidental commercial interests of some members of the ruling group did align them with the lumber-kings of Montreal and Bytown and led to clashes, similar to, albeit less frequent than, the merchant-agriculturalist battles of Lower Canada. The public loans for canal building on the St. Lawrence in the 1820's were carried only against severe opposition. . . .

Even with the collapse of the colonial system, the basic conservatism of the lumber community was little shaken. After it had vented its spleen in the Annexation Manifesto, it drew together once more to salvage what it could from the ruins. Reform, or liberalism, meant retrenchment, slackening of public works. Conservatism, on the contrary, stood for the expansion of business. Agriculture against commerce, the war was still fought out in the arena of politics. Politics meant, preeminently, economics. The chief enemy of lumbering was not Baldwin, not Lafontaine, but Hincks,* the "Ancient Chiseler", the "Port Sarnia Monkey." . . .

Politically, then, lumbering was a stabilizing factor, firmly committed to the status quo. Socially, however, its effect upon the Ottawa Valley was traumatic. The first lumbermen on the Ottawa were French Canadians, apparently reasonably well-behaved and peaceable. "The French *habitans* make the best shanty-men; they are more cheerful and less likely to fight and quarrel, notwithstanding their evil propensities of card-playing and cockfighting." However, after the completion

of the Rideau Canal and the draw of the lumber trade after that time upon the flow of immigration, Irish and Scots began to pour into the camps, replacing the French. The clash of racial groups, with employment rivalry urging them on, convulsed the Valley for a decade. The so-called "Shiners' War" was waged between 1837 and 1845 in the woods, along the slides and in the streets of Bytown. The term, 'Shiner', has been variously described as derived from 'cheneur' or 'oakman', the black silk hats 'shiners', worn by greenhorns arriving in Bytown, or from the newly-minted half crown coins with which the lumberers were paid. At any event, it became universally used of the Irish emigrants who flooded the Valley. Establishing themselves in the area of Bytown known as 'Cork Town', centred about the picturesque 'Mother McGinty's Tavern', the Shiners soon made their presence felt. The first recorded disturbance was on St. Patrick's Day, 1828, when an Englishman, Thomas Ford, clashed with a group of Irishmen, and was slain for his bravado. . . . In 1837, matters came to a head. Irish immigration into the Valley was then at a peak. With the bank crisis of that year, a heavy rise in the cost of provisions and the general financial instability, jobs in the lumber camps were at a premium. The Irish determined to drive the French Canadians from the woods, and by 1845 had succeeded in doing so. . . .

The citizens of the town were forced to unite in "The Association of the Preservation of the Public Peace in Bytown", a vigilante group. But even when the Irish had won their 'war', the disturbances did not end. Freed after long months in the bush, violence erupted whenever lumbermen were in Bytown. "Anything short of murder may be committed with impunity;

---

* Francis Hincks, Inspector-General (Minister of Finance) in the Lafontaine-Baldwin ministry of 1848-1851.

and even murder has been allowed to pass comparatively unnoticed . . . ." [Ottawa *Argus,* 1850]

This violent reaction to freedom was accentuated by the strict regimen of shanty life. In the early period of the trade, the shanty was an unruly haven of the 'rugged individual'. John McGregor, during the 1830's, described a typical camp, with each lumberman enjoying a 'morning'—a drink of raw whiskey—before his breakfast. However, as the timber business became ever more professional, employers could not afford to allow drunkenness and misbehavior among their men. . . . Joshua Fraser assures us that by 1883 there was "government and discipline in shanty life, just as pronounced and strictly carried out as in the most exemplary and well-regulated village, town or city corporation of the Dominion. . . ."

Small wonder, then, that the lumbermen, released from eight months of Spartan life, reacted like proverbial 'wild Indians'. When the drive began, all bedlam broke loose. Under its constant pressure and danger, nerves became taut. Tension was released in drink. "In the matter of scenting out and appropriating whiskey," the lumberman was "as keen as a weasel, as cunning as a fox, and as unscrupulous as a wolf." And every few miles along the Ottawa were to be found taverns dispensing "rank vitrolized poison, under the name of good-whiskey." As the drive swept by, farms near the river were terrorized. [John] Langton reported of the raftsmen, "It is a hard and dangerous life but they are a light-hearted set of dare-devils and the greatest rascals and thieves withal that ever a peaceable country was tormented with. Hen roosts have quite disappeared from the river side and lambs and little pigs have to be kept

under lock and key."

The lumbermen struck Quebec like a cyclone. Having safely delivered their rafts, they received their wages in a lump sum. In the terms of Canada at that time, this was an immense amount of money—perhaps £30. They squandered it all on "the fiddle, the female, or the firewater." Writers of the period delighted in describing the summer roisterings of the colourful woodsmen. . . . The Rev. A. W. H. Rose followed the raftsman to the end of his summer. "He . . . buys a gay suit of clothes, seldom forgetting a particularly smart waistcoat, brushes up ad libitum, and 'sets up for a gentleman,' too often indulging in a life of low debauchery, till his cash is gone, his health perhaps shaken; he parts with his gay apparel, if it has not been already destroyed in some drunken row, shoulders his axe, and sets off again to the wilderness penniless, if not, moreover, in debt." It is no surprise, then, that they constituted a rural proletariat, returning to the woods year after year; few could afford to do anything else. . . .

We thus must disagree with S. D. Clark's generalizations upon the social conditions of Upper Canada. He tells us, "Political unrest was symptomatic of disturbances extending through the entire range of the pioneer society of Upper Canada . . . . The failure of the rural inhabitants to secure cultural status combined with their failure to secure political status." He speaks, too, of Upper Canada as an "agrarian frontier."

The social problems of Upper Canada were far from uniform, and most definitely not exclusively those of an agrarian frontier. The Ottawa was a frontier, but a commercial frontier. Clark has not distinguished between the frontier and rural areas in his generalizations. The "agrarian frontier" of which he speaks was rather the middle area of the province, for example, the Home and Midland districts, where discontent was settled in the Rebellion of 1837. In the Rebellion, the two true frontier areas, the Huron Tract, and the Ottawa Valley, were almost completely quiescent. Commercial prosperity, rather than 'cultural status' or the lack thereof, was the only potent political consideration in the Ottawa frontier.

Part V

The Frontier and the Class System

The frontier thesis is an expression of a general ideology which has captured the imagination of Americans, and to which they still pay at least lip service. If there is any part of that ideology which has had a similar impact on Canadians it is the concept of the "levelling" influence of North American conditions. Like their southern neighbours, most Canadians have seen their society as one of practical equality, one in which there is, and always has been, social mobility. Talent, ambition, drive, these can make the poor boy prime minister as surely as his American counterpart can become president. While there has not been the full articulation of this myth in Canada, as there was in the American frontier thesis, essentially similar ideas have been expressed, over and over again, by scholars and by ordinary Canadians: the class system of the Old World could not exist in Canada, in Canadian conditions, in the Canadian environment.

Again, in scholarly writing, this view obviously has carried a strong moral content. That which contributed to this 'natural' levelling was good, that which attempted to retard it was bad. So, for most Canadian historians, the liberal side of politics has been favoured, alleged anachronisms like the Family Compact have been attacked. Only recently has a more sympathetic, or at least more objective, analysis of those groups which stood for an ordered, hierarchical, society been attempted. The works of historians like S. F. Wise and G. M. Craig have begun the task of understanding the viewpoint of Tory elements, and, perhaps, of showing their defeat was not as complete as the myth has held.

This section continues the conflicts expressed in Part IV, since the class system was an institution imported with the immigrants as were the churches. And somewhat similar problems of interpretation emerge. An analogue for the difficulty of measuring the impact of the various denominations on scattered pioneer communities is that of determining the social attitudes, systems of deference, and so on, of thousands of backwoodsmen—who never thought of recording their attitudes, and probably would have been unable to articulate them if they had thought of it. Similar problems of unravelling cause and effect also emerge. In many Upper Canadian communities, groups with aristocratic pretensions dominated their local societies in the first generation or two after the establishment of their settlements, much as the Family Compact held sway at the provincial level. Most of these groups faded away as the frontier receded. Does this imply that they were destroyed by the inevitable march of the egalitarian ideas sown in the frontier period? Or does it mean that levelling resulted from the conditions of a more settled society, which had more sophisticated needs and more status strivings than the primitive frontier era?

Many of the passages in earlier sections have touched on the class question. Here a group of contemporary comments is collected to illustrate the basic clashes of opinion which have always marked discussion of the issue. No more classic expression of the levelling thesis has been penned than Alexander McLachlan's poem, "Young Canada, or Jack's as Good as His Master." McLachlan was a powerful, if crude, poet of Scottish birth who chronicled and glorified the process of lower class migration to Canada. This poem was originally published in 1861 in a collection called *The Emigrant and Other Poems*. In contrast is the viewpoint of a gentleman migrant of the 1830's, John Langton, who settled at Sturgeon Lake. Langton recognized that the idea of independence was strong, but felt it could be controlled and gave his formula for doing so.

The excerpts from Susanna Moodie and Samuel Thompson show that some members

of the gentry and of the middle class shared McLachlan's judgements. Mrs. Moodie, probably the most important literary figure to emigrate to Canada in the nineteenth century, was more than a little disillusioned by the experience. The hardships of "roughing it in the bush" did not agree with this urbane lady, and she produced a book on backwoods life which was designed to warn off other English folk who might be considering moving to Canada. The frontier, she made clear, was no place for the British gentry: it belonged to the lower classes. The first part of the selection is from her 1871 introduction to a reprint of the book, the second from the body of the text first published in 1852. Samuel Thompson was even more scathing in his assaults on the idea of gentry settlement on the frontier. Thompson, himself, was not one of the horny-handed sons of the soil he glorified, but adjusted very well to the frontier nevertheless. After pioneering successfully, he moved on to a long and profitable career in journalism.

Less frontierist interpretations come from the next four selections. Mary O'Brien, whose journal is quoted here, was one of those gentle pioneers that Samuel Thompson deplored, having moved with her husband from the settled area of Upper Canada near the capital to the wilderness of Lake Simcoe. The O'Briens were an old established British family, with connections in the Family Compact circles at York. As Thompson indicated, the lieutenant governor, Sir John Colborne, urged such people to move into the backwoods to provide a solid and loyal population along the vital interior lakes system in case of an attack by the United States. The O'Briens suffered hardships, but seem to have settled successfully. Some thirteen years after arriving at Shanty Bay they moved to Toronto, perhaps an indication of defeat by the frontier—but if so, late in coming. This section of the O'Brien journal describes the trip to Shanty Bay, and the establishment of their settlement there. John Mactaggart, author of *Three Years in Canada*, was not a resident of the country, but in his three years as an engineer working on the Rideau Canal in the years 1826 to 1828, he was a keen observer of Canadian society. He gives us the reverse side of the social coin: was Canada, as the levellers had it, the haven for the poor? His answer is clearly in the negative. The final two selections are from a brother and sister, Samuel Strickland and Catherine Parr Traill. They are not nearly so pessimistic about the future of the gentle classes as was their other sister, Susanna Moodie, cited earlier. Both agree that society is more mobile in Canada, but they point to economic, not environmental, factors as causing this. And both are confident that superior education and breeding will bring success. In fact, Strickland, Mrs. Traill, and even the sour Mrs. Moodie, all maintained high places in society, prospered financially, and carried on successful literary careers.

Alexander McLachlan, *The Poetical Works of Alexander McLachlan,* (Toronto, William Briggs, 1900), pp. 207-208.

The Forest Destroys the Class System

Young Canada, or Jack's as Good as His Master

I love this land of forest grand!
    The land where labour's free;
Let others roam away from home,
    Be this the land for me!
Where no one moils, and strains and toils,
    That snobs may thrive the faster;
And all are free, as men should be,
    And Jack's as good's his master!

Where none are slaves, that lordly knaves
    May idle all the year;
For rank and caste are of the past,—
    They'll never flourish here!
And Jew or Turk if he'll but work,
    Need never fear disaster;
He reaps the crop he sowed in hope,
    For Jack's as good's his master!

Our aristocracy of toil
    Have made us what you see—
The nobles of the forge and soil,
    With ne'er a pedigree!
It makes one feel himself a man,
    His very blood leaps faster,
Where wit or worth's preferred to birth,
    And Jack's as good's his master!

Here's to the land of forests grand!
    The land where labour's free;
Let others roam away from home,
    Be this the land for me!
For here 'tis plain, the heart and brain,
    The very soul grows vaster!
Where men are free, as they should be,
    And Jack's as good's his master!

W. A. Langton, ed., *Early Days in Upper Canada: Letters of John Langton,* (Toronto, Macmillan of Canada, 1926), pp. 75-76, 90. Reprinted by permission of The Macmillan Company of Canada Limited.

A Gentleman's Advice on Dealing with the Lower Orders

[Langton to his father, February 3, 1834]

As to the desponding which you seem to expect I shall feel in long winter evenings, I can assure you you need feel no alarm; I never felt so little inclined to despond in my life. Your fears lest we should grow bearish in our manners are, I think, needless—at our end of the lake at least; our dress, of course, is not in the style of a town dandy, but we have agreed to keep up a degree of form which sometimes amuses me when I look round on the accompaniments of the scene. You all seem to run upon the subject of danger, as if we were exposed to any here; the fact is, with ordinary precaution, there is nothing in the life of a backwoodsman which is worthy of the name. Fatigue and inconvenience there is in abundance, but danger none, and, as far as I have seen of the two former, there is nothing which novelty, at present, does not make pleasant than otherwise, and to which custom hereafter will [not] reconcile us.

[Langton to his father, April 4, 1834]

Your observation upon servants generally are pretty correct, but I do not, as far as I have yet seen in my own and other establishments, see much difficulty in managing them; but here as in everything else *in medio tutissimus* is the only rule. The working classes here naturally feel an independence which you do not find at home, and which, if you give way as some do, will soon lead them to consider themselves your equals; others again, by endeavouring to keep them under as they call it, only give rise to insolence and make themselves cordially hated. But I have never seen any yet who by a quiet reserve of manner cannot be kept respectful. At particular moments and with particular characters you may unbend occasionally and thereby make yourself liked without losing any authority. The art of managing servants is perhaps the most important one a new settler has to learn; I do not mean to say I am perfect in it, but when I say that, out of the seven people I have at different times had, I never found any difficulty except with one, you must not suppose me the worst manager; and he who did give me annoyance was in all important matters managed easily enough, but in trifles and when not at work too much inclined to be free and easy, which considering that we had lived in the same shanty for six weeks and that I for a great part of the time had acted the menial part of cook, scullion, etc., is not much to be wondered at.

Susanna Moodie, *Roughing It in the Bush; or, Forest Life in Canada,* (Toronto, Hunter, Rose & Co., 1871), pp. 7-10, 14-15, 238-241.

The Tribulations of the Gentry on the Frontier

In the year 1832 I landed with my husband, J. W. Dunbar Moodie, in Canada. Mr. Moodie was the youngest son of Major Moodie, of Mellsetter, in the Orkney Islands; he was a lieutenant in the 21st regiment of Fusileers, and had been severely wounded in the night-attack upon Bergen-op-Zoom, in Holland.

Not being overgifted with the good things of this world—the younger sons of old British families seldom are—he had, after mature deliberation, determined to try his fortune in Canada, and settle upon the grant of 400 acres of land, ceded by the Government to officers upon half-pay.

Emigration, in most cases—and ours was no exception to the general rule—is a matter of necessity, not of choice. It may, indeed, generally be regarded as an act of duty performed at the expense of personal enjoyment, and at the sacrifice of all those local attachments which stamp the scenes in which our childhood grew in imperishable characters upon the heart.

Nor is it, until adversity has pressed hard upon the wounded spirit of the sons and daughters of old, but impoverished, families, that they can subdue their proud and rebellious feelings, and submit to make the trial.

This was our case, and our motives for emigrating to one of the British colonies can be summed up in a few words.

The emigrant's hope of bettering his condition, and securing a sufficient competence to support his family, to free himself from the slighting remarks, too often hurled at the poor gentleman by the practical people of the world, which is always galling to a proud man, but doubly so, when he knows that the want of wealth constitutes the sole difference between him and the more favoured offspring of the same parent stock.

In 1830 the tide of emigration flowed westward, and Canada became the great land-mark for the rich and poor in purse. Public newspapers and private letters teemed with the almost fabulous advantages to be derived from a settlement in this highly favored region. Men, who had been doubtful of supporting their families in comfort at home, thought that they had only to land in Canada to realize a fortune. The infection became general. Thousands and tens of thousands from the middle ranks of British society, for the space of three or four years, landed upon these shores. A large majority of these emigrants were officers of the army and navy, with their families; a class perfectly unfitted, by their previous habits and standing in society, for contending with the stern realities of emigrant life in the back-woods. A class formed mainly from the younger scions of great families, naturally proud, and not only accustomed to command, but to receive implicit obedience from the people under them, are not men adapted to the hard toil of the woodman's life. Nor will such persons submit cheerfully to the saucy familiarity of servants, who, republicans at heart, think of themselves quite as good as their employers. Too many of these brave and honest men took up their grants of wild land in remote and unfavourable localities, far from churches, schools, and markets, and fell an easy prey to the land speculators, that swarmed in every rising village on the borders of civilization.

It was to warn such settlers as these last mentioned, not to take up grants and pitch their tents in the wilderness, and by so doing, reduce themselves and their families to hopeless poverty, that my work *"Roughing it in the Bush"* was written.

I gave the experience of the first seven years we passed in the woods, attempting to clear a bush farm, as a warning to others, and the number of persons who have since told me, that my book "told the history" of their own life in the woods, ought to be the best proof to every candid mind that I spoke the truth. It is not by such feeble instruments as the above that Providence works, when it seeks to reclaim the waste places of the earth, and make them subservient to the wants and happiness of its creatures. The great Father of the souls and bodies of men knows the arm which wholesome labour from infancy has made strong, the nerves that have become iron by patient endurance, and he chooses such to send forth into the forest to hew out the rough paths for the advance of civilization.

These men become wealthy and prosperous, and are the bones and sinews of a great and rising country. Their labour is wealth, not exhaustion; it produces content, not home sickness and despair.

What the backwoods of Canada are to the industrious and ever-to-be-honored sons of honest poverty, and what they are to the refined and polished gentleman,

these sketches have endeavored to show.

The poor man is in his native element; the poor gentleman totally unfitted, by his previous habits and education, to be a hewer of the forest, and a tiller of the soil. What money he brought out with him is lavishly expended during the first two years, in paying for labor to clear and fence lands, which, from his ignorance of agricultural pursuits, will never make them the least profitable return, and barely find coarse food for his family. Of clothing we say nothing. Bare feet and rags are too common in the bush. . . .

While the sons of poor gentlemen have generally lost caste, and sunk into useless sots, the children of the honest tillers of the soil have steadily risen to the highest class; and have given to Canada some of her best and wisest legislators.

Men who rest satisfied with the mere accident of birth for their claims to distinction, without energy and industry to maintain their position in society, are sadly at discount in a country, which amply rewards the worker but leaves the indolent loafer to die in indigence and obscurity.

Honest poverty is encouraged, not despised, in Canada. Few of her prosperous men have risen from obscurity to affluence without going through the mill, and therefore have a fellow-feeling for those who are struggling to gain the first rung on the ladder.

Men are allowed in this country a freedom enjoyed by few of the more polished countries in Europe; freedom in religion, politics, and speech; freedom to select their own friends and to visit with whom they please, without consulting the Mrs. Grundys of society; and they can lead a more independent social life than in the mother country, because less restricted by the conventional prejudices that govern older communities.

Few people [who] have lived many years in Canada, and return to England to spend the remainder of their days, accomplish the fact. They almost invariably come back, and why? They feel more independent and happier here; they have no idea what a blessed country it is to live in until they go back and realize the want of social freedom. I have heard this from so many educated people, persons of taste and refinement, that I cannot doubt the truth of their statements. . . .

All was new, strange, and distasteful to us; we shrank from the rude, coarse familiarity of the uneducated people among whom we were thrown; and they in return viewed us as innovators, who wished to curtail their independence by expecting from them the kindly civilities and gentle courtesies of a more refined community. They considered us proud and shy, when we were only anxious not to give offence. The semi-barbarous Yankee squatters, who had "left their country for their country's good," and by whom we were surrounded in our first settlement, detested us, and with them we could have no feeling in common. We could neither lie nor cheat in our dealings with them; and they despised us for our ignorance in trading and our want of smartness.

The utter want of that common courtesy with which a well-brought-up European addresses the poorest of his brethren, is severely felt at first by settlers in Canada. At the period of which I am now speaking, the titles of "sir," or "madam,"

were very rarely applied by inferiors. They entered your house without knocking; and while boasting of their freedom, violated one of its dearest laws, which considers even the cottage of the poorest labourer his castle, and his privacy sacred. . . .

And here I would observe, before quitting this subject, that of all follies, that of taking out servants from the old country is one of the greatest, and is sure to end in the loss of the money expended in their passage, and to become the cause of deep disappointment and mortification to yourself.

They no sooner set foot upon the Canadian shores than they became possessed with this ultra-republican spirit. All respect for their employers, all subordination is at an end; the very air of Canada severs the tie of mutual obligation which bound you together. They fancy themselves not only equal to you in rank, but that ignorance and vulgarity give them superior claims to notice. They demand the highest wages, and grumble at doing half the work, in return, which they cheerfully performed at home. They demand to eat at your table, and to sit in your company, and if you refuse to listen to their dishonest and extravagant claims, they tell you that "they are free; that no contract signed in the old country is binding in 'Meriky;' that you may look out for another person to fill their place as soon as you like; and that you may get the money expended in their passage and outfit in the best manner you can."

Samuel Thompson, *Reminiscences of a Canadian Pioneer for the Last Fifty Years*, (Toronto, Hunter, Rose & Company, 1884), pp. 84-90.

The Failure of the Upper Classes in Pioneer Settlements

SIR JOHN COLBORNE, as has been mentioned already, did all in his power to induce well-to-do immigrants, and particularly military men, to settle on lands west and north of Lake Simcoe. Some of these gentlemen were entitled, in those days, to draw from three to twelve hundred acres of land in their own right; but the privilege was of very doubtful value. Take an example. Captain Workman, with his wife, highly educated and thoroughly estimable people, were persuaded to select their land on the Georgian Bay, near the site of the present village of Meaford. A small rivulet which enters the bay there, is still called "the Captain's creek." To get there, they had to go to Penetanguishene, then a military station, now the seat of a Reformatory for boys. From thence they embarked on scows, with their servants, furniture, cows, farm implements and provisions. Rough weather obliged them to land on one of the Christian Islands, very bleak spots outside of Penetanguishene harbour, occu-

pied only by a few Chippewa Indians. After nearly two weeks' delay and severe privation, they at length reached their destination, and had then to camp out until a roof could be put up to shelter them from the storms, not uncommon on that exposed coast.

We had ourselves, along with others, taken up additional land on what was called "the Blue Mountains," which are considered to be a spur of the Alleghanies, extending northerly across by Niagara, from the State of New York. The then newly-surveyed townships of St. Vincent and Euphrasia were attracting settlers, and amongst them our axeman, Whitelaw, and many more of the like class. To reach this land, we had bought a smart sail-boat, and in her enjoyed ourselves by coasting from the Nottawasaga river north-westerly along the bay. In this way we happened one evening to put in at the little harbour where Capt. Workman had chosen his location. It was early in the spring. The snows from the uplands had swelled the rivulet into a smashing torrent. The garden, prettily laid out, was converted into an island, the water whirling and eddying close to the house both in front and rear, and altogether presenting a scene of wild confusion. We found the captain highly excited, but bravely contending with his watery adversary; the lady of the house in a state of alarmed perplexity; the servants at their wits' end, hurrying here and there with little effect. Fortunately, when we got there the actual danger was past, the waters subsiding rapidly during the night. But it struck us as a most cruel and inconsiderate act on the part of the Government, to expose tenderly reared families to hazards which even the rudest of rough pioneers would not care to encounter.

After enduring several years of severe hardship, and expending a considerable income in the out-of-the-way spot, Captain Workman and his family removed to Toronto, and afterwards returned to England, wiser, perhaps, but no richer certainly, than when they left the old country.

A couple of miles along the shore, we found another military settler, Lieutenant Waddell, who had served as brigade-major at the Battle of Waterloo; with him were his wife, two sons, and two daughters. . . . Here again the same melancholy story: ladies delicately nurtured, exposed to rough labour, and deprived of all the comforts of civilized life, exhausting themselves in weary struggle with the elements. Brave soldiers in the decline of life, condemned to tasks only adapted to hinds and navvies. What worse fate can be reserved for Siberian exiles! This family also soon removed to Toronto, and afterwards to Niagara, where the kindly, excellent old soldier is well remembered; . . .

Conspicuous among the best class of gentlemen settlers was the late Col. E. G. O'Brien, of Shanty Bay, near Barrie, of whom I shall have occasion to speak hereafter. Capt. St. John, of Lake Couchiching, was equally respected. The Messrs. Lally, of Medonte; Walker, of Tecumseth and Barrie; Sibbald, of Kempenfeldt Bay; are all names well known in those days, as are also many others of the like class. But where are the results of the policy which sent them there? What did they gain—what have their families and descendants gained—by the ruinous outlay to which they were subjected? With one or two exceptions, absolutely nothing but wasted means and saddest memories.

It is pleasant to turn to a different class of settlers—the hardy Scots, Irish,

English, and Germans, to whom the Counties of Simcoe and Grey stand indebted for their present state of prosperity. . . . The settlement was called the Scotch line, nearly all the people being from the islands of Arran and Islay, lying off Argyleshire, in Scotland. Very few of them knew a word of English. There were Campbells, McGillivrays, Livingstons, McDiarmids, McAlmons, McNees, Jardines, and other characteristic names. The chief man among them was Angus Campbell, who had been a tradesman of some kind in the old country, and exercised a beneficial influence over the rest. He was well informed, sternly Presbyterian, and often reminded us of "douce Davie Deans" in the "Heart of Midlothian." One of the Livingstons was a schoolmaster. They were, one and all, hardy and industrious folk. Day after day, month after month, year after year, added to their wealth and comfort. Cows were purchased, and soon became common. There were a few oxen and horses before long. When I visited the township of Nottawasaga some years since, I found Angus Campbell, postmaster and justice of the peace; Andrew Jardine, township clerk or treasurer; and McDiarmids, Livingstons, Shaws, &c., spread all over the surrounding country, possessing large farms richly stocked, good barns well-filled, and even commodious frame houses comfortably furnished. They ride to church or market in handsome buggies well horsed; have their temperance meetings and political gatherings of the most zealous sort, and altogether present a model specimen of a prosperous farming community. What has been said of the Scotch, is no less applicable to the Irish, Germans and English, who formed the minority in that township. I hear of their sons, and their sons'

sons, as thriving farmers and storekeepers, all over Ontario.

Our axeman, Whitelaw, was of Scottish parentage, but a Canadian by birth, and won his way with the rest. He settled in St. Vincent, married a smart and pretty Irish lass, had many sons and daughters, acquired a farm of five hundred acres, of which he cleared and cultivated a large portion almost single-handed, and in time became able to build the finest frame house in the township; served as reeve, was a justice of peace, and even a candidate for parliament, in which, well for himself, he failed. His excessive labours, however, brought on asthma, of which he died not long since, leaving several families of descendants to represent him.

I could go on with the list of prosperous settlers of this class, to fill a volume. Some of the young men entered the ministry, and I recognise their names occasionally at Presbyterian and Wesleyan conventions. Some less fortunate were tempted away to Iowa and Illinois, and there died victims to ague and heat.

But if we "look on this picture and on that;" if we compare the results of the settlement of educated people and of the labouring classes, the former withering away and leaving no sign behind—the latter growing in numbers and advancing in wealth and position until they fill the whole land, it is impossible to avoid the conclusion, that except as leaders and teachers of their companions, gentlefolk of refined tastes and superior education, have no place in the bush, and should shun it as a wild delusion and a cruel snare.

O'Brien Journals, 1828-1838, Journal 67, April, 1832, Ontario Archives.

Maintaining Class Distinction on the Frontier

. . . (4th) breakfasted at a comfortable Inn at the Landing, the last specimen of comfort we were to have for a spell & from then began our journey which was now to lead 30 miles thro' the woods. We went on for some time pleasantly enough but by comparing the lapse of time with the space passed thro' it soon became evident that we could not accomplish our proposed journey—Lucius' waggon, too, was a bad sailer & detained us constantly by various accidents; at last, it broke down just as we who were foremost had reached the hut of an old quaker where, after ascertaining that there was no one sick of measles or scarlet fever of which I journeyed in fear—we determined to stop and await the passing of a storm of wind which was beginning to become alarming—In compliment to the ladies the cloud of tobacco smoke which almost suffocated us at first gave place to the smoke from the chimney & after a little we determined on adding to this the smoke of cookery & when all was ready, sat down with our people to get our dinner, feeling that under such circumstances it was as ridiculous as inconvenient to preserve needless distinctions of rank— . . .

[They are settled on their land and erect a rough shanty]

(Sunday) I had hoped to have much enjoyment in the leisure of to-day—it was, however, necessarily interrupted by the completion of what was most essential to our preservation from cold & wet; happily tho' cold the weather continued dry. I hung up my blankets making our shanty look like a little tent & feel a good deal more comfortable than it had done and on the other side Hunt stopped up a few of the larger holes in their walls & the other men laid up some planks to make a shelter for the mare which, by the way, she kicked down as soon as she was put into it, so was obliged to be taken back to her brush heap. However, we found time to assemble for the worship of the day & from hence forward shall return to our accustomed habits of daily family prayer & (for unlike things are often coupled by circumstances) to our aristocratic habits of separate meals, tho' as yet we have only one dining room but then we have a drawing room, large enough to which we can retire whilst the servants take their meals. . . .

Journal 74, August, 1832

. . . (8th) We have now a good peep at the sky & Ed'd fancies that he already feels the difference—he has been to Capt. O'Brien's today & found him at a stand with his mill works [having] dismissed his Yankee mill wrights. They could not go on without sauces, custard puddings & feather pillows—were they not, they asked, men like himself & would he sleep without a feather pillow? Straw beds they had agreed to endure but feather pillows were indispensible. These neighbours of ours appear to begin at quite a different end from any other people that we hear of— whether beginning in luxury & speculation they will ever arrive at wealth & refinement is a problem.

John Mactaggart, *Three Years in Canada,*
(London, Henry Colburn, 1829), vol. II,
pp. 242-244, 248-249, 253-254.

The British Poor as Pioneers

Travellers in general have set their
faces against *poor people* emigrating to
Canada. There is nothing in which I am
more willing to coincide in opinion with
them than this. Food is not to be had
there merely for the eating; it requires
considerable exertion to make a living, as
it does in almost every other place. Neither
is employment readily obtained; a common labourer can find nothing to do for
almost six months in the year, until he has
learned how to wield the hatchet. He may
then find employment in the woods; but it
takes an Irishman a long time to learn the
art of the hatchet, if he has been used
chiefly to spade and shovel work, which
is quite a different kind of occupation.
When he first commences hewing down
trees, he often hews them down upon
himself, and gets maimed, or killed; and if
he attempts *squaring,* he cuts and abuses
his feet in a shameful manner. The common people of Ireland seem to me to be
awkward and unhandy. What they have
been used to they can do very well; but
when put out of their old track, it is

almost impossible to teach them any thing.
A *Glasgow weaver,* although not bred to
spade and pick-axe, as they are, makes a
much better settler, can build a neat little
house for his family, and learn to chop
with great celerity, so that in a short time
nobody could suppose that he had been
bred amongst *bobbins* and *shuttles.*

It is a singular fact, too, with the
Irish, that if they can get a *mud-cabin,*
they will never think of building one of
wood. At *By-town,* on the Ottawa, they
burrow into the sand-hills; smoke is seen
to issue out of holes which are opened to
answer the purpose of chimneys. Here
families contrive to *pig* together worse
even than in Ireland; and when any *rows*
or such like things are going on, the
women are seen to pop their *carroty polls*
out of the humble doors, so dirty, sooty,
smoke-dried, and ugly, that really one
cannot but be disgusted; and do what we
will for their benefit, we can obtain no
alteration. If you build for them large and
comfortable houses, as was done at the
place above-mentioned, so that they might
become useful labourers on the public
works, still they keep as decidedly filthy as
before. You cannot get the *low Irish* to
wash their faces, even were you to lay
before them ewers of crystal water and
scented soap: you cannot get them to
dress decently, although you supply them
with ready-made clothes; they will smoke,
drink, eat murphies [potatoes], brawl,
box, and set the house on fire about their
ears, even though you had a sentinel
standing over with fixed gun and bayonet
to prevent them.

Living then in such a manner, what
must the consequence be in a climate
such as Canada? It is bad in Ireland, but
there it is worse. They absolutely die by
the dozens, not of hunger, but of disease.
They will not provide in summer against

the inclemencies of winter. Blankets and stockings they will not purchase; so the frost bites them in all quarters, dirt gets into the putrid sores, and surgical aid is not called in by them, until matters get into the last stage. In summer, again, the intolerable heat, and the disregard they pay to their health, by living as they do, and drinking *swamp waters,* if there be none nearer their habitations, instead of spring or river water, bring on malignant fevers of all kinds. . . .

Emigration of the poor may probably answer a good end, as lessening the dense population of Ireland; but it certainly will never do well for Canada, unless some other methods be devised than those now observed. It may perhaps be argued, that they are necessary as labourers at public works; I would say, no such thing. If I had any work to perform in Canada of my own, I would not employ any *Irish,* were it not for mere charity. The native French Canadians are much better labourers, as they understand the nature of the country, can bear the extremes of the climate much better, keep strong and healthy, and always do their work in a masterly and peaceable manner; whereas the Irish are always growling and quarrelling, and never contented with their wages. . . .

Are they any better than if they had remained in *Ireland*? It is true that servants are required, and many would be very willing to employ a great number, but they are unable to pay them adequately for their labour; as agricultural produce will either not admit of being raised beyond what will support the family, or the chance of a crop, and expense of transport to market, deter them from making the attempt. Poor ignorant people, too, when they arrive in such colonies, are apt to feel themselves considerably elevated, and will not condescend to toil for mere *bread* until reduced to the last stage of poverty. Besides, as they have land offered to them for a trifle, the idea of being *proprietors* has a most intoxicating effect. Under this influence, I have seen them hurrying into the woods with a very indifferent hatchet, a small pack on their back, followed by a way-worn female and her children, there to live for a time *on air,* (and if that rise out of the swamps, none of the best either;)—we have met them again crawling out,—and where is the heart that would not melt at the sight—some of the children, most likely, dead, and the rest bit and blindfolded by musquitoes!

[Catherine Parr Traill], *The Backwoods of Canada: Being Letters from the Wife of an Emigrant Officer,* (London, M. A. Nattali, 1846), pp. 80-86, 269-272.

The Basis of Frontier Class Distinction

Peterborough, Sept. 11, 1832.

It is now settled that we abide here till after the government sale has taken place. We are, then, to remain with S—— and his family till we have got a few acres chopped, and a log-house put up on our own land. Having determined to go at once into the bush, on account of our military grant, which we have been so fortunate as to draw in the neighbourhood of S——, we have fully made up our minds to enter at once, and cheerfully, on the privations and inconveniences attending such a situation; and there is no choice between relinquishing that great advantage and doing our settlement duties. We shall not be worse off than others who have gone before us to the unsettled townships, many of whom, naval and military officers, with their families, have had to struggle with considerable difficulties, but who are now beginning to feel the advantages arising from their exertions.

In addition to the land he is entitled to as an officer in the British service, my husband is in treaty for the purchase of an eligible lot by small lakes. This will give us a water frontage, and a further inducement to bring us within a little distance of S——, so that we shall not be quite so lonely as if we had gone on to our government lot at once.

We have experienced some attention and hospitality from several of the residents of Peterborough. There is a very genteel society, chiefly composed of officers and their families, besides the professional men and storekeepers. Many of the latter are persons of respectable family and good education. Though a store is, in fact, nothing better than what we should call in the country towns at home a *"general shop,"* yet the storekeeper in Canada holds a very diffierent rank from the shopkeeper of the English village. The storekeepers are the merchants and bankers of the places in which they reside. Almost all money matters are transacted by them, and they are often men of landed property and consequence, not unfrequently filling the situations of magistrates, commissioners, and even members of the provincial parliament.

As they maintain a rank in society which entitles them to equality with the aristocracy of the country, you must not be surprised when I tell you that it is no uncommon circumstance to see the sons of naval and military officers and clergymen standing behind a counter, or wielding an axe in the woods with their fathers' choppers; nor do they lose their grade in society by such employment. After all, it is education and manners that must distinguish the gentleman in this country, seeing that the labouring man, if he is diligent and industrious, may soon become his equal in point of worldly possessions. The ignorant man, let him be ever so wealthy, can never be equal to the man of education. It is the mind that forms the distinction between the classes in this country—"Knowledge is power!"

We had heard so much of the odious manners of the Yankees in this country that I was rather agreeably surprised by the few specimens of native Americans that I have seen. They were, for the most part, polite, well-behaved people. The only peculiarities I observed in them were a certain nasal twang in speaking, and some few odd phrases; but these were only used by the lower class, who *"guess"* and *"calculate"* a little more than we do. One of their most remarkable terms is to *"Fix."* Whatever work requires to be done it must be *fixed*. "Fix the room" is, set it in order. "Fix the table"—"Fix the fire," says the mistress to her servants, and the things are fixed accordingly. . . .

Persons who come to this country are very apt to confound the old settlers from Britain with the native Americans; and when they meet with people of rude, offensive manners, using certain Yankee words in their conversation, and making a display of independence not exactly suitable to their own aristocratical notions, they immediately suppose they must be genuine Yankees, while they are, in fact, only imitators; and you well know the fact that a bad imitation is always worse than the original.

You would be surprised to see how soon the new comers fall into this disagreeable manner and effectation of equality, especially the inferior class of Irish and Scotch; the English less so. We were rather entertained by the behaviour of a young Scotchman, the engineer of the steamer, on my husband addressing him with reference to the management of the engine. His manners were surly, and almost insolent. He scrupulously avoided the least approach to courtesy or outward respect; nay, he even went so far as to seat himself on the bench close beside me, and observed that "among the many advantages this country offered to settlers like him, he did not reckon it the least of them that he was not obliged to take off his hat when he spoke to people (meaning persons of our degree), or address them by any other title than their name; besides, he could go and take his seat beside any gentleman or lady either, and think himself to the full as good as them.

"Very likely," I replied, hardly able to refrain from laughing at this sally; "but I doubt you greatly overrate the advantage of such privileges, for you cannot oblige the lady or gentleman to entertain the same opinion of your qualifications, or to remain seated beside you unless it pleases them to do so." With these words I rose up and left the independent gentleman evidently a little confounded at the manœuvre: however, he soon recovered his self-possession, and continued swinging the axe he held in his hand, and said, "It is no crime, I guess, being born a poor man."

"None in the world," replied my husband; "a man's birth is not of his own choosing. A man can no more help being born poor than rich; neither is it the fault of a gentleman being born of parents who occupy a higher station in society than his neighbour. I hope you will allow this?"

The Scotchman was obliged to yield a reluctant affirmative to the latter position; but concluded with again repeating his satisfaction at not being obliged in this country to take off his hat, or speak with respect to gentlemen, as they styled themselves.

"No one, my friend, could have obliged you to be well mannered at home any more than in Canada. Surely you could have kept your hat on your head if you had been so disposed; no gentleman would have knocked it off, I am sure.

"As to the boasted advantage of rude manners in Canada, I should think something of it if it benefited you the least, or put one extra dollar in your pocket; but I have my doubts if it has that profitable effect."

"There is a comfort, I guess, in considering oneself equal to a gentleman."

"Particularly if you could induce the gentleman to think the same." This was a point that seemed rather to disconcert our candidate for equality, who commenced whistling and kicking his heels with redoubled energy.

"Now," said his tormentor, "you have explained your notions of Canadian independence; be so good as to explain the machinery of your engine, with which you seem very well acquainted."

The man eyed my husband for a minute, half-sulking, half pleased at the implied compliment on his skill, and, walking off to the engine, discussed the management of it with considerable fluency, and from that time treated us with perfect respect. He was evidently struck with my husband's reply to his question, put in a most discourteous tone, "Pray, what makes a gentleman: I'll thank you to answer me that?" "Good manners and good education," was the reply. "A rich man or a high-born man, if he is rude, ill-mannered, and ignorant, is no more a gentleman than yourself." . . .

I must freely confess to you that I do prize and enjoy my present liberty in this country exceedingly: in this we possess an advantage over you, and over those that inhabit the towns and villages in *this* country, where I see a ridiculous attempt to keep up an appearance that is quite foreign to the situation of those that practise it. Few, very few, are the emigrants that come to the colonies, unless it is with

the view of realizing an independence for themselves or their children. Those that could afford to live in ease at home, believe me, would never expose themselves to the privations and disagreeable consequences of a settler's life in Canada: therefore, this is the natural inference we draw, that the emigrant has come hither under the desire and natural hope of bettering his condition, and benefiting a family that he had not the means of settling in life in the home country. It is foolish, then, to launch out in a style of life that every one knows cannot be maintained; rather ought such persons to rejoice in the consciousness that they can, if they please, live according to their circumstances, without being the less regarded for the practice of prudence, economy, and industry.

Now, we *bush-settlers* are more independent: we do what we like; we dress as we find most suitable and most convenient; we are totally without the fear of any Mr. or Mrs. Grundy; and having shaken off the trammels of Grundyism, we laugh at the absurdity of those who voluntarily forge afresh and hug their chains.

If our friends come to visit us unexpectedly we make them welcome to our humble homes, and give them the best we have; but if our fare be indifferent, we offer it with good will, and no apologies are made or expected: they would be out of place; as every one is aware of the disadvantages of a new settlement; and any excuses for want of variety, or the delicacies of the table, would be considered rather in the light of a tacit reproof to your guest for having unseasonably put your hospitality to the test.

Our society is mostly military or naval; so that we meet on equal grounds, and are, of course, well acquainted with the rules of good breeding and polite life;

too much so to allow any deviation from those laws that good taste, good sense, and good feeling have established among persons of our class.

Yet here it is considered by no means derogatory to the wife of an officer or gentleman to assist in the work of the house, or to perform its entire duties, if occasion requires it; to understand the mystery of soap, candle, and sugar-making; to make bread, butter, and cheese, or even to milk her own cows; to knit and spin, and prepare the wool for the loom. In these matters we bush-ladies have a wholesome disregard of what Mr. or Mrs. So-and-so thinks or says. We pride ourselves on conforming to circumstances; and as a British officer must needs be a gentleman and his wife a lady, perhaps we repose quietly on that incontestable proof of our gentility, and can afford to be useful without injuring it.

Our husbands adopt a similar line of conduct: the officer turns his sword into a plough share, and his lance into a sickle; and if he be seen ploughing among the stumps in his own field, or chopping trees on his own land, no one thinks less of his dignity, or considers him less of a gentleman, than when he appeared upon parade in all the pride of military etiquette, with sash, sword and epaulette. Surely this is as it should be in a country where independence is inseparable from industry; and

for this I prize it.

Among many advantages we in this township possess, it is certainly no inconsiderable one that the lower or working class of settlers are well disposed, and quite free from the annoying Yankee manners that distinguish many of the earlier-settled townships. Our servants are as respectful, or nearly so, as those at home; nor are they admitted to our tables, or placed on an equality with us, excepting at "bees," and such kinds of public meetings; when they usually conduct themselves with a propriety that would afford an example to some that call themselves gentlemen, viz., young men who voluntarily throw aside those restraints that society expects from persons filling a respectable situation.

Intemperance is too prevailing a vice among all ranks of people in this country; but I blush to say it belongs most decidedly to those that consider themselves among the better class of emigrants. Let none such complain of the airs of equality displayed towards them by the labouring class, seeing that they degrade themselves below the honest, sober settler, however poor. If the sons of gentlemen lower themselves, no wonder if the sons of poor men endeavour to exalt themselves above him in a country where they all meet on equal ground; and good conduct is the distinguishing mark between the classes.

Samuel Strickland, *Twenty-Seven Years in Canada West,* edited by Agnes Strickland, (London, Richard Bentley, 1853), vol. I, pp. 81, 134-137, 139-140, 264-266.

The Frontier Aids All Classes

The employments of a respectable Canadian settler are certainly of a very multifarious character, and he may be said to combine, in his own person, several professions, if not trades. A man of education will always possess an influence, even in bush society: he may be poor, but his value will not be tested by the low standard of money, and notwithstanding his want of the current coin of the realm, he will be appealed to for his judgment in many matters, and will be inducted into several offices, infinitely more honourable than lucrative. My friend and father-in-law, being mild in manners, good-natured, and very sensible, was speedily promoted to the bench, and was given the colonelcy of the second battalion of the Durham Militia. . . .

There is no colony belonging to the British Crown better adapted for the poor industrious emigrant than the Canadas, particularly the Upper Province, which is essentially the poor man's country. Twenty-five years ago, the expense of the voyage out to Quebec, and the difficulty,

delay, and additional outlay of the inland journey put it completely out of the power of the needy agriculturist or artizan to emigrate; the very classes, however, who, from their having been brought up from their infancy to hard labour, and used to all sorts of privations, were the best fitted to cope with the dangers and hardships attending the settlement of a new country. The impossibility of the working hand raising funds for emigration, confined the colonists to a set of men less calculated to contend with difficulties—namely, half-pay officers and gentlemen of better family than income, who were almost invariably the pioneers of every new settlement.

Many high-spirited gentlemen were, doubtless, tempted by the grants of land bestowed upon them by the Government, which made actual settlement one of the conditions of the grant. It followed, as a matter of course, that the majority of these persons were physically disqualified for such an undertaking, a fact which many deserted farms in the rear townships of the county in which I reside painfully indicate.

Eighteen or twenty years ago a number of gentlemen located themselves in the township of Harvey. The spot chosen by them was one of great natural beauty; but it possessed no other advantages, except an abundance of game, which was no small inducement to them. They spent several thousand pounds in building fancy loghouses and making large clearings which they had neither the ability nor industry to cultivate. But, even if they had possessed sufficient perseverance, their great distance from a market, bad roads, want of knowledge in cropping after they had cleared the land, lack of bridges, and poor soil, would have been a great drawback to the chance of effecting a prosperous settlement. In a few years not a settler remained of this little colony. Some stayed till their means were thoroughly exhausted; others, more wise, purchased ready-cleared farms in the settlements, or followed some profession more congenial to their taste, or more suited to their abilities.

The only persons fit to undertake the hardships of a bush-life, are those who have obtained a certain degree of experience in their own country upon the paternal estate or farm. Men who have large families to provide for, and who have been successful in wood-clearing, are generally willing to sell their improvements, and purchase wild land for their families, whose united industry soon places them in a better farm than they owned before. They are thus rendered greater capitalists, with increased means of providing for their children, who soon take up their standing in society as its favoured class. Indeed, I would strongly advise gentlemen of small capital to purchase ready-cleared farms, which can be obtained in most parts of the country, with almost every convenience, for half what the clearing of bush-land would cost, especially by an inexperienced settler. In fact, since grants of land are no longer given to the emigrant, there is less inducement to go so far back into the woods. . . .

No person need starve in Canada, where there is plenty of work and good wages for every man who is willing to labour, and who keeps himself sober. The working man with a family of grown children, when fairly established on his farm, is fully on a par, as regards his prospects, with the gentleman, the owner of a similar farm, and possessing an income of 100*l.* per annum. The reason is obvious. The gentleman and his family have been used to wear finer clothes, keep better company, and maintain a more respectable appearance, and if he has children, to give

them a more expensive education.

Then, again, the gentlemen and his family are physically less qualified to undergo the hardships and toil of a practical farmer's life. On the other hand, the working man thinks it no degradation to send his sons and daughters out to service, and the united product of their wages amount, probably to eight or ten pounds per month. He is contented with home-spun cloth, while the spinning and knitting—and sometimes weaving—required by the family, are done at home. Labour, indeed, is money; and hence in a few years the gentleman with his income is soon distanced, and the working hand becomes the man of wealth, while his children eventually form a part of the aristocracy of the country, if the father gives them a suitable education.

There is one thing, however, to be said in favour of the gentleman—namely, his education, which fits him for offices and professions which must remain for ever out of the reach of the half-ignorant. It is, therefore, only in agricultural pursuits, and mechanical operations, that the working man is able to obtain a superiority; and then only if he be sober and industrious, for whiskey has been the great bane of the colony. Hundreds of our cleverest mechanics, and many of gentler blood, have fallen victims to its influence. . . .

There is a very true saying, that necessity is the mother of invention, and in no country is it better exemplified than in Canada. The emigrant has there, especially when distant from a town or settlement, to make a hundred shifts, substituting wood for iron, in the construction of various articles, such as hinges for barn-door gates, stable and barn-shovels, and a variety of other contrivances whereby both money and time are saved.

I have often heard young men say, they "could not" do this or do that. "Did you ever try?" is a fair question to such people. I believe that many persons, with average capacities, can effect much more than they give themselves credit for. I had no more been bred a carpenter than a civil engineer, in which last capacity I was holding office satisfactorily. My education had consisted of Latin, Greek, and French, and the mathematics. My time had been spent in my own country; riding, shooting, boating, filled up with a little amateur gardening.

Want of energy is not the fault of the Americans; they will dash at *everything*, and generally succeed. I had known them contract to do difficult jobs that required the skill of the engineer or regular architect, and accomplish them cleverly too, although they had never attempted anything of the kind before; and they generally completed their task to the satisfaction of the parties furnishing the contract. "I cannot do it" is a phrase not to be found in the Yankee vocabularly, I guess.

It is astonishing how a few years' residence in Canada or the United States brightens the intellects of the labouring classes. The reason is quite obvious. The agricultural population of England are born and die in their own parishes, seldom or never looking out into a world of which they know nothing. Thus, they become too local in their ideas, are awake to nought but the one business they have been brought up to follow; they have indeed no motive to improve their general knowledge.

But place the honest and industrious peasant in Canada, and, no matter how ignorant he may be, when he sees that by his perseverance and industry he will in a short time better his situation in life, and most likely become the possessor of a freehold, this motive for exertion will call forth the best energies of his mind, which had hitherto, for want of a proper stimulus, lain dormant. Having to act and think for himself, and being better acquainted with the world, he soon becomes a theoretical as well as a practical man, and consequently a cleverer and more enlightened person, than he was before in his hopeless servitude in the mother-country.

Part VI

The Politics of the Frontier

The frontier as the birthplace of democ-racy; what image in the frontierist literature has been more pervasive? This is a judgment which flows inevitably from those expressed by frontierists in the last two chapters. If the restraints of traditional institutions are re-moved by the environment, and if a levelling to practical equality taken place, the adop-tion of democratic forms is only a matter of time. The frontier, with its development of individual initiative and self-reliance, with its lesson that all men are equal before nature, becomes the schoolhouse of democracy. In the writings of Turner and his disciples, this has been a central theme. For them, the schoolhouse produced its first graduating class when Andrew Jackson was elected president of the United States in 1828, with the ardent support of the frontier areas, and began the "age of the common man" in American politics.

As with other aspects of the theory, there has been a good deal of controversy over the role of the frontier in producing American democracy. Arthur M. Schlesinger, Jr., in his study *The Age of Jackson* sharply disputed the interpretation that Jacksonian Democracy was an essentially frontier move-ment. Rather, he insisted, it was centred in the East, among the working class and small business interests. More fundamental have been criticisms which have stressed the British and European roots of American democratic thought, and which have argued that western political ideas were derivative, adopted from approaches developed in the eastern sections of the country. The most extreme expression of this viewpoint is in the writings of Louis Hartz. In his studies of the American liberal tradition, Hartz has held that American ideas have remained substan-tially frozen since a liberal bourgeois 'frag-ment' of European society was planted on this continent. The passage from K. D. McRae in Part VII illustrates the application of this approach to Canada.

There has been even more controversy about the so-called "safety-value" theory. Turner explained that the democracy of the United States developed peacefully, without the growth of a revolutionary movement, because the frontier operated as a safety-valve. The discontented were always able to escape from the cities and the settled areas to the freedom of the frontier, and this bleeding off of potential revolutionaries prevented the creation of radical movements like those in Europe. The frontier, then, was at the same time a radical influence—creating democracy and destroying oligarchy—and a conservative influence—preventing revolution. The safety-value theory has been attacked by many historians who have contended that there is no evidence that the frontier drew off potential revolutionaries, no evidence that the poor and suffering could afford to make the long move west. But a variant of the safety-valve concept has gained wide acceptance in Canada. It has been asserted that the United States, especially during the devastating depression of the 1880's, was a safety-valve for Canada, a kind of frontier to which the discontented could move rather than stay and generate radical movements in Canada.

Frontierists have pointed to three major examples of frontier political movements in Canada: the Rebellions of 1837; the Clear Grit movement of the 1850's in Upper Canada; and the western Progressive movement of the 1920's. The first two of these are discussed in this chapter. The problem of illustrating the controversies is the reverse of that in earlier parts. Here it is difficult in find documentary material which covers the main points economically, but there are secondary accounts which do discuss the question adequately.

The first article is a general treatment of the theme of democracy by Canada's best frontierist, A. R. M. Lower. He is concerned not only with explaining the frontier influence on political democracy, but also with why there has been a less thorough-going democratic expression in Canada than in the United States. His interpretation can be placed against that in the brief excerpt from Robert Gourlay's 1822 study, *Statistical Account of Upper Canada*, which points out that American settlers in Canada showed less interest in politics than they did in the United States. It has been argued by some historians that pioneers were far too busy taming the wilderness to have time for politics, democratic or otherwise. Gourlay's opinions should carry some weight, for he was the first major political agitator in Upper Canada, with his ill-fated attempts to bring about fundamental reforms between 1817 and 1819.

Probably the most complete attempt to apply the frontier thesis to Canada was L. S. Stavrianos' article on the Rebellions of 1837. While he admits some serious reservations are necessary, Stavrianos is confident of the general applicability of the hypothesis. More influential have been the views of Donald Grant Creighton, probably Canada's best known historian. In the excerpt from one of his articles, Creighton rejects the idea that the Rebellions sprang from a struggle for democracy by pioneers, and instead discusses them in economic terms. His sympathies clearly lie with the commercial elements who attempted to develop the resources of the St. Lawrence system, and against the agrarians who lacked the vision to grasp the commercial potential of Canada. There is an almost frontierist tone to Creighton's discussion in the 1933 article of the "new men" created by the New World. But there is a vital difference. His "new men" are created by economic opportunity, not the frontier environment, and they are concerned with commercial success, not democracy.

Two selections illustrate the controversy over the Clear Grit movement. Clear Grittism was a radical revolt within the Reform Party in the late 1840's. It adopted advanced liberal ideas on political issues, standing for the extension of the franchise, elected government officials, and a closer control by the people over their representatives. In the 1850's, the bulk of the Clear Grits were reintegrated into a revitalized Reform Party under the leadership of George Brown, publisher of Canada's most influential newspaper of the time, the Toronto *Globe*. The name of the movement lived on, often being applied to the whole Reform Party. Fred Landon, in this passage from his *Western Ontario and the American Frontier*, sees Clear Grittism as a genuine expression of frontier liberalism, in the same agrarian tradition as Jeffersonian and Jacksonian Democracy. This interpretation is consistent with that offered by historians like George

W. Brown and Frank Underhill since the 1920's. It illustrates the way in which the climate of the times can influence historical thought. For Underhill, at least, his enthusiasm for the Grits developed because they resembled the western Progressive movement of the 1920's, in which Underhill placed great hope for a revitalization and a democratization of Canada.

This view is challenged by J. M. S. Careless, with his interpretation of Upper Canadian liberalism as an urban-led movement, more concerned with economics than democracy. One wonders how much the change of the orientation of Canadian society, and Canadian liberalism, between the 1920's when Underhill wrote and the 1960's when Careless' work was published— the change from a rural society with rural protest movements, to an urbanized nation— might have influenced these conflicting interpretations. Indeed, one wonders if Turner himself might not have been an urban historian if he were practicing his craft today.

A. R. M. Lower, "The Origins of Democracy in Canada," *Canadian Historical Association Annual Report,* (1930), pp. 66-70. Reprinted by permission of the Author.

The Natures of Canadian and American Democracy Compared

The historical deductions from geography have been worked out in some detail for the United States by American historians of the school of F. J. Turner and they have shown very well how the frontier has conditioned the whole social setting, manners of thought and political reactions of the people of their nation. Turner's thesis has not yet been thoroughly applied to Canadian history and, indeed, there are factors present in the development of each country which are inconspicuous or absent in that of the other. It must therefore be a modified or adapted version of the thesis which can be fitted to Canada.

Probably the most striking and important aspect of the thesis is that one which dwells on the connection between the frontier and democracy. There can be little question but that American democracy had a forest birth and there also can be little doubt of the validity of the larger thesis that the frontier environment, or life lived on the margins of civilization, tends to bring about an equality of which the political expression is democracy. But it may be doubted whether social equality could work out into political democracy unless the society possessing it had not possessed certain theoretical positions as to its nature before it was projected into its frontier surroundings. The French Canadian and the American before 1763 both were faced with the same frontier conditions and within limits both made the same response to them. Both had much social equality, much rude good comradeship, the virtues of pioneer hospitality, adaptiveness and initiative in meeting the demands of forest life. Both were restive under control, making good scouts but poor regulars. There was infinitely more independence and assertiveness in French Canada, infinitely less readiness to do the will of a superior, than in old France; but it may be safely assumed that once the conditions which made for this independence had passed, the age-old controls of French life, the clergy and nobility, and the pressure of authority which was in the very air of the *ancien régime* would have made themselves felt and the independent Canadian would have had to bow the knee in the same manner as his ancestors.

Not so the American. He had all the independence of the *coureur de bois* and something more: he had behind him the consciousness that he was a free man, that his ancestors had been free men and that his whole society stood for the rights and privileges of the individuals. Thus when pioneer conditions had passed, the attitude toward life which they had induced remained as a conscious philosophy or creed, something to be fought for. It is only with the fading of the memory of the frontier and the elevation of the descendants of frontiersmen into a sort of an aristocracy, at least a plutocracy, over an immigrant and alien bottom layer, that the old framework of American society tends to loosen. It has not loosened much yet but it is doubtful if the political ideals of the original population, reinforced as they were by a most intense frontier experience, can be indefinitely passed on to a citizenry much of which has little of them in its heredity and much of which is slowly becoming a lower class.

In Canada, democracy has been even more of a condition and less of a theory that [than] it has been in the United States. Our political ideas have been British, not American, and in British political idealism, democracy, until a recent date, had no place. In it freedom, it is true, had a large place, but a careful distinction must be made between the old English notion of freedom and the concept suggested by the word democracy. For three quarters of a century after the Loyalists came, lip-service was paid to freedom but "democracy" was discreditable, at least among the people who "mattered". It was something that caused French Revolutions or which was associated with the American tobacco chewers discovered by Martin Chuzzlewit. The whole weight of officialdom and its connections in British North America was thrown against it and only very slowly after the securing of responsible government was the disreputable personage admitted into the drawing-rooms of respectable society. Yet to-day it is the name that is above every name. Here is an interesting historical development which has not yet been traced out as completely as it might be.

The Loyalists brought with them to Canada a bitter experience of popular action. Haldimand said, perhaps truly enough, that they had had all they wanted of Assemblies. Their chief men were aristocrats. Yet in half a century their settlements were being agitated by cries for responsible government. In so far as they supported this agitation and in so far as it did not obtain its chief support from the later comers, the frontier had done its work.

But it is probably necessary to distinguish between responsible government and democratic government. So far as the writer knows, Baldwin, Papineau and Lafontaine were not enthusiasts for democracy. Mackenzie probably was and he more than any other prominent figure represents the frontier at that period. Yet in Canada, the frontier, that is roughly, the countryside as opposed to the little governmental and mercantile centres of power and influence, never scored the ringing victory of Andrew Jackson and his frontiersmen in the United States.

It is curious to reflect how little support Mackenzie received. Logically most of the province should have supported him, for most of the province must have been affected by the grievances for which the ruling class was responsible, the conditions obtaining as to land and land-grants, the Clergy Reserves, the Anglican attempts at an established church, the tyranny of the semi-official Bank of Upper Canada. Similar conditions in the United States, both before and after the Revolution, had caused serious outbreaks. Bacon's Rebellion, the Alemance fight, Shay's Rebellion, the Pennsylvania Whiskey Rebellion, are familiar examples. A similar inspiration, if not actual grievances, had been at the bottom of the triumph of the frontier in 1828. Yet here was Upper Canada and, to a lesser degree, New Brunswick and Nova Scotia, suffering under more severe oppression that [than] these others had been and to a remarkable extent taking it "lying down".

The explanation is two-fold. The character of the population differed from that of the western states. The democratic spirit in its political expression was a post-Revolutionary development in which the Loyalist migrants had not shared. Later immigrants were not completely emancipated from old world modes of life and thought. The pioneer in his day-to-day life manifested all the characteristics of his American brother except the fierce desire of the latter to control the political situation. Mackenzie, a pioneer only by courtesy, a pioneer born in Scotland and seeing the frontier from the windows of a York printing house, was not an Andrew Jackson. Again, the provincial unit was small and control in various forms was easily exerted.

Both of these factors come together and are nicely illustrated in the case of Egerton Ryerson and the Methodists. Methodism was essentially a religion of the frontier, a fact which accounts for its rapid spread through an originally non-Methodist population, and if they had been left to themselves, its adherents, many of them of Loyalist origin, would almost certainly have gravitated into the rebel camp. But it happened to have Ryerson at its head and he also was Loyalist but a Loyalist and Methodist of a more sophisticated type than the simple pioneer. Consequently, old sentiments and the old allegiance triumphed in his person and grievances or no grievances, Strachan or no Strachan, he retained the loyalty of frontiersmen and Methodists.

The events of the rebellion period are not particularly creditable to a proud people. It should logically have been a great popular movement against undoubted grievances. Instead of that, its inherited social alignments, from which much of the meaning had evaporated, took all the fire

out of it.

Though, partially as a result of the rebellion, self-government came, democracy did not prevail and as late as 1867, Sir John Macdonald could vigorously and without condemnation champion a property suffrage. Property and privilege is written into the British North America Act to a much greater extent than it is written into the American constitution, itself a document far from democratic. . . .

Despite the continuance in the west down to the present of democratic phenomena . . . the present democratic tone of our institutions cannot be looked upon as having been an inevitable political evolution. In 1867 there was no body of opinion in favour of democracy. In fact, as has been said, opinion was in the other direction. Yet to-day our governments are responsive to the slightest breath of the air of public opinion and sometimes in their efforts to anticipate it, move ahead of it. Providing it be vocal enough, there is no class in the community that cannot force government's hand. This would not have been true sixty years ago. The problem is to account for the change.

Democracy both as a theory and a condition made great headway in Great Britain after 1867 but it is impossible to believe that British political practice had any important influence on Canadian. There was no echo in Canada of John Bright's famous campaign preceding the Second Reform Bill and no echo of the bill itself. Our democratic evolution must have come from elsewhere.

Robert Gourlay in his day made excellent fun of the provision in the Constitutional Act for a hereditary nobility in Canada and pictured the Marquis of Erie as a petty lawyer in a small country town or the Duke of Ontario observed by some passer-by in the act of getting in his own hay. Descriptions exist of the unconventionality of the Canadian Legislatures of the early days and of the illiteracy (and worse) of their members. In the state of society reflected in matter[s] such as these, surely lies the key to the problem. You cannot make a silk purse out of a sow's ear and you cannot make class distinction in a country where there is not much wealth and where everybody has started in the race for its accumulation from approximately the same point and started very recently. In other words, society in a new country is almost necessarily equalitarian and democratic, and therefore sooner or later politics must become so. If they do not, it is because the long arm of an old polity is felt stretching out toward the new. France stretched out such an arm towards Canada before 1763 and kept the country mildly feudal. But even in feudal New France, the seigneurs had little to distinguish them from the habitants except their pride and poverty. England stretched out such an arm after 1763 and for many years kept the institutions of the new country mildly aristocratic. But when self-government came, the regime of privilege rapidly evaporated in the sun of economic equality.

It need not necessarily have been so. In a small and isolated community, where opportunity was narrow, privilege might easily have maintained itself. Probably eastern Canada was alone large enough to have avoided this, certainly the Dominion as at present constituted is, but in any case the influence of the outside world would have prevented it. With our traditions of political freedom working in the modern world, we must have come out somewhere near the point at which we have in fact arrived. Moreover we lay close to a country in which during the nineteenth century democracy was, so to speak, being continuously re-manufactured, recreated anew with every belt of new country opened up. In the tone of society as in every other particular, we were influenced by the United States and there is no doubt that the march of democracy in the United States influenced its march in Canada. The back-wash of western democracy forced political equality in all the eastern states and by the 'forties the last property qualifications and the last established church had disappeared from New England. Its effect on Canada must have been similar, for while the boundary tends to retard the spread of ideas northward it does not stop it. It may be concluded that our own pioneering era plus the influence of American pioneer life brought about political democracy in Canada.

Despite American influence, there are observable differences between our democracy and that of the United States. We have never erected democracy into a creed in Canada and consequently we endure without even feeling their inconsistency, let alone injustice, such undemocratic remainders as the property suffrage in municipal politics and property qualifications for the Senate. We endure or did endure until recently, distinctions of rank that have never been tolerated in the United States. We like to think that our democracy does not shout as loud as that of America. These differences, for the most part small, probably proceed from three causes. The first is that our frontier experience, owing to differences in habitable area, has not been as intense and prolonged as has that of the United States. We have not been ground up quite as fine by it as the United States. Sir John Beverley Robinson was able to keep his coach and four and to pose as grand seigneur in "Muddy York" but it is unlikely that he could have done so in contemporary Cincinnati. The second cause is that the old world sentiment has been much stronger in Canada and the old world connection much more recent than in the United States. And the third lies in our monarchical form of government; in the old days we were governed and we have never quite got accustomed to governing ourselves. Government to many of us still seems a thing apart, not quite our own concern. The perpetuation of monarchical forms, even though the life has long since gone out of them, doubtless tends to act as a curb to the fullest expression of democracy. At any rate, the differences just mentioned between our democracy and that of the United States consist in a general way in this, that democracy in Canada has not had quite as thorough-going an expression as it has had amongst our neighbours.

Robert Gourlay, *Statistical Account of Upper Canada,* I, (London, Simpkins & Marshall, 1822), 248-249.

Pioneer Disinterest in Politics

The tide of emigration naturally flows from old to new settlements. These causes, combined with the fertility of the Canadian soil, the relative cheapness of land and lightness of public burdens, have induced many Americans, from year to year, to move into the province. Here they have generally acquired farms and engaged in business, not as a distinct people, like the French population in Lower Canada, but blended and intermixed with the former inhabitants.

The intermixture produces no effervescence, personal or political. Politics, indeed, are scarcely named or known among them. They have very little agency in the affairs of government, except that the freeholders once in four years elect their representatives. The people are not agitated by parties, as they are in the United States, where all branches of government depend, directly or indirectly, upon frequent popular elections.

L. S. Stavrianos, "Is the Frontier Theory Applicable to the Canadian Rebellions of 1837-1838?", *Michigan Magazine of History*, vol. XXII, (1938), pp. 326-335. Reprinted by permission of *Michigan History*.

A Frontierist Interpretation of the Rebellions of 1837

Some forty years ago, Frederick Jackson Turner first presented his thesis that the continual expansion of the United States into new regions shaped the course and the nature of American civilization. To this day the majority of historians find this hypothesis ". . . as easily to be accepted as it was when launched." Strangely enough, students of Canadian history have practically ignored this theory, despite the parallels in certain aspects between the developments of the two countries. What efforts have been made in this direction have been denounced as an ". . . attempt to deform the story of our own development to fit the Procrustes bed of the frontier theory."

As in most generalizations, there is a certain amount of truth in this statement. The growth of Canada has been influenced by a number of modifying factors not present in the American frontier, which have made impossible the acceptance of the Turner thesis with all its economic, social and political implications. It does not necessarily follow, however, that the frontier theory is wholly inapplicable to Canadian history. This is especially true of the period leading to the rebellions of 1837-38, when the Canadas were influenced by the prosperous American republic with its Jacksonian democracy, as well as by a frontier environment similar in many respects to that on the American frontier. The purpose of this study, therefore, is to estimate to what extent, if at all, the Turner hypothesis is applicable to the Canadian rebellions.

Considering first the revolts in lower Canada, the peculiar racial limitation of the frontier theory immediately becomes evident. The reaction of the French Canadians to the frontier environment was quite unlike that of the Anglo-Americans. This difference constitutes the major factor in the history of Lower Canada and the principal reason for the outbreak of the rebellion there. The struggle between the French Canadians and the Anglo-American merchants in Lower Canada was due, not to the fact that the latter were English speaking Protestants, but to the more fundamental fact that they were the representatives of the commercial seaboard and the British-American land frontier, as against the tepid colonial society which they found on the banks of the St. Lawrence. This was clearly realized by Stuart Derbishire, a London lawyer and journalist who came out with Lord Durham as a special agent. "The rebellion had its foundation in two opposing philosophies, the British element represented industrial enterprise while the French Canadians, with a few exceptions, were opposed to all measures which would encourage the growth of commerce and looked back to a state of society in which an almost 'pastoral' existence had been the rule."

Considering next the situation in

upper Canada, there is to be found no such clash of conflicting civilizations as existed in the lower province. The history of Upper Canada seems rather to have been the result of the interplay of three forces, the moderating effect of the imperial tie, the levelling tendency of the frontier environment and the democratic influence of the neighboring republic.

The instrument of the imperial power in Upper Canada was the constitution provided by the Canada Act of 1791 by which the affairs of the province were strictly subordinated to the central government, so that the moderating influence of the imperial connection constituted one definite force in the dynamics of Upper Canadian politics. The second factor in the history of Upper Canada is to be found in the frontier environment of the province. Many accounts, both contemporary and recent, have been written of pioneer life in the backwoods of Upper Canada so that this point need not be elaborated upon. It should be noted, however, that at the time of the rebellions a far greater percentage of the population lived under frontier conditions in Upper Canada than in the United States as fully one-half of the population consisted of immigrants who had arrived in the country within the previous ten years and who necessarily still lived in a frontier environment.

The historical significance of this environment lies in the fact that it produced a society in many respects similar to that existing in the American west. On both sides of the border there was the same tradition of individualism, independence and equality. There was a common dislike of military discipline and authority, the Canadian settler brandishing umbrellas and walking sticks rather than corn-stalks, at the annual militia parade. The same eagerness for bees, dances and societies, especially temperance societies, was to be found in Upper Canada, most of these institutions, in fact, having originated in the United States and spread across the border. Excessive drinking, as travellers invariably remarked, was characteristic of both countries. In the field of religion there was the same tendency towards emotional worship and sectarianism, the American frontier being the origin of the circuit riders, the camp-meetings and the numerous obscure sects which swept Upper Canada during this period. In the diary of Joseph Richard Thompson, one can even find a picture of a settlement in Upper Canada which, confronted with the lack of satisfactory law and order, formed its own compact, unconsciously and naturally following the example of the Pilgrim Fathers and the settlers of Transylvania, Franklin and the Watauga.

Thus, under the influence of a similar environment, there had grown up in Upper Canada a society resembling in many respects that on the American frontier. In the United States this had resulted in conflict between the trans-Alleghany west and the tidewater east, but in Upper Canada where the scene was much more limited, there was no corresponding rise of geographic sections. It does not follow, however, that there were no conflicting interests in the province. A provincial oligarchy, the so-called Family Compact, had grown up in Upper Canada, and in practically every field it came into conflict with the popular assembly. Religion, immigration policy, the crown and clergy reserves, the Upper Canada Bank and the imperial trade regulations all furnished points of dispute. Thus this struggle between the democratic frontiersmen and the landed city oligarchy constituted the second force in the dynamics of Upper Canadian politics.

Finally account must be taken of the neighboring republic, especially in view of the large influx of American settlers stimulated by the low price of land in Upper Canada. The actual migration of the settlers cannot be traced because of the lack of records yet its extent was realized when the war of 1812 revealed that the American settlers in Upper Canada constituted about two-thirds of the total population. The political significance of this close relationship between Upper Canada and the United States lies in the influence of the latter upon the former. The family relationships and everyday contacts between the people of the two countries, the large number of American owned inns in Canada, the extensive circulation of American newspapers, the large percentage of American teachers in the backwoods schools, the wide use of American text books and the constant stream of pedlars, showmen, circuses and ministers which included Upper Canada in their travels all aided, consciously or unconsciously, in spreading the doctrines of Jacksonian democracy throughout the province.

In the decade that preceded the rebellion, this catalytic influence of the United States grew increasingly more potent, due largely to the flourishing prosperity of the United States. It was during these years that the rise of "King Cotton" provided a home market for northern manufacturers, permitted the United States to import the necessary European goods, and above all, provided a market for western farmers and thus inaugurated the "Mississippi Valley Boom." In Upper Canada, on the other hand, there was no counterpart to this progress of the western states. The absence of any great, export-able, staple product, the lack of adequate markets and the fifteen hundred miles of barren lands between the province and the central prairies, all combined to place Upper Canada during these years in much the same position as the American west before the development of the south and the rise of internal commerce.

The resulting contrast between the prosperity in the United States and the relative backwardness of Upper Canada played an important part in the political history of the province. "Suppose, for instance," argued the reformer Mackenzie in his paper, the *Constitution*, "that the Mississippi River had been the western boundary of Upper Canada. What would Michigan, Indiana, Illinois or the Wisconsin Territories have been at present? Would they, in the short space of a few years, have been swarming with hundreds of thousands of inhabitants actuated by the industry, public spirit and enterprise characteristic of the people of the Western States? Or would they have been held back, and their energies crippled by the same accursed drag chains which have hitherto withered the prospects, and retarded the progress of our own misgoverned Province?"

Such then was the background of the rebellion in Upper Canada. In the decade before 1837 the internal conflict between the reformers and the Family Compact was heightened and colored by the influence of the United States with its Jacksonian democracy and its flourishing prosperity. In the struggle over the crown and clergy reserves, the Upper Canada Bank, the responsibility of government and the numerous other points of conflict, the reformers tended more and more to point to the United States as a model. Thus the conservatives turned reactionary and the reformers grew increasingly radical, until finally a series of aggravating events goaded the radicals to open resistance and transformed the political struggle into armed conflict.

The events leading to the outbreak of the rebellion are well known and need not be repeated here. The significance of the revolt, however, is worthy of examination, particularly in view of its similarity in certain respects to the numerous American frontier uprisings.

In the first place, the potentiality of the rebellion, and the discontent which followed it, were far greater than is generally realized. Concrete evidence is to be found in the escape of practically all the rebel leaders, in the reports of numerous informers and loyalists sympathizers to the military authorities and in the alarming increase of emigration from Upper Canada to the United States that followed the rebellion. This latter movement had been going on for some years but now it assumed such proportions that observers and newspapers in both the United States and Canada were commenting throughout this period on the extent of this exodus.

In the second place, the rebellion was representative, not only of a large portion of the population, but also of a definite section. This is clearly revealed in the analysis of the prisoners taken after the rebellion, in the contrasting attitudes of the tories and reformers towards the principles of Jacksonian democracy and in the division of public opinion in Upper Canada over the internal policies of the United States. The tory journals consistently criticized Jackson's administration, bitterly blamed Van Buren for the financial panic of 1837 and then adopted an extremely bellicose tone toward the United States during the post-rebellion border difficulties. During this period the reformers' viewpoint found little support as

practically all the reform newspapers disappeared. The following article, however, published in the liberal Toronto *Mirror* during the Congressional elections of September 1838, reveals the sense of identical interest on the part of reformers with Democrats and tories with Whigs.

"A Canada editor, it may be said, has nothing to do with the politics of the United States. It may be so, but we cannot look on, and see the great struggle that is going on, at our doors, between the privileged hundreds and the advocates of 'a clear coast and no favor', without expressing an anxious wish to see the true Republican democratic cause prevail. . . . Like begets like. The Whigs of the United States, and the Tories of Canada, salute each other: They shake hands across the lines—May they both experience the same vote."

Finally, in considering the other aspect of the question, that is, the attitude of the American public towards Upper Canada, the situation is found to correspond to a striking extent. Before the outbreak of the rebellion, Americans as a whole were relatively ignorant of Canadian affairs, but even then there was noticeable a tendency among the commercial classes and the large eastern newspapers to favor the tories of Upper Canada, while the lower classes and the small journals in the northwestern states sympathized with the reformers. Once the revolt broke out this difference of opinion became marked and distinct especially after the Caroline incident of December 29, 1837. The New York *American*, for example, attempted to soothe its readers with the advice, "Let us do as we would be done by, and judge others as we would be judged," but the Rochester *Democrat* demanded revenge, ". . . not simpering diplomacy either,— BUT BY BLOOD . . . ."

In addition to this sectional difference, there was also apparent a class division in the American attitude to the Canadian rebellions. The masses of ordinary people, especially along the border, were distinctly pro-rebel in their sympathies, whereas the commercial, industrial and official circles were strictly neutral or pro-tory. It can be seen, therefore, that just as the reformers in Upper Canada were pro-American and pro-Democrat and the tories were anti-American and pro-Whig, so the population of the northwestern states was pro-reformer and pro-"Patriot" while the eastern vested interests and the upper classes in general were pro-tory and anti-"Patriot". Just as the liberal Toronto *Mirror* referred to the Whigs of the United States and the tories of Canada as saluting each other and shaking hands across the lines, so the Buffalo *Star* pointed to the similarity between them.

". . . the portion referred to as the respectable part of the Canadas are the aristocracy—the titled aristocracy and the pensioned agents of a foreign government —persons who have interests as well as feelings, distinct from those of the mass— and differ only in their outward political condition from the Moneyed Aristocracy in the United States. The same feelings which induce the Tories of Canada to claim to themselves all the 'respectability', induce the aristocracy of the United States to claim all the decency, religion, talents and lastly, the 'charity' of the country."

From this analysis of the rebellion in Upper Canada, it is apparent that it was neither an accident nor an insignificant affair but rather a movement similar in many respects to the numerous frontier revolts in the history of the United States. In view of this fact, one would have expected a more formidable uprising than that which occurred, especially since the farmers in Upper Canada constituted such a large majority of the population. The explanation is to be found in a number of modifying factors present in Upper Canada but not in the United States. The most important of these was the effect of the Laurentian Plateau and the international boundary which effectively checked the expansion of the Canadian frontier. Thus while the American settlers during the thirties were pouring across Michigan, Indiana, Illinois and Wisconsin, the Upper Canadians were hemmed in both to the west and to the south. Accordingly, although a large proportion of the settlers in Upper Canada had but recently arrived, yet at the time of the rebellions there was no replica in Upper Canada of the American fringe of settlement constantly pushing westward. As a result, the Upper Canadian frontier, if it may be so called, lacked the vitality, the expansive force and, therefore, the influence of the American.

This comparatively slow advance of settlement resulted in a second point of difference between Upper Canada and the United States, namely, the Indian problem. The history of the rapidly expanding American west has been largely one of constant warfare between the advancing settlers and the Indians whereas in Canada the slower rate of expansion and the greater utilization of the Indians in the economic life of the country precluded any trouble outside of the half-breed Riel Rebellion of 1868 [*sic*]. The importance of this contrast between the two countries lies in the fact that it produced two different types of frontiers. Constant Indian fighting in the United States engendered a general spirit of lawlessness in which the posses and gun-toting frontiersmen disregarded the central authority and made their own law. In Upper Canada, however, Indian warfare was absent and the control of the government was far more stringent, so that the irresponsible, lawless type of frontiersman was not present in the province. Thus the conditions for a successful revolt were far less favorable in Upper Canada than in the United States.

Another factor that tended to produce a more orderly and law-abiding society in Upper Canada was the moderating influence of the imperial connection. This link created, in the first place, a powerful and conservative class consisting of half-pay officers, imperial officials, provincial administrators and United Empire Loyalists. These formed a definite provincial society which was quite as pretentious and dignified as any of the Old World, and which exerted a powerful moderating influence that was not to be found on the American frontier. In addition the imperial government exerted a strict control over the affairs of the province, thus eliminating the disorder characteristic of the American west. Irresponsibility and lawlessness were reduced to a minimum and the possibility of a successful rebellion was correspondingly diminished.

Finally, account should be taken of the difference in the nature of the population of the two countries. The American frontiersmen of this period were usually the descendants of a long line of backwoodsmen and were continually pressing on to new frontiers, the average settler moving six times in a life-time. [In] Upper Canada, however, the immigrants from the mother country were usually unfitted for frontier life and they either drifted on to the American cities or fell back on government aid. The result of this situation was that there was no class of restless, independent and intensely individualistic, frontiersmen in Upper Canada as in the United States. Instead of resenting the control of the authorities, the Upper Canadian settler insisted upon law and order and often he was dependent upon the government for assistance in his struggle against the wilderness. The average settler in Upper Canada, therefore, was much more amenable to governmental control and far less likely to revolt than the individualistic backwoodsman of the American frontier.

In conclusion there arises the problem of ascertaining the extent to which the frontier theory, in view of these limitations, is applicable to Upper Canada. It is apparent, in the first place, that the slower advance of settlement, the absence of Indian wars, the powerful influence of a conservative upper class and the general tractability of the population of the province all contributed to form a society distinctly different from that of the United States. It cannot be said, therefore, that the true point of view in the history of Upper Canada or of the rebellion, is "the Great West". Neither can it be said, however, that the environment exerted no influence or that the rebellion was an accidental or incidental affair. Rather it was the quintessence of the whole history of the province, the product of three conflicting forces: the egalitarian influence of the frontier environment, the moderating influence of the imperial tie and the catalytic effect of the neighboring republic.

D. G. Creighton, "The Commercial Class in Canadian Politics, 1792-1840," *Papers and Proceedings of the Fifth Annual Meeting of the Canadian Political Science Association,* Ottawa, 1933, pp. 43-44, 46-51, 54-55. Reprinted by permission of the Canadian Political Science Association and the Author.

An Economic Interpretation of the Rebellions

There were two occupations of Canada at the conquest, the military and the commercial. And this dual occupation sums up much of the history of the past and suggests the development of the future. The long struggle on the North American continent had not only been a war between two great European powers, France and England; it had also been a conflict between two purely American societies—the society of the St. Lawrence and that of the Atlantic seaboard; and the significance of the conquest lies less perhaps in the fact that it extended British imperial control over the old Province of Canada as it does in the fact that it made possible the conjunction of these two dissimilar colonial societies within the confines of a single state. British control might mean either arrogance and ineptitude or impartiality and wisdom. But the great issues in Canada, as in all America, were not to be decided by imperialistic virtues and vices; they were to be decided by American capacities and by the promptings of the American spirit.

And this American spirit was, fundamentally, materialistic. It was the response of a middle class population in a commercially-minded age to the apparently unbounded possibilities of an unworked continent. On the Atlantic seaboard, this spirit was, perhaps, best typified by Massachusetts, where the New Englanders were creating a commercial prosperity with that ingenious efficiency which, in the seventeeth century, had been devoted to the establishment of a Puritan paradise. It was this energy and commercial aggressiveness which the "miserable sutlers and traders" brought to Quebec and Montreal. They came to the newly-conquered province with the single, simple, and essentially American objective of making money by trade. And they were to be an incalculably disturbing force, not, in the main, because they were English-speaking Protestants, but because they were the pure, distilled spirit of British American commercialism dropped into the tepid colonial society of the St. Lawrence.

The most important products of the New World were its new men. The French, like the Spaniards, Dutch, British, and Germans, crossed the Atlantic Ocean as Europeans; but they and their descendants remained in the new continent as Americans. It is impossible, in comparing the society of the St. Lawrence with that of New England, to insist exclusively upon such old-world factors as race, language or religion. The French Canadians were also distinguished from their southern neighbors by the peculiar responses of their spirit and by the characteristic adjustments of their social heritage, to the promises and demands of a vast and empty continent. The population—a scant sixty-five thousand—huddled together comfortingly along the lower reaches of the river. The inward pull of church, family and seigniory was enormous. The little colony peopled itself slowly without expanding and the earthy solid frontier of New England and Virginia was replaced here by the vast unsubstantial empire of the fur trade. In that trade the courage and resource of the French Canadians had been lavishly expended. Their use of the St. Lawrence river system, their transportation units, their commercial techniques and their cultural borrowings from the Indians, were all distinctive features of their colonial civilization. So was their economic dependence on the fur trade; for efforts at more extended and diversified commercial enterprises had been unsuccessful. And back in the seigniories between Quebec and Montreal, the habitant, ruled by an old-world system of tenure, sale and inheritance, toiled tranquilly away at his subsistence farming. It was a curious little society, stolid, comfortable and unaspiring; and to the commercial seaboard and the land frontier of British America it appeared—in all its aspects—alien and almost incomprehensible. . . .

The period from 1783 to 1821 witnessed the first great economic revolution in Canada. It opened, on the morrow of the Peace of Paris, with the appearance of the Loyalists on the shores of Lake Ontario, and it closed appropriately in 1821, with the collapse of the vast fur trading organization centralized in Montreal. French Canada, which had survived the American Revolution, succumbed to the Peace; and the Loyalists, who entered where the Republicans had been repulsed, brought equally a revolution to the old life of Quebec. They were followed by the first American settlers in the Eastern Townships; and before

1821 forces were at work in Scotland and Northern Ireland to produce the great Canadian immigrations of the 'twenties and 'thirties. While the first frontiersmen in Upper Canada began to produce and to consume, the North-West organization, centralized to pursue a retreating trade across a half-continent, was directed inevitably into the last furious struggle with Hudson Bay. But, already, years before the long contest between the canoe and the York boat had been concluded, capital and labor were being shifted to the new staples, timber and wheat. Population grew; farmers settled where fur traders had roved; the whole commercial technique and transportation system of the French was altered and then abandoned. Gradually the limitations and deficiencies of the St. Lawrence system of communications became startingly distinct to a new population in which optimism, restless energy and materialistic ambition were the dominant traits.

The slow course of this revolution masked for a time its inevitable consequences; but it was from the beginning big with menace for the French Canadians. And it ended by completing the divorce between the merchants and the colonial society of the St. Lawrence. By 1821 the fur trade had passed away; but while the merchants who had directed it grasped eagerly at fresh opportunities, the society which had been based upon it endured unchanged on the lower reaches of the river. Aloof and dogged, the French Canadians clung to the nerve centre of a communication system which restless aliens were determined to exploit in new and unfamiliar ways; and the merchants began to feel annoyance at the very time when the Canadians experienced their first cool thrill of apprehension. The attack was no longer against single features of their culture, such as their commercial law or their devotion to the paternalistic form of government; it was an attack from all sides, against the position as a whole, and it was led by merchants whose commercial interest, which had once directed them to maintain the economic system of the St. Lawrence, now forced them to undermine it. Immigration threatened to submerge the culture of the French Canadians. Freehold tenure in the Eastern Townships menaced the seigniorial system in the very province which they believed their own. Merchants and land speculators began sharply to question their system of notarial records, their bankruptcy laws, their fines on sales of land. The slowly elaborated programme of banks, land companies, roads, canals, harbors and ship channels was conceived to gain objectives which they did not cherish and was to be implemented by methods of which they did not approve. Private enterprise on a grand scale through banks, and public works on a grand scale through taxation and credit were alien to them and distrusted instinctively. By 1821 the issue was joined between a peasant community producing for consumption and led by lawyers and priests, and a frontier community producing for export and led by a business class whose primary interest was trade.

During this period, the commercial class was adapting its programme and its methods of political action to the slowly changing exigencies of the situation. Their demand for an Assembly, reinforced now by the petitions of the Loyalists, was satisfied at last by the Constitutional Act. But the projected division of the province robbed the concession of much of its savour; and Lymburner, the merchants' agent, fought to

the last to preserve the economic unity of the country. His defeat and the division of the old province of Quebec into Upper and Lower Canada conditioned largely the economic and political activity of the merchants for the next half-century. Political division became inevitably the chief check upon their commercial programme, just as union became the chief article of their political creed.

Rapidly, their political position under the Constitutional Act became paradoxical in the extreme. Cut off from their friends in the Upper province who in all essentials accepted the same gospel of expansion and prosperity, surrounded by a peasant and professional society at once dormant and suspicious, the merchants acquired an outward aspect of extreme political conservatism as naturally as they developed a revolutionary economic creed. In 1792, when the first legislature opened, they were weak in the Councils and fairly strong in the Assembly. But in 1821, when the Canadian commercial revolution had run its course, all this had altered. The governors of the 'teens and early 'twenties turned to the traders as the French Canadians turned away from them; and the commercial class, along with the bureaucrats, judges and French Canadian landowners, became intrenched in the Legislative and Executive Councils as it was extruded from the Assembly. This union with governors and councillors, not often intimate, was frequently interrupted. The interests of the merchants were immensely practical and unemotional; they could scarcely sympathize with Ryland's unreasoning bigotry nor could they understand, later on, Lord Gosford's feeble wooing of French Canadian popularity. In the Councils, moreover, they could not always win their point. They were unable, in 1805, to persuade the Legislative Council to vote down the new customs duties and they failed to induce it to support the Union Bill of 1822. But while the Council was a defective institution for their purposes, it was the only institution which they could hope to dominate. And the whole trend of events from 1783 to 1821 was forcing them to depend less upon their private capacities and more upon the public instruments of legislation and finance.

But if their union with government was never perfect, their divorce from French Canada became inevitably complete. But it was not until the crowding economic changes had begun this alienation and had stamped the commercial minority with a faint tinge of red, that symptoms of serious trouble first appeared. It is surely significant that the first embittered clash in Lower Canada occurred, not during the governorship of Craig, the terrorist, but during the administration of the mild and ineffective Milnes; and that it concerned, not the lofty questions of religion and language, but the prosaic problem of financing the construction of jails. It was a straight dispute between a peasant community which hated all taxation and land taxation in particular and a commercial class which wished to escape part of a burden, which rested, in the first instance, almost entirely upon its shoulders. The abusive articles in the Quebec *Mercury* and the founding of *Le Canadien* followed the quarrel; and thereafter the war of newspapers and pamphlets never really ceased. While *Le Canadien* attacked the fur traders and criticized the American frontiersmen in the Eastern Townships, British publicists began to laud American enterprise and prosperity and to reflect sadly that unprogressive Canada "exhibited its

infant face, surcharged with all the indications of old age and decay." The merchants, as they established steam-boat services and founded banks, realized acutely that they had only half escaped from a society which remained unchanged to provoke and to impede them. As this period closes, they began to organize for the repeal of the Constitutional Act and the establishment of Union.

In rapid succession, at the beginning of the new period, the North-West Company passed from existence, the first little canal at Lachine was started, the financial struggle in Lower Canada broke out and the ill-fated Union Bill was debated and withdrawn. These apparently haphazard events constitute at once a warning and a prophecy; they reveal the basic problems of the period only to suggest their final solution; and they symbolize the intimate and vital connection between new staples, transportation, public finance and union which dominates the situation and which creates the maladjustments, efforts and tensions of the next few years. The period of gradual change is over; the pace is enormously accelerated. A new world confronts the men of 1821 imperiously. Its opportunities and problems crowd in upon them faster than the immigrants who land by thousands in the ports of Quebec and Montreal. And beneath all the shifting perplexities of immigration, settlement, roads, staples, currency and credit, lay the immense problem of the St. Lawrence, which complicated all the joint and several difficulties of the provinces and upon the solution of which their future, as a going American concern, depended.

But if the new age produced problems, it created confidence to meet them. The country was full of hope, naïve optimism and driving ambition; exhortations and grandiose programmes crammed the press; an army of surveyors, engineers and promoters invaded the provinces, and land companies, canal companies, railway organizations and banks sprang into existence. Inevitably men were driven back to the provincial and imperial parliaments; and, as the political pressure increased, as the petitions and programmes continued to rain upon the heads of unhappy governors and recalcitrant assemblies, the antagonisms, deep and irremediable between the spirit of colonial France and colonial America, was now at length completely revealed. The American culture, expressed by merchants and frontiersmen, was in the ascendant; and, as the tide closed in around them, the French Canadians realized its menacing significance and were driven into violence and hysteria. . . .

The rebellions in Upper and Lower Canada were both, to a considerable extent, the result of the efforts made by two politically divided colonies to adjust themselves to a geographical background which demanded their union. But, while the basic economic problem was the same for both colonies, the two societies which wrestled with it were profoundly different and the resultant political struggles were fundamentally distinct. The conflict in Upper Canada conformed to a type which the history of the Thirteen Colonies had made wearisomely familiar; but the origins of the dispute in Lower Canada are more mysterious and obscure. One theory, that the conflict was a quarrel between frontier liberalism and a conservative obligarchy, Lord Durham speedily rejected; another, that the dispute was a racial struggle between French and English, he confidently believed. But surely both theories are inadmissible; the first because, as we have seen, it is a patent misinterpretation of the facts, the second because it is an undue simplification of them. When Lord Durham found in race a *primum mobile* external to the facts, he became a victim to the monotheistic determinism common to most philosophers of history. Race, as a universal, automatically operating constant, is a myth. There were two races and two religions in Quebec in 1763; but there was no rebellion until 1837. And North America, in this case as in others, has proved tolerant of religions and races, when those races have accepted its social uniformity and bowed to the materialistic gospel of its inhabitants.

It was precisely this that the French Canadians refused to do. Their programme was essentially a broad social programme—the preservation of a distinct colonial society unimpaired in all its basic essentials; and they insisted, not merely upon their racial purity, their religion and their language, but also upon the legal system, the land system, the agrarian social structure and the simple economic activities which had always distinguished their community. The Quebec Act, to which they began to appeal, is an instrument for the preservation of an old order, just as the Declaration of the Rights of Man and the Citizen is an instrument for the creation of a new. Decades after the French Revolution and the Napoleonic regime had transformed the land and legal systems of continental France, the French Canadians were still descanting upon the nobility and simplicity of the Custom of Paris and earnestly debating the advantages and disadvantages of the feudal system. They saw greed in American commercialism; and turbulence in the American frontier; and they desired to protect their little society from the onslaught of both. Their methods varied, but their purpose remained the same. Distrustful at first of democracy, they learnt to use it, and later demanded its extension. But they opposed an elective Assembly in the seventeen-eighties and demanded an elective Council in the eighteen-thirties for basically the same reason—the preservation of the old colonial society of the St. Lawrence.

F. Landon, *Western Ontario and the American Frontier,* (Toronto, McClelland and Stewart, 1967), pp. 231-237. Reprinted by permission of The Canadian Publisher, McClelland and Stewart Limited and the Author's Estate.

Frontier Democracy and the Clear Grits

The Reform party in Upper Canada, despite the charges of disloyalty lodged by its political opponents (charges widely believed in England), quickly recovered its place after the union of the provinces in 1841. During the forties it was led by Robert Baldwin, who, though ready to fight to the last ditch for what he believed to be the right, was in no sense an extremist. Within the party, however, there was a radical wing whose political programme was definitely influenced by American theory and practice. To this group the name Clear Grit was applied, at first derisively but later in more respectful manner. Boastful of their democracy, the Clear Grits demanded wider suffrage, the secret ballot, and abolition of property qualifications for candidates for Parliament. They also called for biennial Parliaments, popular election of many officials, abolition of all special privilege to any group, and direct taxation. This programme, with its American tinge, was regarded in conservative circles as radical and dangerous, and was even viewed with sus-

picion by many within the Reform party itself. George Brown, editor of the *Globe,* once described the group as "a miserable clique of office-seeking, bunkum-talking cormorants" and on another occasion classified them as "radicals, republicans and annexationists." By the early 1850's, however, he had cast in his lot with them and soon became their recognized leader. The chief area of circulation of the *Globe* was the western peninsula and it was there that Clear Grit sentiment was most in evidence. Among the Scottish farmers, so numerous in this section, the *Globe's* views were read and accepted as having almost inspired authority. In the cities Clear Grit principles made little headway and it was noticeable also that they were less in evidence as one travelled eastward, becoming almost non-existent in the more easterly counties of the province. The party's suspicion of cities and bankers and railway interests bears a likeness to other progressive and agrarian movements in Canada and the United States. As F. H. Underhill has observed: ". . . the essential thing about the *Globe* and the move- ment it led is that it represented the aspir ations and the general outlook on life of the pioneer Upper Canadian farmer. The 'Clear Grit' party in Upper Canada was an expression of the 'frontier' in our Canadian politics just as Jacksonian Democracy or Lincoln Republicanism was in the politics of the United States. It was to 'the intelligent yoemanry of Upper Canada' that the *Globe* consciously made its appeal." An added characteristic of the Clear Grit movement after Brown assumed leadership was its hostility to the Roman Catholic Church. This anti-Romanist attitude bore some resemblance to that of the contemporary Know Nothing party in the United States but there is no evidence that the Upper Canadian group was influenced by the American propaganda, though Thomas D'Arcy McGee noted the influence in another direction. In a letter written to the *Globe* in 1861, he said: "Since the era of the Know Nothing movement the last vestige of political preference for the United States has disappeared among the Irish."

For a time John A. Macdonald, Brown's chief opponent, was inclined to minimize the effects of the Clear Grit movement but by the end of 1856 he was less sanguine. Writing to the editor of the Montreal *Gazette*, he said: "The Peninsula must not get control of the ship. It is occupied by Yankees and Covenanters, in fact the most yeasty and unsafe of populations." Macdonald here recognized what the Toronto *Leader* had once described as the "eternal restlessness of the Peninsula," a temper of mind in which democratic ideas found congenial soil.

The Reform convention of 1859, the first great party convention ever held in Canada, clearly demonstrated where the strength of the Clear Grit movement lay, If the "Peninsula" did not have control of the ship of state, a danger which Macdonald had suggested, it did at least have numerical control of the convention of 1859, for of the 520 delegates who attended no less than 273 were from the western counties and the Niagara Peninsula, with 178 others from York and the central counties and less than 70 from the eastern section of the province. It was a clear proof that Clear Grit strength was greatest where most remote from Montreal. Another interesting aspect of the convention was the prominence in it of the newspaper editors of the province. The notice calling the convention was signed by sixty-two persons, of whom no less than forty-two were connected in some way with newspapers. Editors were likewise prominent in the convention itself. The *Globe* specifically mentioned twenty-eight in its list of delegates and there is good reason to believe that there were others present who were not so identified. Of the twenty-eight mentioned by the *Globe*, twenty-three were from what Macdonald called "the Peninsula."

The Reform convention of 1859 is one of the turning points in Canadian political history and its decisions form one of the milestones on the high road towards the federation of 1867. The union of Upper and Lower Canada brought about in 1841 had long been a cause of heart-burning to the Clear Grits who believed their province to be the victim of an unscrupulous and unprincipled government which maintained itself in power by gross corruption and the votes of Lower Canada. "Were human ingenuity," said the *Globe*, "exercised to the utmost to discover a political machine by which one section—and that section Lower Canada —should inflict the greatest possible amount of insult, injury, and costly injustice upon its partner in the business of legislation, no better contrivance than the union could be devised." Reform newspapers boiled over with charges of governmental extravagance, railroad peculation tariff discrimination against the farmer in favour of the commercial class, and general cynical indifference to the farming class and its needs. Criticism was extended even to the representative of the Crown. When Sir Edmund Head in 1858 gave sanction to the famous "Double Shuffle," Brown and his friends waxed highly indignant and in the London *Free Press* its editor Josiah Blackburn wrote:

The governor-general ought to keep in mind that acts such as the black one so recently chronicled in Canadian history have a very complex bearing and might have a direful issue. Loyal as we Canadians are, we are not intoxicated with crowns; and, indeed, it is a notorious fact that in this age crowns are not ascending in power and value. . . . We can be independent—we might prosper as an independent power, and less than a "heads or tails" may decide the issue of events. The cords that bind us to England are strong, but they can be severed, and what if Governor Head is teaching us to sharpen the scissors.

The Reform convention of 1859, following closely upon the political scandal of 1858, assembled in a mood far from complacent. Rather, it was "a political avalanche of outraged virtue" which descended upon Toronto. The convening circular stated that its object would be to consider the whole aspect of public affairs and seek the best remedy for the evils complained of "unfettered by any restriction." Opportunity was to be afforded for the discussion of written constitutions, dissolution of the union of the two provinces, a federal union of all the British North American provinces, a federal system for the united province of Canada alone "or any other plan calculated . . . to meet the existing evils."

Of the several alternatives to be presented to the convention, dissolution of the union was by far the most dangerous. Adoption of this idea would promptly have split the Reform party in two since the whole eastern section of the province was economically dependent upon Montreal. Moreover, it would leave the province cut off from a sea port and thereby produce a situation where it would tend at once to move down an inclined plane into close relations with the United States.

The chief protagonist of dissolution was George Sheppard and chief support for this radical proposal came from the delegates representing the western section of the province. But even they were by no means unanimous. Hope Mackenzie, of Sarnia, expressed the opinion that dissolution was supported only by those holding "American ideas" and he predicted that dissolution would create a desire for annexation to the United States. This view also found expression in the editorial columns of the London *Free Press*. To George Brown, however, must go the chief credit for heading off a proposal which would have been disastrous to the Reform party and probably also to the country. It was one of his great services to Canada. As a recent writer on this period has observed:

The stake was high—nothing less than half a continent, but if the union of the provinces was dissolved, if the Grit party turned its eyes inward to fight the battle of constitutional reform within the bounds of Upper Canada, everything might be lost. The unity of the party on some basis of co-operation with Lower Canada was the one essential of the moment to be preserved at all costs. To imagine that Brown saw nothing of this is to him an impossible injustice and indeed the whole record of these months makes it clear that this was his guiding principle.

Sheppard, as the chief advocate of dissolution, deserves some attention. An Englishman of radical views, he had migrated to America in 1850 where, after an unsuccessful colonizing venture in the West, he became associate editor of the *Daily Republican* at Washington. In 1857 he was in Toronto as editor of the *Daily Colonist* but soon transferred his energies to the *Globe*. To that newspaper, during the summer of 1859, he contributed a series of editorials enunciating policies which were more extreme than George Brown himself favoured. Sheppard was an ardent admirer of the political institutions of the United States and firmly convinced that the Grit party must commit itself whole-heartedly to the cause of constitutional reform even though that meant the damning of its prospects for office. Sheppard's influence, as exercised during the summer of 1859, was distinctly mischievous, as Brown was to find out during the Reform convention.

Brown and the more conservative element in the party favoured the idea of a federal system for Upper and Lower Canada by themselves, believing that a federation of all the provinces in British North America was a still somewhat remote possibility. Resolutions along this line were presented to the convention on the evening of the first day and precipitated a debate that lasted until eleven o'clock on the following evening. Of that debate it has been written:

. . . every phase of Grit thinking was elaborated at length. One cannot but be struck by the fact that the voice of the assembly was that of an agrarian democracy. There were present many town-dwellers, but the movement was essentially of the soil. Here we listen to the farmer of Canada West voicing his suspicions of merchants, bankers and politicians who fattened themselves at the expense of the honest toilers of the frontier. There was a sturdy belief in the essential virtue of a free and enfranchised citizenry. Government, it was felt, should be near at hand and always under the scrutinizing eye of the sovereign people: it should be simple, inexpensive, and entrusted with as few

responsibilities and powers as possible.

This was Jeffersonian democracy in earnest. Government was to rest in the hands of the producing class where intelligence and sanity chiefly dwelt, and democratic progress was to be attained by preserving and extending political and economic liberty. "A government vigorous, frugal and simple," Jefferson's formula in the election of 1800, was what the Clear Grits of 1859 hoped to see achieved. It was not easy to keep American political theory out of the discussions but any mention of annexation met with immediate disapproval while generous applause greeted all expressions of loyalty to the British connection. The Reform convention of 1859, like many Reform gatherings since, had to be on guard against statements that might be twisted by political opponents into some semblance of disloyalty.

Sheppard's speech was the critical point in the convention. "I appear here as the advocate of the simple, unadulterated dissolution of the Union," was his introductory sentence, and as he pursued his way through the subject it was clear that he was the voice of a large section of the delegates present. His amendment favouring complete dissolution of the Union with Lower Canada meant a split in the party if it were accepted. This the leaders of the party knew full well. Reform ranks would be broken on almost straight geographical lines since the more easterly portion of the province, with its close ties to Montreal, was bound to reject a proposal that meant economic ruin.

In the end the Reform convention of 1859 did exactly what conventions of later days and of both parties have done in the face of a troublesome issue—it compromised on an amendment which offered a means of saving its face. And, as has so often happened since, the amendment which offered a way out was carried with "immense enthusiasm." What the convention approved after long hours of debate was a proposal that there should be two or more local governments to care for matters of local sectional character with "some joint authority" charged with the care of matters of common interest. The whole proceeding bore the stamp of practical party tactics. Words were uttered but none could define precisely what they meant—their value lay in their vagueness. Nevertheless, Brown's success in securing adoption of the rather meaningless amendment meant a victory over Sheppard and those who favoured dissolution. Their policy would have left the western wing of the party divorced from the central and eastern groups. Brown's success in carrying the convention forestalled the possibility of Upper Canada being separated from Lower Canada and forced into closer relations with the United States by being cut off from the sea. However vague might be the ideas of federation enunciated in 1859, there was embraced in them a principle which was to widen out during the next few years to take in not merely two but all the British provinces. Here

may be seen the importance of the decisions arrived at in 1859. Upper Canada Reformers had clearly grown in their political thinking. The Reform convention of 1857 had seen only one feasible solution for its woes, representation by population. Two years had changed the point of view. This is clearly seen in the editorials which appeared in the *Globe* during the summer of 1858. Brown and his party were becoming more national in outlook and it was such an outlook that coloured his speech before the Reform delegates assembled in 1859. "I do hope," he said on that occasion, "that there is not one Canadian in this Assembly who does not look forward with high hope to the day when these northern colonies shall stand out among the nations of the world as one great confederation." He could scarcely dream as he uttered those words that within ten years this high hope would be realized and that in its accomplishment he would be one of the leading figures. The decisions arrived at by the Reform convention under the influence of his convincing arguments were a prelude to greater developments to come and determined the road along which these developments were to proceed.

J. M. S. Careless, "The Toronto *Globe* and Agrarian Radicalism, 1850-67," *Canadian Historical Review*, vol. XXIX, no. 1, (1948), pp. 14-19, 34-39. Reprinted by permission of the author and of the publisher, University of Toronto Press.

Urban Liberalism and the Clear Grits

It is well established in Canadian tradition that the Toronto *Globe* of the Confederation era spoke above all for the farmers of Canada West. The *Globe*'s constant care for the "intelligent yeomanry of Upper Canada" was repaid by the flattered members of that community in steadfast devotion to George Brown, his party and his journal. An anecdote of the time sought to illustrate this when it depicted a farmer of the Huron Tract replying warily to a remark that it was a fine day, "I can't say till I've seen my *Globe*." . . .

One can scarcely question the essential validity of this well established interpretation of the *Globe*'s opinions and activities. And yet if followed too narrowly it may tend to obscure other significant characteristics of the *Globe* and the movement it represented. The whole "agrarian approach," if one may so call it, needs qualification. To explain the complex opinions of the *Globe* even generally in terms of the outlook and aspirations of the pioneer farmers is to overemphasize one aspect of the journal and to neglect or misconceive other aspects of considerable importance. For instance, it would be unwise to assume too much from a premise of agrarianism about the *Globe*'s attitude toward democracy, or its views on commerce and manufacturing or banking and railways. It would not be sufficient to identify the *Globe*—and George Brown himself—with the aims and interests of a farming population. And it would be dangerous to accept its Liberal creed simply as an expression of frontier democracy. Of course, cautions of this sort have not gone wholly unregarded. But they have had little weight in judging the policy of the *Globe* as a whole.

Moreover, it may be questioned whether the *Globe* was speaking, as has been affirmed, for a "pioneer agricultural settlement." There is good reason to doubt whether this is a satisfactory description of the western portion of the Province of Canada, during the fifties and sixties of the last century, and therefore to doubt whether it provides the proper frame for examining the newspaper. In many ways the pioneer era was rapidly passing away in Upper Canada by 1850. Even in the western Ontario peninsula, the stronghold of agrarian radicalism and a major source of *Globe* support, the fast dwindling supply of fertile wild land foreshadowed the disappearance of the frontier. In the next decade, the growth of the grain export trade, the increase in local commerce, the rise of towns, and the coming of the railway began the transformation of the western region. A scattered community of backwoods settlements was becoming an integrated commercial agricultural society, in which the business class was steadily rising to prominence, and through which the metropolitan pull of the city of Toronto was making itself felt ever more strongly. Toronto in 1850 was merely "a fair-sized commercial town," mainly distinguished from other Upper Canadian centres by its administrative functions and its past as a seat of government. By 1867 it was well advanced on its way to economic as well as political hegemony over the entire western section. Between these years Toronto invaded territory formerly subject to the trade of rival Ontario towns, spread out a railway network, became a leading Canadian manufacturing centre, and established capital facilities capable of serving a wide area. It even began to contend, on not too unequal terms, with the older metropolis of Montreal. One could scarcely suppose that the *Globe* would remain isolated from the turbulence, the aggressive self-confidence, and the grand designs of its native city. In fact, its own expanding influence throughout Upper Canada in this period may be read as one striking manifestation of Toronto's rise to metropolitan status. The city's press was coming to dominate the West.

In similar fashion in politics "tory Toronto" became the headquarters of Grit radicalism—not a surprising development, for this expression of Upper Canadian sectionalism found a natural focus in the rising western metropolis. In the middle fifties the Clear Grit agrarian movement thus fell under the control of an urban and professional group led by George Brown which was chiefly to be identified with Toronto. The many-headed, loosely led Clear Grit movement was gradually organized under a party hierarchy centred in that city. The mass of agrarian support was joined with influential western business interests, numbers were linked with economic power,

and a strong sectional block was built up. The *Globe* played a major role in this process as the voice of the Toronto leadership, and did a good deal to put its views, full of care for business considerations, before the rural community. The proprietor of the journal was himself far from being a member of the farm community. George Brown was a fairly typical member of the Toronto business world; and many leaders of Toronto business were prominent in the party which he dominated. Among them were William McMaster, whose extensive financial interests made him the dean of Toronto business, John Macdonald, head of the city's leading wholesale house, A. M. Smith, an urban real estate owner and one of Toronto's wealthiest citizens, John McMurrich, a prominent city merchant and president of two insurance and investment companies, and W. P. Howland, one of the Howland family then outstanding in Toronto finance and industry. All these men appeared as Liberal members of the Assembly or Legislative Council in the decade after 1857; and all but W. P. Howland were in 1867 members of the party's Central Committee (which, however, included H. S. Howland).

Brown had close business ties as well as political affiliations with these urban Liberals. He was one of the leading members of the Toronto group, captained by McMaster and including John Macdonald and the Howland brothers, that formed the Bank of Commerce in 1867 to meet the threat of a Bank of Montreal monopoly. His brother, Gordon Brown, editor of the *Globe* during much of this period, was associated with McMaster, W. P. Howland, and McMurrich in financing the Kennedy expedition "of commerce and exploration" to the Northwest in 1856; and he was again associated with them in the directorship of the North West Transportation Company, organized in 1858. George Brown was also affiliated with A. M. Smith and two other prominent Toronto magnates, William Gooderham, Sr., and J. C. Worts, as a major stockholder in the Toronto Linseed Oil Manufacturing Company. Shortly after Confederation he appeared with McMaster and John Macdonald in the directorate of the Toronto Isolated Risks and Farmers Insurance Company. His private holdings during the eighteen-fifties and sixties, apart from the most widely circulated newspaper in Canada (in 1862 it claimed three times the circulation of its nearest rival,) included a large amount of speculative real estate, lumber workings, saw mills, a cabinet factory, a village, and oil lands in the heart of the western oil-boom districts of Kent and Lambton. From the material interests of its proprietor alone, it would seem to be safer to identify the *Globe* with the Toronto business man than with the pioneer farmer. Without swinging to this other extreme, however, it does become necessary to consider the journal with reference to the growth of western business generally and of Toronto business in particular. To put it simply, the *Globe*'s dealings with "urbanism" must be treated no less than its dealings with agrarianism.

The fact that the *Globe* had these diverse interests does not necessarily imply any contradiction in its views. One need not look for any inevitable conflict between urban and agrarian interests in Canada West during this stage of transition from the frontier era. Instead, dividing lines between town and country were somewhat blurred. Prosperous Toronto citizens turned from their offices to practical farming, as did George Brown on his Bow Park stock-breeding farm, and

not to golf clubs or summer homes in beautiful but barren Muskoka. Wealthy farmers like the prominent Clear Grit, Joseph Gould, invested in banking, railway promotion, and new factories in or about the towns. In general, as in the case of Winnipeg and the prairie West in a later age, the farming populace and the local business community that lived by its trade shared many important points of view, particularly in opposition to outside metropolitan forces which sought to dominate the whole region. Accordingly, in Upper Canada of the Confederation era one could find an "agricultural interest" representing the West as a whole in its struggle against Lower Canadian domination, but made up of both urban and agricultural elements. Its prevailing tone might be that of an agricultural society. Its leadership would come largely from town-dwellers, commercial and professional men, and well-to-do-farmers with close ties with the urban world of business.

In this context, the *Globe* might speak generally on behalf of the western farming classes; but it would look specifically to the interests of the leaders of western agricultural society, which involved a good deal of concern for matters of commercial significance outside the ken of the ordinary farmer. Approaching the journal by way of agrarianism and frontier democracy obscures the significance of its constant care for business affairs. The final picture of the *Globe* should not be that of an agrarian radical oracle making common cause, on occasion, with the essentially foreign world of Toronto business; but rather one of an urban Liberal newspaper seeking to carry its viewpoint to the rural masses—and generally succeeding. . . .

Regarding the general pattern of the

Globe's thought, one must say that its political ideas could not fairly be called "democratic," as the word was understood in North America of that day. . . . The *Globe* condemned the American system where, at elections, "The balance of power is held by the ignorant unreasoning mass." It agreed that the franchise in Canada undoubtedly should be widened, but thought increased education should go with its extension, since, "the lower we go in the scale of suffrage the more we add to that dangerous element." "In view of these facts we are not willing to travel quite so fast or so far in the democratic path as some of our friends." This cautious position, tying education and the recognition of property and intelligence into franchise reform, is reminiscent of middle class Liberalism in Victorian England; . . . In Canada, there was no need for the *Globe* to look so definitely to a similar middle-class, propertied group, because, as it often said, in Canada all could be men of property. Yet its attitude towards the rising urban and industrial proletariat, which contravened that statement, showed that essentially it did not take a democratic position but believed in the political virtues of property. It saw its rural followers as property-owners—they were not "mere leaseholders," it said—and its confidence in their intelligence was largely because they did have property.

Yet does this trust in rural property-owners bring the *Globe* in line with North American democratic thought as expressed by Jefferson? One could say that once again it demonstrated the journal's reliance on agrarian support; but it did not constitute an expression of Jeffersonian beliefs. The *Globe* had none of Jefferson's distrust of industrialism, or of the commercial classes, and, far from deploring the great power of urban communities, was associated with the rise of the chief city in Canada West. It did not look to the placid rule of simple farm proprietors, and a sort of bucolic Utopia, but to a hard-driving partnership of rural and urban men of property in which the latter led. And, of course, the *Globe*'s feelings for democracy itself were decidedly qualified. Nor does Jacksonian frontier democracy fare any better as a frame for *Globe* opinion. There is too much that will not fit; its rejection of the elective principle —a frequent frontier solution for political domination by propertied groups—its close associations with the business world, its stress on the interests of capital and sound finance rather than on those of an agrarian debtor community. . . .

If, however, the *Globe* does not fit in easily with the ideas of North American agrarian democracy, it falls in readily with the Liberalism of Cobden, Bright, and other middle-class business men in mid-Victorian British politics—the men the journal so much admired. Its admiration for Cobden himself was somewhat restrained by his anti-imperial views. But the imperialist *Globe* found in Gladstone a worthy exponent of all that was best in the Manchester School, together with a proper acceptance of the imperial bond. The *Globe*'s interest in material development and retrenchment at the same time, its stress both on popular rights and on the danger of an unpropertied, uneducated democracy, its concern for laissez-faire business enterprise and its distrust of the labour movement, its devotion to free trade—all these leading aspects of *Globe* opinion accorded perfectly with the doctrines of British middle-class Liberalism of the mid-nineteenth century. The views of the *Globe* represented the transfer of mid-Victorian

Liberal thought to the North American scene.

This transfer of ideas is partly to be explained by the character of the men behind the newspaper. George Brown himself was raised in the atmosphere of Nonconformist, middle-class British Liberalism. Associated with him in the early years of the *Globe* was his father, Peter Brown, a Scots merchant turned journalist and a veteran Liberal of the days before the great Reform Bill. The two Browns were Free-Kirk Presbyterians. They entered eagerly into the battle for the separation of church and state in Canada, a question that was exercising Nonconformist Liberals in Britain too, although it was hardly echoed in the contemporary American climate of opinion. The *Globe* was kept in close touch with British Nonconformity. This contact, together with others—plentiful copying from English journals, regular correspondence with England, and frequent visits there by *Globe* representatives to cover special events—helps to explain further how British doctrines were transmitted through the pages of the newspaper. Nevertheless, even its close contact with British sources does not fully explain the fact that the *Globe* was such a ready medium for transferring urban British Liberalism to a fundamentally agricultural North American society. If, as the agrarian approach has held, the *Globe* represented the outlook of a pioneer farming community, would this be a favourable environment for doctrines that stemmed from a highly developed industrial and commercial society? However, if instead the *Globe* represented urban business and professional elements in Upper Canada, as well as back-country farmers, then this problem in the transference of ideas disappears. The journal

found itself not in the midst of the agrarian frontier, but at the centre of a thriving business community, within a rising metropolis; and it had its interests very much at heart. This is not to equate Upper Canada merchants with the mighty *entrepreneurs* of Victorian Britain, nor to consider Toronto as a backwoods Manchester. It is enough that the doctrines of urban, middle-class British Liberalism would be naturally qualified to express the interests of the urban, middle-class *Globe*.

The original manifestations of the clear Grit movement may have expressed democratic impulses common to the North American agrarian frontier, though one might ask how far the transference of British ideas also operated here, to infuse Grit radicalism with the views of the Chartists and philosophical radicals. In any case, even granting that the ordinary Clear Grit was a North American farmer, naturally affected by the common western American environment, the fact remains that the *Globe*, despite its strong rural interests and close rural affiliations, dwelt in an urban setting and in a city traditionally devoted to all things British. In such a position, it was particularly open to the transfer of British Liberal ideas, which it then expounded to a western constituency that did not find them alien. In fact, thanks to the *Globe*'s prestige in Upper Canada, and to the political eminence of its proprietor, it could do much to direct and re-shape the thoughts of the farming population which it led. That, at least, is one explanation for the decisive change in the character of the Clear Grits between 1850 and 1867. Beginning in 1850 as an extreme radical faction, displaying sympathy for American ideas (for which "Yankee Republicanism" they were roundly attacked by the *Globe* among others), by 1867 they had become a respectable colonial Liberal party, devoted to the Crown and the British constitution, and for nearly a half-century after Confederation they controlled Ontario, the most vociferously loyal and British of all provinces. Surely it is probable that the great influence of Brown and his newspaper over the Clear Grits had a good deal to do with this metamorphosis. . . .

Part VII

New Approaches

How many times over the last fifty years have Turner and his thesis been given up for dead? And yet always new life stirs in the body, new aspects of the theory are emphasized, new implications are discovered. In the American tradition the approach has maintained its vitality unimpaired. The most stirring appeal of the 1960's for Americans was John F. Kennedy's call to explore the 'new frontier'. It was a call that Americans responded to, as they have responded to the frontier lure for generations. On the eve of the moon landing in July, 1969, newspapers across the continent carried an article by Thomas O. Paine, head of the United States space agency, which dramatized the moon landing in terms of a great new frontier opening to mankind, a frontier which would renew the vitality of men, which would create of mankind a vigorous "frontier brotherhood." There indeed is life in the body yet.

The frontier thesis fell on hard times in the 1930's and 1940's. Scholarly reaction against the excesses of nationalism made the Turnerian emphasis upon the greatness and uniqueness of the American national character suspect. The impact of the social sciences upon history led to a rejection of simple environmentalism; sociology, psychology, anthropology, these convinced historians that society was too complex to be understood by any single interpretative tool. And, increasingly, liberal scholars were questioning the very bases of American society and with them Turner, who had glorified and sanctified these traditions. The theory came under a similar onslaught in Canada, and gave way to the Laurentian approach and later to the metropolitan thesis. Yet, even in its darkest days, frontierism had its adherents, and its influence upon the general climate of thought was clear.

In recent years there has been a revival of interest in the frontier problem. One reason may be a new concern with social history, and a belated recognition of both the significance of the frontier development process in North American social history, and of the enormous contribution Turner made to opening up this field of historical study. Frontierism as an orthodoxy is little practiced. But the approach has been adjusted and adapted to fit new knowledge and has emerged in a number of interesting new variations. Some of them are illustrated here.

Stanley Elkins and Eric McKitrick of Columbia University attempted in the early 1950's to inform the study of the frontier with the techniques of modern social science. The problem they chose to cope with was the core of the Turnerian faith—the contribution of the frontier to the growth of American democracy. Two articles in the *Political Science Quarterly* treated first the Midwestern frontier, and then those of the South and of New England. Passages from the treatment of the Midwest, the 'Old Northwest', of the United States are reproduced here. There is a major redefinition of the frontier in this treatment, a redefinition in terms of problems, and in terms of business and urbanism. They are broadening out the frontier approach, making it generally applicable rather than tied to a necessary relationship to free land. Sociology and political economy have added their techniques to that of history. But there is much of the old moral tone, too, and the authors clearly accept the general validity of Turner's ideas. Jack Eblen's demographic approach, however, challenges the frontier hypothesis. This brief excerpt demonstrates some of the new scientific techniques which are now moving beyond traditional social science methods and which are increasingly being applied to the study of history.

Canadians, too, have returned to consideration of their wilderness experience. An intellectual approach is to be found in a bril-

liant essay by Canada's distinguished literary critic, Northrop Frye, in his conclusion to the *Literary History of Canada*. Drawing on the earlier chapters of the book, in which a variety of authors have discussed the schools and periods of Canadian literature, Frye ranges widely over the problem of how the environment has affected Canadian character and Canadian literature. There is much here of which Turner would approve; but there is a striking contrast to American frontierism, too, in the emphasis on the ambiguous, often negative, tone taken by Canadian writers toward the wilderness. There is little of the heady optimism of the American frontier. There is rather more of this optimism in K. D. McRae's contribution to the book *The Founding of New Societies*. The book, as mentioned earlier, is an attempt to apply the theories of Louis Hartz to the colonial societies thrown off by England. Each of these societies, in the theory, is only a "fragment" of the older society. The United States, founded by businessmen, is a "bourgeois" fragment. Isolated from the interplay of all the fragments of the total mother society—the feudal fragment, the proletarian fragment, etc.—the nature of the American bourgeois, liberal fragment has remained relatively static. In applying the theory to Canada, which is seen as an offshoot of the American liberal tradition, McRae has modified the approach somewhat by attempting to integrate the Hartz and the frontier approaches.

The final selection, appropriately, illustrates the most complete attempt to adjust frontier theory to the conditions of Canada. Starting from a radically different definition of the frontier—the frontier "is taken . . . to refer to the development of new forms of economic enterprise."—sociologist S. D. Clark broadens the thesis to embrace many other factors than the environment. And yet, despite these factors, despite discussion of commercial frontiers, despite the tone of modern sociology, is the end product so very different from the essay which began this book?

With every fresh attack, with every demolition by critics, Turner and his thesis seem to rise phoenix-like from the ashes.

Stanley Elkins and Eric McKitrick, "A Meaning for Turner's Frontier, Part I: Democracy in the Old Northwest," *Political Science Quarterly*, Vol. LXIX, No. 3, (1954), pp. 322-336. Reprinted by permission of the Authors.

Social Scientists Defend Turner

A new phalanx of critics has now demolished the Turner conception. His vagueness, his abstraction, his hopeless imprecision, his poverty of concrete examples, have each been held up to the scientific eye. . . .

And yet, though conviction now burns so low, it remains to be noted that even the unkindest of Turner's critics have conceded, with a kind of bedeviled monotony, that *some* relation most likely does exist between our history and our frontier. The fact thus stands that, in this direction at least, no advance has yet been made beyond Turner's own dazzling abstraction. The problem is still there, its vitality unextinguished. It is no further resolved than ever.

If we examine with suspicion the body of critical work, we discover an interesting paradox. Turner and his teachings have been approached with deadly seriousness on their own terms—no other —and handled with what turns out to be *textual* criticism: a method which is illuminating but whose value for the analysis and correction of theoretical material is acutely limited. The result has been to demonstrate the absurdities of Turner's internal logic—which is an undoubted contribution to perspective. Yet it should be recognized that no concrete attempt to restate Turner's idea has ever actually been undertaken. Now might there not, after all, be a way of rescuing Turner? Is it possible to ask the great question itself in a form permitting a concrete answer?

Turner's critics may be allowed the most sweeping of concessions. Nearly everything could be sacrificed—everything, that is, except the one thing that matters: the development of political democracy as a habit and the American as a unique political creature. This was the supreme fact which overwhelmed Tocqueville in the 1830s; every American still knows in his heart that the frontier had something to do with it. "What?" is, of course, the crucial question. It has always been difficult to ask it, if only because it has never seemed very important to discover a working, functional definition of "political democracy." "Democracy" is alluded to, invoked, celebrated, its collapse predicted daily. Democracy, in our traditions, has rich connections with the yeoman farmer (involving, as it were, "grass roots" and freedom from the urban banker); it is at once individualistic and coöperative, equalitarian and fraternal; hand in hand with stout self-reliance goes the civic exercise of universal suffrage. For most of our daily purposes democracy is a synonym for all that is virtuous in our social traditions and on the public scene.

Yet it still appears that we need a *working* definition of political democracy. It should in some way account for concepts central to most traditional notions, but it should also be functional, in the sense that its terms may be tested. . . .

Suppose that political democracy be regarded as a manipulative attitude toward government, shared by large numbers of people. Let it be thought of as a wide participation in public affairs, a diffusion of leadership, a widespread sense of personal competence to make a difference. Under what conditions have such things typically occurred? When have the energies of the people been most engaged? What pushes a man into public activity? It appears that nothing accomplishes this more quickly than the formation of a settlement.

Our national experience, indeed, furnishes us much material for a hypothesis. Political democracy evolves most quickly during the initial stages of setting up a new community; it is seen most dramatically while the process of organization and the solving of basic problems are still crucial; it is observed to best advantage when this flow of basic problems is met by a homogeneous population. Now "homogeneity" should here involve two parallel sorts of facts: not only a similar level of social and economic status and aspirations among the people, but most particularly a lack of, or failure of, a traditional ready-made structure of leadership in the community. A simple test of the effectiveness of structured leadership is its ability to command acceptance and respect. . . .

Before turning to history for a trial of this so simple yet interesting idea, let us set it in yet another dimension by examining a series of extremely important findings in contemporary sociology. Robert K. Merton has conducted a study, whose results are soon to be made public, of social behavior in public housing communities. A theory of political democracy which would meet all our criteria may be derived from Mr. Merton's work; there is little we shall say from a historical viewpoint which has not already, in a present-day setting, been thoroughly documented by him.

He and his associates have observed two public housing projects, one being designated as "Craftown" and the other as "Hilltown". Craftown, located in southern New Jersey, administered by the Federal Public Housing Authority, and set up originally to house warworkers, was much the more active and interesting of the two. The key to the activity there was a "time of troubles" in the initial stages of the community's existence. The people who settled in Craftown ("homogeneous" in the sense that a majority were employed in nearby shipyards and defense plants) were immediately faced by a staggering series of problems of a fundamental sort, affecting the entire community. These bore on law and order, government, public health, housing, education, religion, municipal services, transportation, and markets. Slovenly construction had resulted in leaky roofs, flooded cellars, and warped floors. There were no schools, no churches, no electricity, no community hall, no grocery stores. Bus service was irregular and the nearest depot was a mile away. There were no hard-surfaced roads or side-walks and much of the area was flooded during the rainy season. There was a wave of vandalism and no organization for its suppression. There was an epidemic of poliomyelitis. There were no municipal services of any kind; the environing township did not want to assume the cost of such services and by legislative action Craftown was gerrymandered into an independent township—which meant that it had to set up its own institutions for government and for the maintenance of law and order.

Craftown did have a ready-made structure, as it were, of leadership; its affairs were under the administration of a federal bureau, the Federal Public Housing Authority, and handled by a resident manager and staff. Under stable conditions such a structure would have been adequate for most of the community's basic concerns. Yet the problems in Craftown were so overwhelming, so immediate, so pressing, that the residents could not afford to wait upon the government for action. They were therefore forced to behave in that same pattern which so fascinated Tocqueville: they were driven to "the forming of associations". Mass meetings, committees and subcommittees were organized, a township board was set up, officials of great variety were elected; a volunteer police force, fire department and local court were established, with residents serving as constables, firemen and judges. A coöperative store soon came into existence. An ambulance squad, a nursery and child care center, and a great variety of organizations devoted to community needs made their appearance during this critical period. Pressures brought upon the bus company and the government agencies resulted in the improvement of transportation, the paving of the streets, repair of houses, drainage of swamps, and the erection of buildings for education, worship and other functions of the community.

This experience resulted in an extraordinary level of public participation by people who for the most part had never had previous political experience; and it produced a political life charged with the utmost energy. Many jobs were created by the crisis—by the flow of problems—and they had to be handled by someone; many

rôles were created, someone had to fill them. The key was necessity. Persons who had previously never needed to be concerned with politics now found themselves developing a familiarity with institutions, acquiring a sense of personal competence to manipulate them, to make things happen, to make a difference. Thus the coin of necessity had its other side: there were compensations for the individual. With many offices to be filled, large numbers of people found themselves contending for them; the prestige connected with office-holding, the sense of energy and power involved in decision-making, became for the first time a possibility, a reality, an exploitable form of self-expression. . . .

One more reference to the Craftown episode should be made, in order to note two interesting subsidiary consequences of this problem-solving experience, this wide participation, this sense of individual competence spread among such great numbers. One was a close supervision of the officialdom which the Craftowners themselves had created—and a lesser degree of respect for it than had apparently been the case in their previous communities. The other was a body of shared "traditions," with a common vocabulary, rich with meaning, whereby the experience might be relived and re-shared. Although the level of activity was never as high in later times as it was in the beginning—the problems by then had been solved—the intensity of the "time of troubles" served to link the "pioneers" and the later-comers together by a kind of a verbal bond. Talking about it was important: once this experience had been undergone, it was not lost. In such a usable fund of tradition, resources for meeting a new crisis, should one appear, would remain always available.

How might such a contemporary

model square with the pioneer frontier? No sorcery of forest or prairie could materialize the democrat, yet it should be safe to guess that the periods of wholesale migration to the West forced a setting in which such an experience as that just outlined had to be enacted a thousand times over: an experience crucial in the careers of millions of Americans. Frederick Jackson Turner has stated the undeniable fact—that an organic connection exists between American democracy and the American frontier. The insight is his. But Turner never offered a conceptual framework by which it might be tested. We are proposing such a model; it involves the establishment of new communities. Its variables are a period of problem-solving and a homogeneous population whose key factor is the lack of a structure of leadership. . . .

"The frontier," to Turner and his followers, as well as to most others, seemed almost automatically to mean the Old Northwest—the "valley of democracy"—whose settlement took place during the first third of the nineteenth century. To discover why the connection should be made so naturally, let us select this region, with its key states Ohio, Indiana and Illinois, as the first frontier to be observed.

The chronicles of these states abound with reminiscences of the pioneer; close upon them in the county histories came haphazard statistics which proudly mark progress from howling wilderness to fat countryside and prosperous burgs. Between these points come many a crisis, many a relished success. We should consider not the solitary drifters, the Daniel Boones, but the thousand isolated communities each of which in its own way must have undergone its "time of troubles." There, the basic problems of organization were intimately connected with matters of life and death. They were problems to be met only by the united forces of the community. Think of the basic question of housing itself, and how its solution was elevated by necessity, throughout the Old Northwest, to the status of institution and legend: the cabin-raising. The clearing of the forest and the manner in which this was accomplished gave an idiom to our politics: the logrolling. Defense against the Indians required that the experience of the Marietta settlers, forced to raise their own militia in the 1790s, be repeated elsewhere many times over at least until after the War of 1812. And there was the question of law and order: the traveler Elias Fordham, stopping one night in 1818 at a cabin near Paoli, Indiana, found himself in the midst of preparations by the citizenry for apprehending a gang of brigands. How often must such a scene—the formation of *ad hoc* constabularies, the administration of emergency justice—have been enacted in those days? . . .

Now as these communities toiled through the process of stabilizing their affairs, what effect must such an experience have had upon the individuals themselves, exposed as they were to the sudden necessity of making great numbers of basic and vital decisions, private and public? With thousands of ambitious men, predominantly young men, looking for careers, pouring into vast unsettled tracts, setting up new communities, and being met with all the complex hazards of such an adventure, the scope and variety of new political experience was surely tremendous. A staggering number of public rôles was thrust forward during such an enterprise, far too many to wait upon the appearance of seasoned leaders. With the organization of each wilderness county and pioneer township, the roster of offices to be filled and operated was naturally a perfect blank (how long had it been since this was so in Philadelphia?); somebody, willing or unwilling, must be found to fill each one. . . .

. . . the first settlers anywhere, no matter who they were or how scanty their prior political experience, were the men who had to be the first officeholders. This meant that the pioneers, in the very process of establishing and organizing their settlements, were faced with a burden of decision-making disproportionate to that exacted of the late-comers. The political lore, the manipulative skills, which must have been acquired in that process should somehow be kept in the foreground when judging the ferocious vitality, the extravagant energy, of early political life in the Old Northwest. . . .

Thus the extraordinary animation with which the people of Craftown flung themselves into political activity may be seen richly paralleled in the life of the Old Northwest. Every militia muster, every cabin-raising, scow-launching, shooting match, and logrolling was in itself a political assembly where leading figures of the neighborhood made speeches, read certificates, and contended for votes. Sometimes at logrollings rival candidates would take charge of opposing sections of workers, fitness for office having much to do with whose group disposed of its logs first. The enterprising farmer understood, it is said, that this political energy could be

exploited at its height about a month before election time, and tried to schedule his logrolling accordingly.

Our concept of political democracy, it may be remembered, involved a homogeneous population. Can it be asserted that these early Northwest communities were characterized by such a population? There is striking evidence that both attributes of "homogeneity"—a similar level of aspiration and status, and conditions rendering impossible a prior structure of leadership—were widely present here, just as they were in Craftown. A leading symptom of this may be found in the land arrangements. Beverly Bond has made calculations, based on lists of lands advertised for delinquent taxes, as to typical holdings in the Northwest about 1812, and concludes that the "average farm" at that time was probably less than 250 acres. Though such tentative statistics are embarrassing in themselves, the limiting conditions which make them plausible are clear enough—uniform conditions not only permitting but forcing a reduced scale of holdings. Much has been made of large engrossments of land by speculators in the Northwest Territory, yet before the admission of Ohio in 1803, and many years before that of Indiana and Illinois, it was apparent to all that the day of the great land magnate was at an end. His operations were doomed by the very techniques of settlement and by the measures taken by the settlers themselves to thwart his designs.

Jack E. Eblen, "An Analysis of Nine-teenth-Century Frontier Populations," *Demography*, II, (1965), pp. 412-413. Reprinted by permission of the Community and Family Study Center of the University of Chicago.

A Social Scientist Disputes the Turner Thesis

The frontier did not last long—within a decade the population characteristics were moderated rapidly and after two decades census data would hardly bear witness to the frontier experience—but during the first half-decade of settlement within new areas along the farming frontiers, 85 percent of the agricultural van of American civilization was native-born, coming from New England, the Middle States, and states contiguous to the frontier. Within an average sample of the people settling along the frontier, there would be 10 percent more children under ten years of age than in most other parts of the country, but the number of women between twenty and thirty years of age would be the same as within an equal sample taken to represent the nation. In the latter age group there would be 150 men for every 100 women; the percentage of men in their twenties was about 25 percent higher in the frontier agricultural county than the national average and the same percentage lower than the territorial average. In the ages from thirty to forty

there would be a similar differential of 20 percent between the numbers of men, and the number of women in the new farming settlement would be about 10 percent below the comparable figure for the nation. The casual observer probably would not even notice that there were fewer adults over forty in the West than elsewhere in the United States and might be expected to point to their presence in such numbers as something of a curiosity.

Occasionally, as they proceeded, census takers provided copious marginal notes in which they discussed the people coming to the frontiers and indicated their time and mode of arrival, the rate of settlement in their areas, and the settlement patterns. But, even without such notes, the most casual survey of the manuscript censuses furnishes abundant evidence of the significance of the family unit on the frontier. If it were assumed that all the women between twenty and thirty, in the typical county created in this study, were married to men the same age, not more than a third of the men would have remained single. A survey of census manuscripts, however, suggests that such an estimate would probably be conservative, because there were few widows on the fringes of settlement and the few single women who appeared on the frontiers invariably married quickly, regardless of their attributes, whereas widowers with their children were present in impressive numbers. Therefore, to conclude that not over a quarter of the adult males were single, in the ordinary sense, would probably be more realistic. This, too, omits consideration of the men who went west alone with the intention of starting a farm before marrying or bringing out a wife and family—settlers who further emphasize the familial nature of American expansion. Thus, if one accepts the assertion that the American frontiers placed a premium on a high degree of cultural malleability and tenacity, he must also recognize that the deeply entrenched ideal and institution of the family provided the mechanism by which people were bound together during the process of cultural transplantation and adaptation.

In conclusion, the findings of this study suggest a need for further studies of the demographic characteristics of other types of populations in the United States during the same time period. For example, tentative surveys indicate that a similar analysis of commercial farming areas well east of the frontier—such as central Ohio, Indiana, or Kentucky—would yield characteristics which would further reduce the significance of the special features of the agricultural frontiers, whereas an analysis of the Negro populations of the South Atlantic states' slave-breeding areas or of the southern frontiers would likely produce population pyramids quite similar to those found in this study.

Northrop Frye, "Conclusion", in Carl F. Klinck, ed., *Literary History of Canada: Canadian Literature in English,* (Toronto, University of Toronto Press, 1965), pp. 824, 826-831. Reprinted by permission of the University of Toronto Press. © University of Toronto Press 1965.

The Frontier and Literary Imagination

Canada began . . . as an obstacle, blocking the way to the treasures of the East, to be explored only in the hope of finding a passage through it. English Canada continued to be that long after what is now the United States had become a defined part of the Western world. One reason for this is obvious from the map. American culture was, down to about 1900, mainly a culture of the Atlantic seaboard, with a western frontier that moved irregularly but steadily back until it reached the other coast. The Revolution did not essentially change the cultural unity of the English-speaking community of the North Atlantic that had London and Edinburgh on one side of it and Boston and Philadelphia on the other. But Canada has, for all practical purposes, no Atlantic seaboard. The traveller from Europe edges into it like a tiny Jonah entering an inconceivably large whale, slipping past the Straits of Belle Isle into the Gulf of St. Lawrence, where five Canadian provinces surround him, for the most part invisible. Then he goes up the St. Lawrence and the

inhabited country comes into view, mainly a French-speaking country, with its own cultural traditions. To enter the United States is a matter of crossing an ocean; to enter Canada is a matter of being silently swallowed by an alien continent. . . .

The mystique of Canadianism was, as several chapters in this book make clear, specifically the cultural accompaniment of Confederation and the imperialistic mood that followed it. But it came so suddenly after the pioneer period that it was still full of wilderness. To feel "Canadian" was to feel part of a no-man's-land with huge rivers, lakes, and islands that very few Canadians had ever seen. "From sea to sea, and from the river unto the ends of the earth"—if Canada is not an island, the phrasing is still in the etymological sense isolating. One wonders if any other national consciousness has had so large an amount of the unknown, the unrealized, the humanly undigested, so built into it. Rupert Brooke, quoted by Mrs. Waterston, speaks of the "unseizable virginity" of the Canadian landscape. What is important here, for our purposes, is the position of the frontier in the Canadian imagination. In the United States one could choose to move out to the frontier or to retreat from it back to the seaboard. The tensions built up by such migrations have fascinated many American novelists and historians. In the Canadas, even in the Maritimes, the frontier was all around one, a part and a condition of one's whole imaginative being. The frontier was primarily what separated the Canadian, physically or mentally, from Great Britain, from the United States, and, even more important, from other Canadian communities. Such a frontier was the immediate datum of his imagination, the thing that had to be dealt with first. . . .

It is not much wonder if Canada de-

veloped with the bewilderment of a neglected child, preoccupied with trying to
define its own identity, alternately bump-
tious and diffident about its own achievements. Adolescent dreams of glory haunt
the Canadian consciousness (and unconsciousness), some naïve and some sophisticated. In the naïve area are the predic-
tions that the twentieth century belongs
to Canada, that our cities will become
much bigger than they ought to be, or,
like Edmonton and Vancouver, "gate-
ways" to somewhere else, reconstructed
Northwest passages. The more sophisticated usually take the form of a Messianic
complex about Canadian culture, for
Canadian culture, no less than Alberta,
has always been "next year country." The
myth of the hero brought up in the forest
retreat, awaiting the moment when his
giant strength will be fully grown and he
can emerge into the world, informs a good
deal of Canadian criticism down to our
own time. . . .

The sense of probing into the distance,
of fixing the eyes on the skyline, is something that Canadian sensibility has inherited from the *voyageurs*. It comes into
Canadian painting a good deal, in Thom-
son whose focus is so often farthest back
in the picture, where a river or a gorge in
the hills twists elusively out of sight, in
Emily Carr whose vision is always, in the
title of a compatriot's book of poems,
"deeper into the forest." Even in the Maritimes, where the feeling of linear distance
is less urgent, Roberts contemplates the
Tantramar marshes in the same way, the
refrain of "miles and miles" having clearly
some incantatory power for him. It would
be interesting to know how many Canadian novels associate nobility of character
with a faraway look, or base their perora-
tions on a long-range perspective. This
might be only a cliché, except that it is

often found in sharply observed and distinctively written books. Here, as a ran-
dom example, is the last sentence of W. O.
Mitchell's *Who Has Seen the Wind*: "The
wind turns in silent frenzy upon itself,
whirling into a smoking funnel, breathing
up top soil and tumbleweed skeletons to
carry them on its spinning way over the
prairie, out and out to the far line of the
sky." Mr. Pacey quotes the similarly long-
sighted conclusion of *Such is My Beloved*.

A vast country sparsely inhabited naturally depends on its modes of transportation, whether canoe, railway, or the
driving and riding "circuits" of the judge,
the Methodist preacher, or the Yankee
peddler. The feeling of nomadic movement over great distances persists even
into the age of the aeroplane, in a country
where writers can hardly meet one other
without a social organization that provides
travel grants. Pratt's poetry is full of his
fascination with means of communication,
not simply the physical means of great
ships and locomotives, though he is one of
the best of all poets on such subjects, but
with communication as message, with
radar and asdic and wireless signals, and,
in his war poems, with the power of rhetoric over fighting men. What is perhaps
the most comprehensive structure of ideas
yet made by a Canadian thinker, the structure embodied in Innis's *Bias of Communication*, is concerned with the same
theme, and a disciple of Innis, Marshall
McLuhan, continues to emphasize the
unity of communication, as a complex
containing both verbal and non-verbal
factors, and warns us against making un-
real divisions within it. Perhaps it is not
too fanciful to see this need for continuity
in the Canadian attitude to time as well
as space, in its preoccupation with its own
history (the motto of the Province of
Quebec is *je me souviens*) and its relent-

less cultural stock-takings and self-inventories. The Burke sense of society as a continuum—consistent with the pragmatic and conservative outlook of Canadians—is strong and begins early. Mr. Irving quotes an expression of it in McCulloch, and another quotation shows that it was one of the most deeply held ideas of Brett. As I write, the centennial of Confederation in 1967 looms up before the country with the moral urgency of a Day of Atonement: I use a Jewish metaphor because there is something Hebraic about the Canadian tendency to read its conquest of a promised land, its Maccabean victories of 1812, its struggle for the central fortress on the hill at Quebec, as oracles of a future. It is doubtless only an accident that the theme of one of the most passionate and intense of all Canadian novels, A. M. Klein's *The Second Scroll*, is Zionism.

Civilization in Canada, as elsewhere, has advanced geometrically across the country, throwing down the long parallel lines of the railways, dividing up the farm lands into chessboards of square-mile sections and concession-line roads. There is little adaptation to nature: in both architecture and arrangement, Canadian cities and villages express rather an arrogant abstraction, the conquest of nature by an intelligence that does not love it. The word conquest suggests something military, as it should—one thinks of General Braddock, preferring to have his army annihilated rather than fight the natural man on his own asymmetrical ground. There are some features of this generally North American phenomenon that have a particular emphasis in Canada. It has been remarked—Mr. Kilbourn quotes Creighton on the subject—that Canadian expansion westward had a tight grip of authority over it that American expansion,

with its outlaws and sheriffs and vigilantes and the like, did not have in the same measure. America moved from the back country to the wild west; Canada moved from a New France held down by British military occupation to a northwest patrolled by mounted police. Canada has not had, strictly speaking, an Indian war: there has been much less of the "another redskin bit the dust" feeling in our historical imagination, and only Riel remains to haunt the later period of it, though he is a formidable figure enough, rather like what a combination of John Brown and Vanzetti would be in the American conscience. Otherwise, the conquest, for the last two centuries, has been mainly of the unconscious forces of nature, personified by the dragon of the Lake Superior rocks in Pratt's *Towards the Last Spike*:

On the North Shore a reptile lay
    asleep—
A hybrid that the myths might have
    conceived,
But not delivered.

Yet the conquest of nature has its own perils for the imagination, in a country where the winters are so cold and where conditions of life have so often been bleak and comfortless, where even the mosquitoes have been described, Mr. Klinck tells us, as "mementoes of the fall." I have long been impressed in Canadian poetry by a tone of deep terror in regard to nature, a theme to which we shall return. It is not a terror of the dangers or discomforts or even the mysteries of nature, but a terror of the soul at something that these things manifest. The human mind has nothing but human and moral values to cling to if it is to preserve its integrity or even its sanity, yet the vast unconsciousness of nature in front of it seems an unanswerable denial of those values. I notice that a sharp-witted Methodist preacher quoted by Mr. Cogswell speaks of the "shutting out of the whole moral creation" in the loneliness of the forests.

If we put together a few of these impressions, we may get some approach to characterizing the way in which the Canadian imagination has developed in its literature. Small and isolated communities surrounded with a physical or psychological "frontier," separated from one another and from their American and British cultural sources: communities that provide all that their members have in the way of distinctively human values, and that are compelled to feel a great respect for the law and order that holds them together, yet confronted with a huge, unthinking, menacing, and formidable physical setting—such communities are bound to develop what we may provisionally call a garrison mentality. In the earliest maps of the country the only inhabited centres are forts, and that remains true of the cultural maps for a much later time. Frances Brooke, in her eighteenth-century *Emily Montague*, wrote of what was literally a garrison; novelists of our day studying the impact of Montreal on Westmount write of a psychological one.

A garrison is a closely knit and beleaguered society, and its moral and social values are unquestionable. In a perilous enterprise one does not discuss causes or motives: one is either a fighter or a deserter. Here again we may turn to Pratt, with his infallible instinct for what is central in the Canadian imagination. The societies in Pratt's poems are always tense and tight groups engaged in war, rescue, martyrdom, or crisis, and the moral values expressed are simply those of that group. In such a society the terror is not for the common enemy, even when the enemy is or seems victorious, as in the extermination of the Jesuit missionaries or the crew of Franklin (a great Canadian theme, well described in this book by Mr. Hopwood, that Pratt pondered but never completed). The real terror comes when the individual feels himself becoming an individual, pulling away from the group, losing the sense of driving power that the group gives him, aware of a conflict within himself far subtler than the struggle of morality against evil. It is much easier to multiply garrisons, and when that happens, something anti-cultural comes into Canadian life, a dominating herd-mind in which nothing original can grow. The intensity of the sectarian divisiveness in Canadian towns, both religious and political, is an example: what such groups represent, of course, vis-à-vis one another, is "two solitudes," the death of communication and dialogue. Separatism, whether English or French, is culturally the most sterile of all creeds. . . .

Kenneth D. McRae, "The Structure of Canadian History", in Louis Hartz, *The Founding of New Societies,* (New York, Harcourt, Brace & World, 1964), pp. 234-247. © 1964, by Louis Hartz. Reprinted by permission of Harcourt, Brace & World, Inc.

Fragment Cultures and the Frontier

When we turn to the English-speaking fragment in Canada, there is something about it that is strangely but elusively familiar. At first this feeling of re-living a faintly remembered experience is disturbing, baffling, perplexing, until finally the truth hits home. As the central figure of the English-Canadian tradition we encounter once again the American liberal. To be sure, he is not quite on his home ground, and this accounts for our initial difficulties in recognition. He appears first as an exile, a political refugee from his own land, a fragment torn once again from the original American fragment. He settles in a land where his religious feelings are once again hypersensitized by an attempt, ultimately unsuccessful, at church establishment, and by the presence of a large Catholic majority. He lives through a period of government by narrow colonial oligarchies which aspire to become full-fledged aristocracies. Yet through all this he retains, no matter how far obscured or submerged, much of the original liberal heritage of the American colonies.

It is easy to show that the scanty English-speaking population of Canada-to-be before the American Revolution was fundamentally American in outlook. We have already noted the typical clash that ensued when the fledgling merchant community of Montreal confronted Governors Murray and Carleton. Nova Scotia, an even more forceful example of the same phenomenon, is a new New England whose failure to join the other colonies in revolt was the result of economic, geographic, and military factors rather than of any significant difference in outlook. But can we make the same judgment of the American Loyalist refugees who poured into Upper Canada and the Maritime Provinces in the seventeen-eighties? To do so is to deny traditions which have become cherished myths in both the United States and Canada. For in the American view the Loyalists were unregenerate Tories, place-men, servile monarchists, enemies of the notion of liberty upon which the new republic was founded. In the Canadian view they become heroes who endured exile and hardship to demonstrate their attachment to the Crown and the British connection and their abhorrence of mob violence and democratic excesses. When the emotional content is allowed to boil away, the two traditions are not very far apart.

Before examining the facts, let us consider for a moment the theoretical problem. The key to the puzzle is the interpretation to be placed on the American Revolution. For if the United States achieved its present liberal ethos through the expulsion of genuine preliberal or feudal elements at the Revolution, then it is logical to look for those elements in Canada. But if, as is argued elsewhere in this book, the American experience is fundamentally a liberal one from its earliest origins, and if the American Revolution was not a social revolution, then it is folly to represent the Loyalists as a genuine Tory aristocracy or a privileged class. For how could America cast off a social order that it had never really possessed? And if the American experience was basically a liberal one, how could the main Loyalist heritage be anything else? The logic alone is compelling in its clarity, but behind it stands a wealth of empirical evidence. . . .

In Upper Canada we scent at once the atmosphere of the American frontier. The Loyalist influx is described by one of the commissioners investigating their losses claims as "mostly farmers from the back parts of New York Province," and indeed five-sixths of the claimants were from New York. Their losses had been correspondingly small. The typical claimant might have left behind a hundred-acre farm, either owned or leased of which ten acres or less might be cleared land. Many of these men were illiterate, or nearly so, as the records of their signatures and marks subscribing to the oath of allegiance show. Perhaps it is also typical of the still-fluid frontier society that of some six hundred whose claims were examined in Canada only about half were American born. Many of the rest arrived in America only a few years before the Revolution. Only the barest handful of the Upper Canadian Loyalists belonged to the professions, and large landholders seem to have been almost as scarce. But the crowning fact is that this political migration of some 6,000 persons in the late seventeen-seventies and seventeen-eighties was soon far outnumbered by a continuing flow of American settlers moving westward in search of free land. The Upper Canadian Loyalists became sim-

ply a phase in the unrolling of the North American frontier, living in harmony with the new arrivals, and undistinguishable from them in any social sense.

All this may seem rather puzzling, but two cardinal facts must be remembered. The first is that there is no simple criterion to explain the incidence of Loyalism during the Revolution. American society split vertically almost from top to bottom. Factors of geography, military campaigning, local politics, and private vendettas all added their weight to political and economic considerations. Many, as the Loyalist claims amply prove, changed allegiance during the war, and families were often split within themselves. All of which demonstrates that we are not dealing here with a simple social revolution of class against class.

The second point is that out of the vast numbers who supported the Loyalist side, which many estimate as high as a third of the population of the colonies, only a small fraction actually went to Canada. The great majority made their peace and returned home, or settled elsewhere in the new republic. Many of the wealthy and the well-connected found more attractive opportunities in Britain or in the West Indies. Thus frontier conditions in Canada and the Maritimes operated selectively, and in a liberal direction, in attracting immigrants. They also exerted a powerful leveling force upon those who did come. Even the well-educated, the cultivated, and the well-to-do learned unforgettably the meaning of equality as they faced the untamed wilderness. Though the social composition of the Maritime migration might be more varied than its Upper Canadian counterpart, neither offered promising foundations for an aristocratic tradition.

Indeed the American Loyalist undoubtedly never understood his own basic liberalism until the circumstances of his exile thrust it upon his consciousness with unmistakable clarity. Those who went to Upper Canada made the discovery most dramatically, for here they found their new townships still part of the old province of Quebec, administered according to the Quebec Act. During the first few critical years, the absence of a legislative assembly and of English common law did not greatly bother them, for of what use was either in the midst of the wilderness? But they found the feudal tenure of their lands more than a little disquieting, since in law each township was a seigneury under the direct lordship of the Crown. They then discovered, with mounting anger, that the Crown proposed to alienate the milling *banalités* as monopolies to private individuals, with reversion of the mills to the Crown after fifteen years. When rumors began to circulate that the half-pay officers were planning to perpetuate the feudal system and to make themselves seigneurs, grumbling unrest flared into hysterical resentment and near-rebellion. The settlers called unequivocally for freehold tenure and "the British constitution." But this storm passed quickly, and their aspirations for liberal institutions were satisfied by the separation of Upper and Lower Canada in 1791. . . . .

If the American Loyalists who came to Canada were representative of their fellow-Americans in social background and social outlook, this is not to say that they were exactly like them in all their convictions. For a second process of fragmentation or quasi-fragmentation is at work here, and the principle of selectivity in the composition of the fragment has served to differentiate the English-Canadian tradition from the American in certain subtle, minor ways from the very beginning.

Most Loyalists believed fervently in monarchy and in Empire unity. Indeed, this belief was the principal cause of their vicissitudes, and its influence can be traced extensively in Canadian history. In the War of 1812 it proved an important and perhaps decisive factor in stiffening the wavering loyalty of the Upper Canadian population under American attack. In 1837 it seems to have deterred many Reformers from following William Lyon Mackenzie all the way into overt rebellion, although characteristically, and in keeping with their liberal heritage, we find just as many Loyalists and sons of Loyalists among the Reformers as on the government side in the Legislative Assembly of 1835. In the longer run it is difficult not to attribute to the Loyalist tradition much of that hyperloyalism to Britain, Crown, and Empire which has exacerbated French-English relations in Canada. In summary, while loyalism is a differentiating quality that distinguishes the Canadian fragment from its American origins, for many historians it has obscured the all-important parental relationship between them.

But there are other, more subtle differences. The American opponents of the Revolution, though they often disapproved strongly of imperial policy, had been advocates of moderation, gradualism, compromise, and preservation of the existing political order. They had a faith in the rule of law that amounted almost to a passion, and in many these beliefs were fortified by years of military discipline. It is not difficult to show that these qualities passed into Canada, where they became elements in the English-Canadian tradition. Among other effects, they frustrated the Upper Canadian rebellion of

1837, dominated the struggle for responsible government, and even influenced the pattern of westward expansion. There is an instructive contrast between the informal folk law of the American frontier and the federal criminal law imposed by the North-West Mounted Police on the Canadian prairies, between the tumultuous rush to the California gold fields and the curiously regulated race to the Klondike. . . .

In the meanwhile government had to be carried on. The period down to the eighteen-forties was marked in all the British North American colonies by the rule of small, tightly knit colonial oligarchies, to which Canadian history has applied the vivid but somewhat misleading term Family Compacts. It is not too difficult to explain the emergence of oligarchic control. The demands of the frontier left little time or energy for participation in politics, and the desperate lack of educational facilities was soon reflected in a lack of effective leadership. In the beginning the Family Compacts simply filled a political vacuum.

Their composition was extremely varied. In New Brunswick the ruling group were cultivated Loyalists, who preserved, more than in any other colony, an aura of patrician gentility. In Nova Scotia the Loyalists were initially outsiders, and the oligarchy consisted in leading Halifax families established before the Revolution, as well as British career officials. Upper Canada reflected its raw frontier condition in the variegated quality of its elite. Fewer than a third were original Loyalists, although a few of the latecomers were from New Brunswick Loyalist families. If the Upper Canada Compact was a rather nondescript group in its origins, there was no very broad social basis from which to select it. Even

Lower Canada had its oligarchy, although by a reversal of its earlier history it was the representatives of the English minority that surrounded and influenced the governor from the seventeen-nineties onward.

To understand the significance of these Family Compacts is by no means a simple task. The complexity begins even in describing them. To risk a broad generalization for a fifty-year interval, they include, characteristically, the heads of departments in the colonial administration, judges, most barristers, and the bishop or ranking churchman of the Church of England. But this is not all, for closely associated with this official oligarchy we find the leaders of the commercial and banking community. In the microcosm of colonial society there is no clear differentiation between the political and the economic elite. And frequently it made for a strange amalgam, compounded of patrician principles and self-made men, of Old World polish and frontier crudity, of public spirit and naked greed.

In British North America the Family Compacts developed no appreciable interest in landed estates. There is no parallel in Canadian history to the pastoral ascendancy in Australia. Though they might speculate in unimproved land, the Compacts showed no inclination to retain and develop it. And this was just as well, for there could be no rural tenantry in a land where freehold farms could be had almost for the asking. But it was left to the unsuspecting English gentleman immigrant to make this discovery; the Family Compacts never made the experiment. Their interests were overwhelmingly in the commercial and governmental activities of the emerging cities.

Contemporary observers perceived the commercial role of the Compacts, but they did not always correctly assess its significance. They merely cited this aspect to illustrate how ridiculous were their aristocratic pretensions. Judge Thorpe, one of the earliest critics, wrote scornfully in 1806 of a "Shopkeeper Aristocracy" of "scotch Pedlars . . . there is a chain of them linked from Halifax to Quebec, Montreal, Kingston, York, Niagara and so on to Detroit." Lord Durham noted in 1839 that the Upper Canada Compact practically monopolized banking and owned much of the undeveloped land of the province. Even Sir Francis Head, replying to Lord Durham's criticisms, defended rule by a small group "who by their own industry and intelligence, have amassed wealth." There is little flavor of Old World aristocracy here. The much-traveled Mrs. Jameson, who certainly could tell a true aristocracy from a false one, referred to the Upper Canada group as "a petty colonial oligarchy, a self-constituted aristocracy, based upon nothing real, nor even upon anything imaginary." For in European eyes a mercantile aristocracy is no aristocracy at all. The trouble is that the Family Compacts of British North America have been judged—and found ridiculous—in the light of what, in their most imaginative moments, they aspired to become. But it is far more realistic to assess them in the light of what they actually were: ambitious mercantile oligarchies that were not above using whatever measure of privilege they could get to perpetuate their position.

If we pursue this point a bit further, we find illuminating parallels. The first and most obvious is the substantial similarity between the Family Compacts and the American colonial oligarchies before the Revolution. But this parallel, while useful in many respects, is incomplete in

that it ignores the crucial fact of the Revolution that separates the First and Second Empires. British North America, it has been suggested, was constructed out of the reaction to the American Revolution; it is therefore the land par excellence of the counter-revolution. There is truth in this view, provided it is properly understood. But if, as we have already noted, the American Revolution was a mere political revolution executed within a social framework already basically liberal, what sort of reaction would it engender? If the American reaction at its height could only produce a Whig-Girondin type of liberalism in the shape of the Federalists, is it any wonder that the more primitive societies of British North America could scarcely do more? Neither the original European inheritance nor the North American environment would permit the successful planting of anything genuinely aristocratic. It is true that sustained attempts were made in all the colonies to establish the Church of England, and for Upper and Lower Canada the Constitution of 1791 even visualized for a fleeting moment a prospect of hereditary aristocracy, but these measures remained hopelessly unattainable. In the North American setting the blackest sort of reaction possible was commercial oligarchy and the petty religious, educational, and social privileges to which these groups clung so desperately serve only to underline the essentially nonaristocratic nature of their ascendancy.

When we understand this basic nature of the Family Compacts, we begin to discover the clues to their prolonged success. As miniature aristocracies modeled on the Old World, they would be inexplicable. But as mercantile oligarchies of ability and drive in colonies where these qualities were in short supply, they provided the banking and commercial facilities necessary to economic progress. As groups substantially involved in the economic development of their own province, they were often the most articulate spokesmen for provincial interests on the broad imperial stage. Finally, and simply because of their position as oligarchies, they soon found a profitable role for themselves in saving the colonial masses from the specter of republicanism and democracy.

Here a second parallel comes into view which may be even more revealing. It is the fate of their American contemporaries, the Federalists and Whigs. Because the latter found it impossible to impress the American masses with the dangers of democracy, they went down helplessly before the onslaughts of the Jeffersonians and Jacksonians. But the insoluble problem of the American Whigs proved the salvation of the Family Compacts. For in British North America democracy still held many terrors. Nothing was easier than to cry up the perils of demagoguery, lawlessness, and Yankee republicanism. In Loyalist tradition the memory of these persisted from Revolutionary days and had been rekindled by the War of 1812. This deep, unreasoning fear of unqualified democracy, carefully nurtured by the ruling groups, was the weakest link in the armor of the Loyalist liberal, and it led him to acquiesce uncertainly in the many inconveniences of oligarchical government rather than to run the risk of mob rule.

Thus while the Federalists and Whigs were tasting the bitterness of defeat, the Family Compacts, operating on very similar social premises, were enjoying an unbroken ascendancy that lasted half a century. And luck was with them, at least for a time. For when a combination of offi-

cial intransigence and temperamental instability led Mackenzie and Papineau into rebellion in 1837, did this not show that all the direst warnings of the Compacts had come true? Their luck ran out, however, when the Reform leadership passed into the hands of moderates like Baldwin and Howe, for then their claim to a monopoly on loyalism was patently ridiculous and their defeat became inevitable.

And yet, except in a narrow political sense, there was no complete repudiation of the Compacts and what they stood for, no flight of exiles to other lands, no real revolution at their overthrow. When responsible government came, members of the oligarchy simply adapted themselves to the new rules of democratic politics and in time found other means to return to power. The transition has a Hegelian flavor, sustaining and preserving something of the old order even while superseding it. And in New Brunswick, the purest example of the Loyalist mentality, the change was so smooth as to be difficult to date.

The British North America poised on the threshold of self-government in 1850 is not the same British North America whose foundations we have traced down to the War of 1812. One factor that greatly helped to overthrow oligarchic rule was the dramatic growth of the society by immigration. If the first wave of English-speaking settlement in modern Canada was American in origin, the second stemmed from the great outpouring of population from the British Isles after 1815. Between 1815 and 1850 almost a million immigrants left Britain for British North America. Their impact on the new society was far-reaching indeed. An English fragment of perhaps 350,000 in 1815 was more than doubled in twenty years, tripled in thirty, more than quadrupled in forty. Nor was the rate of growth equal in all colonies. The populations of Nova Scotia and New Brunswick almost quadrupled between 1815 and 1851, but that of Upper Canada increased tenfold, from an estimated 95,000 in 1814 to 952,000 in 1851. This poses an interesting problem. What will be the fate of the original fragment when exposed to such conditions? Upper Canada, born of American liberalism, isolated from the rest of British America, and flooded by a tidal wave of almost wholly British migration, offers almost a classic testing ground for the survival of an original fragment in a rapidly growing society.

The social background of this wave of immigration is significant. The records of arrivals at Quebec and Montreal during the early eighteen-fifties provide a valuable picture of male occupations. Approximately half are designated simply as laborers, and the proportion was probably higher during the worst famine years of the eighteen-forties. Roughly thirty per cent are listed as farmers and farm servants, and practically all the rest are skilled artisans. The middle and professional classes are virtually unrepresented. Thus while the British middle classes figured largely in the colonies' literary and cultural development down to the eighteen-fifties, they were statistically insignificant, and their supposed influence on social development may well have been considerably overestimated.

Down to the eighteen-fifties Upper Canadian society was overwhelmingly rural. The agricultural frontier dominated. And yet upon this simple foundation arose a social pattern of bewildering complexity. Settlement of the land was tried in almost every conceivable form. Direct grants, land companies, paternalistic despotism, and even squatting, all made their appearance. The census figures of 1851 and 1861 show that more than half of the British-born population were of Irish stock, the balance being fairly evenly divided between English and Scots. In many areas immigrant groups homogeneous in religion and ethnic origin created distinctive pockets of rural settlement whose imprint remains clearly visible today. The new arrivals brought with them all their clannishness and native animosities, most notably the deep-rooted antagonism between Irish Catholics and Ulster Orangemen. In the Canadian setting such a struggle was highly inflammatory, and it spread like a forest fire to non-Irish groups.

It would be inaccurate to say that this wave of migration was absorbed into the original fragments; an influx of these proportions does not permit of simple assimilation. And yet the original North American liberal heritage was working with irresistible force upon it in at least two basic respects. The first was the universal urge to own property. Though raised in a society where property belonged to the few, the vast majority of immigrants gravitated to the land—to their own land—at the earliest possible opportunity. The second influence of the liberal heritage lay in the immigrants' discovery of the classlessness of North American society. For the first time in their lives they experienced a feeling of freedom, of independence, of camaraderie, of escape from a system of class differences. All too frequently they abused their new-found freedom. The accounts of English travelers are full of the swaggering impertinence of their ex-compatriots as they indulged in what they imagined to be Yankee manners. However, offensive or not, this behaviour is the answer to our emerging question: the immigrant, despite his overwhelming numbers, quickly forgets his old notions of social hierarchy and becomes an egalitarian.

Landed property and equal social condition, the two key elements of the North American liberal tradition: though they may have been unfamiliar at first, it was inevitable that the British immigrant should embrace them both without reservation. For in their discovery he fulfilled in full measure the very hopes of bettering his condition that had first sent him in trembling anticipation to the New World.

Despite the flood tide of immigration, then, the original liberal inheritance of English-speaking Canada survived and dominated. Though the society had become more complex, its spirit was unchanged. The phenomenal growth down to 1850 showed that the liberal tradition could be diversified without being deflected from its course. After mid-century the rate of immigration fell off sharply, and for a generation English Canada had the same chance to harden and consolidate its tradition that French Canada had had following the Treaty of Utrecht. More challenges lay ahead: further waves of immigration, which would include new ethnic groups bringing with them alien traditions; the rise of industrial society; some epic battles with French Canada. The English fragment could look on all these issues with a confidence that bordered on complacency, for it was now ready to confront any challenge from a well-established position of its own.

S. D. Clark, *The Developing Canadian Community,* second edition, (Toronto, University of Toronto Press, 1968), pp. 3-11. Reprinted by permission of the University of Toronto Press, © University of Toronto Press, 1965.

The Commercial Frontier: A Sociological Interpretation

The importance of the opening up of new areas of economic exploitation in the economic history of Canada serves to justify concern with the effects of such developments upon the development of social organization. If some of the older settled areas in Canada early reached a state of economic maturity, and if at times economic recession halted the pushing out into new areas, these developments did little more than punctuate the sweep of frontier economic expansion. The drying up of resources or the loss of markets resulted in a shift to new economic activities rather than in a prolonged economic regression; the succession of export staples provides evidence of the importance in the economy of Canada of new techniques of production rather than of techniques of conservation. The establishment of the fishing industry in the Gulf of St. Lawrence led to the traffic in furs with the Indians and to the settlement of the Annapolis and St. Lawrence valleys. To fish and fur was later added the important staple of timber, opening up for agricul-

tural exploitation the interior of New Brunswick and the new Province of Upper Canada. Expansion of the fur trade to the West brought about the sudden rush for gold in British Columbia, and eventually in the Yukon, and the settlement of the wheat lands of the prairies, and these developments hastened the growth of industrial capitalism in the East. The pushing out of the frontiers of manufacturing, and the exploitation of the mining and pulp and paper resources of the North, mark the final phases of the frontier expansion of economic life in Canada.

Social problems in Canada, accordingly, have been largely associated with frontier economic developments. The opening up of new areas or fields of economic exploitation made certain special kinds of demands upon social organization, and the failure to meet fully these demands resulted in disturbances in social relationships which may be described as social problems. Centres of new economic activity became the points of origin of forces of disturbance, and these forces extended to the peripheries of such activity. The areas of greatest social disturbance were to be found where the impacts of the new techniques of production were most felt, and the intensity of the disturbance reached its peak during the interval in which the new economic developments were most rapidly taking place. As the economy became more mature, the social organization adjusted itself to the conditions of production, and an approximate state of equilibrium was attained by the time the economy passed beyond the frontier stage.

Frontier economic expansion involved the recruitment of capital and labour from outside, and this growth of population made necessary the extension of institutional controls and often their establishment beyond customary boundaries. Since institutions are essentially a body of trained functionaries performing specialized services, organization had to be widened and personnel enlarged if the needs of growing populations were to be adequately served. The considerable distance which often separated new areas of development from centres of control and supply made difficult the maintenance of effective supervision from the homeland in establishing institutional agencies and also imposed severe limitations upon the recruitment of personnel. In addition, conditions within such areas discouraged the financial support of institutions which did not directly promote economic exploitation and the immigration of professionally trained workers. The drain of capital into economic enterprise left little for community services while the demand for labour meant that even those who possessed specialized training of some sort were attracted into economic vocations. The failure of churches or educational institutions to secure adequate financial support, problems of public finance, and the lack of sufficient school-teachers, clergymen, and medical practitioners were characteristic features of Canadian frontier communities. The stronger pull of economic enterprise meant that capital and labour flowed beyond the boundaries of institutional systems. Where economic development took place rapidly and considerable additions to the labour force could be immediately absorbed, as in mining frontiers, the lag of such systems was most conspicuous, but even when development took place slowly and the exploitative process did not require great numbers of workers there was a considerable interval before social organization could catch up with the movement of population. . . .

To some extent, the failure of economic enterprise to provide an agency for the transfer of social institutions to frontier areas was offset by efforts put forth by the state. Imperial, or later, national forces promoted the extension of political agencies into new areas of development in Canada. Frontiers have always assumed considerable strategical importance in the political organization of the northern half of the continent, and, for this reason, never became unrestricted areas of economic exploitation. The presence to the south of a rapidly expanding nation served to emphasize the need of maintaining close political contacts with the frontier. The police force and courts of law, or at any rate the army, pushed out with the frontiersmen. The maintenance of military garrisons in New France and later in the British American colonies, the construction of roads and canals to serve as military routes, the dispatch of a force of Royal Engineers to Victoria in 1859, and the organization of the North West Mounted Police in 1874 were instances of efforts to promote imperial or national interests in outlying areas of economic development. To some extent the political controls imposed by the state were paralleled by controls of a social or cultural character. Land grants to favoured individuals or organizations, financial subsidies, preferments in political appointments, or measures restricting the operation of competitive interests were means employed to build up privileged social institutions such as an aristocratic class or established church. The object was to assure the loyalty of frontier populations to the mother country, and such aids therefore served the same purpose as military garrisons or police forces. However, even when such supports of the state were extensive, there remained in new areas of development many needs not immediately taken care of by institutions. The coercive controls of the state, or of privileged social institutions, tended to be of a negative rather than positive character. The instruments of law provided no direction to behaviour outside of prohibitions, while institutions such as established churches supplied leadership only to those who were their adherents. For the large number of people who committed no infractions of the law or who did not owe allegiance to the formally constituted social institutions, authority was for the most part morally indifferent. The extension of social organization into all areas of social behaviour required the active participation of the population itself, and this involved more than simply the transfer of formal machinery.

The lack of institutional agencies securing the active participation of frontier populations increased the reliance upon individual resources, and the greater the lack the greater was this reliance. As frontier populations were left without leadership, they tended to become less dependent upon traditional institutions even after they were established. The weakened state of social organization thereby tended to perpetuate itself. Habits of independence were converted into attitudes of nonconformity, and what was first perhaps missed came later to be resented. New patterns of behaviour inevitably developed which did not fit into traditional systems of institutional control, and efforts of institutions to secure greater conformity led to a conflict of social values and to a condition which might be described as one of social disorganization. The difficulty faced by churches in reviving habits of worship after a considerable interval during which religious

services were not provided and other ways of occupying the time on the sabbath day had developed illustrate the kind of problems resulting from the extension of social organization into new areas of development.

The character of the population which moved to frontier areas tended to strengthen nonconformist attitudes and to make more difficult the establishment of institutional systems. If the very fact of movement resulted in a considerable dislocation in habits and beliefs, this dislocation was greater when the population was recruited from a number of different cultural milieus. Conflicts emerged between opposing systems of control; the folkways, mores, and social codes of the various groups strove for supremacy. The efforts of some institutions to strengthen their position by privileges secured from the state were offset by the vigorous propaganda of less favoured organizations. The disturbances resulting from associations with strange people, in weakening traditional habits and beliefs, increased the area of cultural indifference and intensified as a result institutional competition. To the extent that segregation could not be achieved and long-established attachments preserved, frontier populations tended to be indifferent as to the particular institutions to which they gave their support. The effects were evident in a large, culturally detached population in new areas of development which floated from one institution or group to another, their momentary attachments depending largely upon circumstances of convenience and waves of enthusiasm.

This tendency was accentuated when the population contained elements which had joined the movement to new areas as means of escape from restraining influences at home. In some respects, this was characteristic of all frontier populations in Canada. Those people migrated who were most exposed to economic, political, or cultural pressures. New areas of economic development provided greater opportunities to realize potentialities of certain kinds. The worker, peasant, entrepreneur, and the religious or political heretic found there an outlet for their particular aptitudes or beliefs. These types of people made more difficult the establishment of certain forms of social organization. The extension of institutions is facilitated by the presence of a body of receptive attitudes and a favourable set of social customs, and, where these were lacking, dependence had to be placed upon the exercise of powers of coercion or upon propaganda. The weaknesses of economic monopolies, colonial class systems, established churches, or authoritarian systems of government, and the steady drain of the United States upon the population of Canada, were directly related to these characteristics of the settlers in Canadian frontier communities. When the nonconformist elements included those who sought escape from moral codes or agencies of law enforcement, the strains upon social organization in the newly settled areas were even greater. Habits of resistance of such groups to authority were carried over from the old to the new society and increased the general tendency of frontier populations to become independent of traditional institutions. The emigration of social misfits resulted partly from the social pressures applied to get them out of the way and partly from the opportunities of escape or freedom from restraint provided within rapidly growing and largely inaccessible communities. Though the nature of the frontier economy determined to a con-

siderable extent the particular character of these people, in all of the newly developing Canadian communities there were outcasts of some sort from older societies.

Similarly, the presence in frontier areas of people who had emigrated because they were failures at home, whether because of economic adversity, ill health, or some other reason, made more difficult the establishment of community organization. It is true that the rehabilitation of the individual's economic, physical, or mental condition often accompanied settlement in new areas, but this did not relieve the strain upon social organization in the interval before such rehabilitation was accomplished. The inability of such persons to provide for their needs meant that they could not fully participate in community life but were rather a burden upon frontier society. Numbers of such socially dependent persons have invariably accompanied the movement of population into Canadian frontier communities; if some found their way to such communities in the hope of bettering their state, others were sent there as a means of reducing the burdens of relief faced by local and national agencies in the home community. Efforts of France and later of Britain to secure through overseas colonization a solution to the problem of mounting poor-rates were paralleled by attempts on the part of Canadian cities to reduce burdens of relief by the promotion of settlement in the West and in recent years a back-to-the-land movement.

Other characteristics of the population served to make more difficult the establishment of orderly social relationships. Movements of people into new areas almost invariably involved disturbances in the equilibrium of age and sex groups. Though the nature of the economy largely determined the extent of these disturbances, migration ordinarily cut through the population structure to eliminate the very young and the very old and to secure a considerable predominance of men. Hazards of travel discouraged the migration of women, children, and old people, while the frontier society placed an emphasis upon productive as distinguished from service occupations and favoured as a result adult males who could take part directly in the process of economic exploitation. The age and sex composition of the population had considerable significance with respect to the stability of social organization. The absence of the older age groups in frontier areas relieved the pressure upon health and welfare institutions but removed the steadying influence of tradition and deprived the communities of the leadership of those who were not strenuously engaged in making a living. Since there were relatively few children among the early settlers, recreational and educational facilities were not required in the first years of development, but, where settlement of young persons of both sexes took place, problems of maternity and infant welfare quickly assumed considerable importance, and, in later years, an abnormally high proportion of school-age children imposed a heavy burden upon elementary educational institutions; it was not until after the passing of the first generation of settlers in frontier communities that a stable balance was secured between the school-age and total population. A predominance of men in the population raised problems of institutional adjustment of an even more critical character. Social organizations which depended upon the family unit, or which chiefly served the needs of women or children, failed to become established or remained largely ineffective. The result was that a large

proportion of the normal controls of society were absent or greatly weakened. Apart from the mores of the family, religious and neighborhood institutions were most affected. Devoutness tended to disappear when female influences were absent, while most of the niceties and refinements of social relationships depending upon companionship within the family group were disregarded or coarsened when such companionship was lacking. Where conditions were favourable, prostitution developed as a substitute for familial relationships, and the prevalence of drinking, gambling, and certain forms of crime in many frontier areas was indicative of general weaknesses of social organization resulting largely from the disproportionate number of men. In brief, the age and sex composition, like other characteristics, of the population intensified problems of institutional adjustment which resulted from the opening up and peopling of new frontier areas.

Such problems were still further accentuated by the contact of frontier populations with strange environmental influences, since adjustments to these influences were made much more quickly on the individual than on the institutional level. More strictly, adjustments took place most rapidly among that section of the population most exposed to strange environmental influences and were most resisted by that section least exposed, and it was those people least exposed who had chief voice in the direction of traditional institutional policies and activities. The dignitaries, priests, or official classes of the community were very largely sheltered from disturbing influences; the very nature of their roles meant that their employments were not directly related to frontier economic enterprise. It was the new occupational groups who faced the full force of new economic developments, and these groups had few claims upon the offices or emoluments of established social institutions. Individuals participating in frontier economic enterprise came in contact with new problems of life for which new solutions were necessary; the application of new techniques of production, and the development of new ways of living, involved a rational appraisal of the relation of means to desired ends and required the formulation of new habits of behaviour and thought. In a sense, such people moved out to the margins of society, and, while they carried with them some of the habits of thought and behaviour which had been implanted by previous forms of control, they had to leave behind, or cast off on the way, the great body of habits not fitted to the new conditions of life. Habits, like tools, were abandoned through non-usage because they failed to work. Whether this represented a failure to maintain conditions of life which had been considered desirable, or a release from social obligations which had been felt as irksome, the effect was to emancipate the individual from controls to which he had been accustomed. He was left to work out by himself a code of conduct and philosophy of life which more nearly satisfied his present needs. The immediate reaction was one of uneasiness, relieved partly by a feeling of exhilaration. The ultimate result, if new group attachments failed to be forged, was complete personal disorganization. Problems of mental health and suicide, and to some extent of intemperance, in periods of rapid social development, were an indication of the failure of individuals to resolve the personal crisis in face of radically new conditions of living.

Suggested Reading

The literature on the American frontier and on the frontier thesis is staggeringly profuse. Good bibliographies of the literature can be found in: George Rogers Taylor, ed., *The Turner Thesis*, Problems in American Civilization Series, (Boston, 1956); Ray Allen Billington, *Westward Expansion*, (New York, 1949); and Nelson Klose, *A Concise Study Guide to the American Frontier*, (Lincoln, Neb., 1964).

Among the best studies of Turner are Richard Hofstadter's excellent *The Progressive Historians*, (New York, 1968); *Turner and Beard*, (Glencoe, Ill., 1960), by Lee Benson; James C. Malin's *Essays on Historiography*, (Lawrence, Kan., 1946); and Wilbur R. Jacobs, ed., *The Historical World of Frederick Jackson Turner*, (New Haven, Conn., 1969). A good collection of pro-frontierist thought is found in *Wisconsin Witness to Frederick Jackson Turner*, (Madison, Wis., 1961), edited by O. Lawrence Burnette, Jr. Still worth reading is the masterwork of Turner's most ardent disciple, Frederic L. Paxson, *History of the American Frontier, 1763-1893*, (Boston, 1924). So, too, is the intelligent and readable criticism of frontierism by Carlton Hayes, "The American Frontier—Frontier of What?", *American Historical Review*, vol. LI, (1946), pp. 199-216. A thoroughly devastating assault on Turner is found in Francis S. Philbrick, *The Rise of the West, 1754-1830*, (New York, 1965).

In recent years there have been many reinterpretations of the American frontier experience, some favourable to Turner, some unfavourable. The most striking of the neo-Turnerian approaches is that of Ray Allen Billington, in his brilliant book, *America's Frontier Heritage*, (New York, 1966), one of the finest studies of the problem since the work of Turner himself. Urban history has been on the rise in the last fifteen years. An instructive study of frontier cities, which sharply challenges traditional frontierist views, is Richard C. Wade, *The Urban Frontier*, (Cambridge, Mass., 1959). David Potter reinterprets the frontier experience in terms of material abundance, a useful approach in Canadian history, in *People of Plenty*, (Chicago, 1954). Two excellent literary approaches are: Henry Nash Smith, *Virgin Land: The American West as Symbol and Myth*, (Cambridge, Mass., 1950); and Leo Marx, *The Machine in the Garden: Technology and the Pastoral Idea in America*, (New York, 1964).

The best general treatments of Canadian frontierism are: Morris Zaslow, "The Frontier Hypothesis in Recent Historiography", *Canadian Historical Review*, vol. XXIX, (1948), pp. 153-167; and J. M. S. Careless, "Frontierism, Metropolitanism and Canadian History", *Canadian Historical Review*, vol. XXXV, (1954), pp. 1-21. Walter Sage's article, "Some Aspects of the Frontier in Canadian History", *Canadian Historical Association Annual Report*, (1928), pp. 67-72, was one of the earliest full-scale applications of the theory to Canada. Another good example was A. L. Burt, "The Frontier in the History of New France", *Canadian Historical Association Annual Report*, (1940), pp. 93-99. French Canada and the frontier is created more critically in a recent volume by W. J. Eccles. Other uses of the theory in Canada include: Edmund H. Oliver, *The Winning of the Frontier*, (Toronto, 1930), a study of religious development; Marcus Lee Hansen and J. B. Brebner, *The Mingling of the Canadian and American Peoples*, (New Haven, 1941); Mason Wade, "Social Change in French Canada", in Ralph Braibanti and Joseph J. Spengler, eds., *Tradition, Values, and Socio-Economic Development*, (Durham, N.C., 1961); Wilfrid Eggleston, *The Frontier and Canadian Letters*, (Toronto, 1957);

William Bennett Munro, *American Influences on Canadian Government*, (Toronto, 1929), a rather crude treatment of common frontier influences in North America; George W. Brown, "The Reform Convention of 1859", *Canadian Historical Review*, vol. XVI, (1935), pp. 245-265, a Turnerian treatment of Upper Canadian radicalism; W. A. Mackintosh, "Economic Factors in Canadian History", *Canadian Historical Review*, vol. IV, (1923), pp. 12-25, the article which began the staple approach to Canadian history, but which expressed a strong debt to Turner.

J. B. Brebner criticized frontierism in "Canadian and North American History", *Canadian Historical Association Annual Report*, (1931), pp. 37-48, as did George Stanley in the same journal in 1940, in a paper called "Western Canada and the Frontier Thesis", pp. 104-114.

S. D. Clark has advanced his special treatment of the frontier in several volumes: *Church and Sect in Canada*, (Toronto, 1948); *Movements of Political Protest in Canada*, (Toronto, 1959); *The Social Development of Canada*, (Toronto, 1942).

Frontier social life in the Canadas has as yet received little attention from historians. A. R. M. Lower's social history of Canada, *Canadians in the Making*, (Toronto, 1960), has some provocative ideas. More directly relevant is his *Settlement and the Forest Frontier in Eastern Canada*, (Toronto, 1936). There is little available on institutional problems or the theme of law and order, and the response of the lower classes to frontier conditions has been largely ignored. However, there are several instructive articles on the experience of elite groups in pioneer Upper Canada. S. F. Wise has produced a number of excellent studies, among which is "Tory Factionalism: Kingston Elections and Upper Canadian Politics, 1820-

1836", *Ontario History*, vol. LVII, (1965), pp. 205-225. More immediately concerned with frontier problems is M. S. Cross, "The Age of Gentility: The Creation of an Aristocracy in the Ottawa Valley", *Canadian Historical Association Annual Report*, (1967).

did Frontier Thesis
apply to settlement
of Upper Canada